Fire & Grace

Stories of History and Vision

edited by Jim Taylor

UNITED CHURCH PUBLISHING HOUSE

Toronto, Canada

Fire & Grace
Stories of History and Vision

Copyright © 1999 United Church Publishing House

Canadian Cataloguing in Publication Data

Main entry under title:

Fire & grace : stories of history and vision

Includes bibliographical references and index.
ISBN 1-55134-101-8

1. United Church of Canada. 2. United Church of Canada — History.
I. Taylor, James, 1936-   . II. Title: Fire and grace.

BX9881.F57 1999   287.9'2   C99-931777-6

United Church Publishing House
3250 Bloor Street West, Suite 300
Etobicoke ON
Canada M8X 2Y4
416-231-5931
bookpub@uccan.org

Design, Editorial, and Production: Department of Publishing and Graphics

Cover photos: United Church mission plane CF-FBK, Alert Bay, BC, 1965 (HUC-92); *The Basis of Union* (882336, M-2-15); Captain Oliver and the *Udal* (122, BC 350); Nellie McCung (Mc23); hands (40 AFL-28); Union Service at Mutual Arena, June 10, 1925 (HUC-07); Korean children (K65-466 #29); Missionary couple (glass slide no number) published with permission of Berkeley Studio. The Creed in Cree from *Voices United* with permission.

Photos on page 6: June 10, 1925, 92.185P/346 N with permission of The United Church of Canada/Victora University Archives, Toronto. August 14–21, 1997, 970072 published with permission of Berkeley Studio.

Photos on page 43 published with the permission of Marguerite Nicolson.

Printed in Canada
5   4   3   2   1   03   02   01   00   99

 980279

Contents

With thanks to the following contributors and sources:

Rod Booth, Judith Edith Maxted Brewer, Marion D. Christie, Philip A. Cline, Annie Crowell, *Currents* magazine, Constance Deiter, Ted Dodd, Caryn Douglas, T. M. Russell Dunham, Maitland Evans, J. Rae Grant, Henry and Christine Hansen, Fleming Holm, Noreen Hull, Grace Tuer Jacklin, Elinor N. Kent, Betty Marlin, Marguerite Miller, Ralph Milton, F. Marguerite Nicolson, Beth Parker, Bill Phipps, Alfred Alexander Radley, Florence Perry Shephard, Ross Skuse, Linda Slough, Morton B. Stratton, William S. Taylor, Fred J. Thompson, K. H. Ting, Evan Tonin, and Mary Welch.

Preface

In the fall of 1996, in response to requests from the United Church constituency, the Executive of General Council asked the United Church Publishing House to publish a "historical book" in commemoration of the seventy-fifth anniversary of Church Union (1925–2000).

After talking with many United Church members, surveying potential readers, and holding two separate consultations, the objectives for the book became clear:

- To identify and reflect on this turning point in the United Church's life;
- To recount those issues attended by the church and contemplate their far-reaching social and political implications within Canada;
- To produce a publication celebrating seventy-five years as the United Church and looking forward to the next century;
- To offer a "popular" publication that employs storytelling as a primary tool with which to re-visit our history as a denomination.

We were excited and challenged by the task to produce a book that was thoughtful and significant, but at the same time readable and entertaining!

We greatly appreciate that so many talented and busy people took the time to write the essays that make up the chapters in this book. Your words and insights give all of us much to ponder, and encourage us at different points to offer a grateful acknowledgement, a word of forgiveness, a smile, or a silent prayer.

We were also delighted that so many people responded to our request to submit anecdotes and personal memories of Church Union and of other significant places along the way to this anniversary.

Finally, our thanks to Jim Taylor, long-time United Church member and highly respected Canadian editor, whose thoughtful and careful work brought the stories together.

Beth Parker
Director
Department of Publishing
and Graphics

Linda Slough
General Secretary
Division of
Communication

Commissioners and delegates attending the inaugural service of The United Church of Canada held in Mutual Street Arena, Toronto, June 10, 1925.

Commissioners at the Thirty Sixth General Council, Camrose, Alberta, August 14–21, 1997.

This Church of Ours

A love affair with
what we are and
how we got here

The Church I Love

by Bruce McLeod

The unity of the church starts with the unity of God. We see it when we learn to look up from the ruts so that we can see those "high white following birds."

Three-quarters of a century ago the thousands of people, some of whom still remember being there, who jam-packed Toronto's old Mutual Street arena witnessed three distinct and ancient church traditions, to the world's (and their own) amazement, combine in the Inaugural Service of what we've known ever since as The United Church of Canada.

Forty-nine years later, near the end of my term as moderator, I met a terminally ill United Church elder in a Regina hospital. He was a farmer. He told me how he used to ride his combine through the fresh earth, how blessed he felt to have spent his life's energy turning fields of grain to bread, knowing the satisfaction of tiredness for a good purpose, moving through open gates onto rich land in clear air, and ploughing in the seasons' rhythm beneath the tracking of white following birds.

He had a sense, he said, of having participated in the ongoing spirit of creation that worked through him during his strong years, and to which he gladly gave his life, as a trumpet gives itself to the breath of one who blows it. His accustomed way of naming that spirit was to call it Christ, as in poet John Masefield's lines:

> *O Christ who holds the open gate,*
> *O Christ who drives the furrow straight,*
> *O Christ the plough, O Christ the laughter*
> *of holy white birds flying after.*

He didn't have to name the spirit for it to blow in him. But the elder, like Masefield, called it Christ. He learned to do that in the United Church. It was Christ he rested back in as he took bread from me that day in Jesus' name. But the Christ Spirit, he knew, is broader than Jesus or Jesus' churches. It waits in the earth by open gates and ploughs, and lifts laughter out of tired men. "It holds all things together," Paul said (Colossians 1:17).

The Many Faces That Make Home

For two millennia people have come together in Jesus' name and made themselves available to that Spirit and its world-warming power. In The United Church of Canada, we've done that now for seventy-five years. I love the United Church; almost as though I'd chosen it. But I didn't. I was born into it four years after 1925. If I'd been born Presbyterian or Catholic or Muslim, I'd probably have loved those communities just as much. But the

United Church is my home. It has nourished me, put up with me, held me, and encouraged me. It has given me open gates and plough handles and laughter and, some days, glimpses of flying birds.

And people's faces, gone now, but not really gone. A Sunday school teacher teaching us to sing how Jesus "chided the billows and hushed the wind"—"Rhyme it with 'kind,'" she said—while her eyes shone on us with love. My father winding his watch during the long prayer, but in church week by week, together with other apparently sane people, bowing his heart before something greater than he. Stanley Russell, the only minister I ever had, preaching at Toronto's Deer Park Church for twenty-nine years, teaching me from the beginning, once I began to listen, that God wants minds as well as hearts so that, unlike some who grew up in narrower circles, problems about the Bible and science, or Christianity and other religions, were never problems for me.

Other faces later, in congregations of my own. A weathered man in a country church, watching weekly by the old stove as I clambered into cassock, belt, tabs, gown, hood, stole. After six months he finally commented, "Takes about as much equipment to preach these days as it does to farm!" Fragile faces down the years stunned by tragedy and somehow, through it all, sustained. A woman bright with welcome at a winter door, a table set for two behind her, and I there with the police to tell her that her husband was dead in a car accident. Hands clammy, not knowing what to say, I learned suddenly that nothing had to be said; it was enough to be there and somehow be enveloped by a presence that hurt with her hurt and that held us both with love.

And children, always children, interrupting our rehearsed solemnity, running through sanctuaries like gifts just before funerals begin. Bread broken and passed to faces old and young in congregations large and small. The farmer who grew it holding dying hands out for it that day, as though for life, then smiling as though hearing holy laughter from flying birds.

"Someone Like That" with Us

Memories tumble down the quick years. *The Observer*'s Al Forrest, his lopsided grin, unruly forelock, stubborn courage, and journalistic skill. Controversial Moderator Jim Mutchmor, "the last of the ranting Methodists" as he loved to be called—gracious, outspoken, and perfectly groomed. Senior church executive Harriet Christie on an *Observer* cover surrounded by her all-male colleagues in the national office, the first woman in a man's world. The Board of Women's Beatrice Wilson who was never fooled. Another moderator,

I Remember
by *Judy Edith Maxted Brewer*

I remember Church Union. I was eight years old. Before their marriage, my mother was Presbyterian and my father was a loyal Methodist. My father won the first decision, but later the whole family moved down the street to Mount Dennis Presbyterian.

Dr. C. A. Gowans was our minister in 1925 and our church became Chalmers United (later, Mount Dennis United). What a joy there was in our home! My parents were delighted to have a place of worship where they both had roots. Church Union became a personal experience to me.

Arthur Moore—passionate, trusted, and always remembering your name. General Secretary George Morrison, smiling and energetic, always with time to talk. Division Secretary Jack Leng, blue-blazered and approachable in Church House halls.…Someone phoned the CBC not long ago, recalling Leng as a United Church chaplain in Europe shoring up frightened boys, wrapping their dead bodies, writing their families, holding their comrades. "Wouldn't we all like to have someone like that with us when we die?" host Peter Gzowski said.

Time fails to name the faces that well up in our hearts, of people we all know who've ploughed and driven straight furrows and left the gate open for us, their lives attesting the spirit that blew through them like trumpets while they were here.

That's the strength of the United Church. Not eloquent preachers or good people (though we've had plenty of both). But a Spirit here and holding us. A loving earth-growing Spirit that has harvest in mind for the world's broken ground, creating among us meanwhile a community of hope in the midst of incompleteness, a place of singing and laughter and holy bread and celebration of white birds ahead of time though pain still stalks around.

A Church That Can Change Its Mind

I love the United Church, its potluck suppers and Christmas pageants. I love its conciliar system—at our best, we live in circles, not on ladders. In 1964 the General Council Judicial Committee retired in all its dignity to consider whether One-Board systems could legally replace Session and Stewards. The next day they returned, and solemnly announced that no, that couldn't happen.

Wide-eyed at my first General Council, I sat beside a minister whose church in Calgary already had a One-Board system. "What will you do?" I whispered.

"Nothing at all," he whispered back.

And he didn't have to. By the next General Council there were forty or fifty One-Board systems across the church. The Judicial Committee was again asked for its opinion on their legality. They announced this time that yes, One-Board systems were allowed. I learned there about the United Church, and loved what I learned.

I love the inclusivity of the United Church. On our tenth anniversary—in a statement reaffirmed in 1950 and included ever since in *The Manual*—we renewed our commitment to what we called "inclusive Christian fellowship." Ever since those three distinct traditions combined and compromised in 1925 to form one church, we've been suspicious of any person or school of thought that claims to have the only way. On our best days we gather around Jesus' table and listen for God's voice in lives and views that differ from ours.

We know not every church is like that. Some Christian communities began as split-offs from larger denominations that, they thought, didn't give sufficient importance to some point of doctrine or practice that they then made central. People in those groups don't look for too much diversity; they like everyone to think and act alike.

A Wider Gate

The United Church, like most large churches, casts a wider net. From the beginning we've encompassed in our membership an amazing variety of opinions, styles of life, and practice. We have United Church people who take the Bible quite literally and others who read it with the help of modern scholarship. We have those who might be called conservative and others who are more liberal. We have those who love liturgical responses and those who really hate them. We have those who speak in tongues and those to whom it would never in the wide world occur to do that. We have the grouchy, the open, the tired, the talkative, the hopeful, the nay-sayers—sometimes all in the same person, depending on which day you ask.

The love of God surrounds us all, we believe. It works beneath the worst we do and the best we do to make this Earth a home. What holds us together as a family is never our agreement on how to describe God doing all that. Peter and Paul differed sharply many times. Christians often disagree. The unity isn't in us; it's in God, and the steady presence of God's inclusive love. That's what holds us as we gather our family differences around a table. Passing bread, our hands touch, our eyes lock, and we listen together for the blessing of high white following birds.

And it's from that table we take decisions about what open gates Christ is beckoning us towards in our communities. Decisions, on a national level, about who is allowed to begin the rigorous and years-long path towards ministry in our church. Despite much pressure to elbow whole groups of people off that path in 1988 [the year that the United Church decided that all persons regardless of their sexual orientation were eligible to become members of the church on profession of faith in Jesus Christ, and that all members could offer themselves as candidates for the order of ministry], our *Basis of Union* reminded us that it is Jesus, not the church, who chooses

Splits in the Family
by J. Rae Grant

Our church in rural Ontario, about eighteen miles northeast of Guelph, was formerly Presbyterian. The local vote for Church Union carried, so it was thereafter known as Mimosa United Church. However, my maternal grandfather had emigrated from Scotland and was not in agreement with Church Union. So in 1925, he and my grandmother transferred their membership to the Presbyterian church in Fergus, some twelve miles distant. But to the best of my knowledge, they seldom attended there. Instead, they maintained their activity in the local congregation.

My own parents seemed in full agreement with Church Union and readily adapted to the change—although I did hear a few grumpy remarks about subsequent ministers of Methodist background who did not always conduct the affairs of the church in the way to which my good Presbyterian parents had become accustomed.

ministers; the church's task is only to recognize those whom he has chosen. In the end, we couldn't risk being more exclusive than Jesus, and so remained (not without anguish) an inclusive church.

Not to Convert But to Listen

In the same way, we sat down in the sixties to consider our attitude towards people of other faiths. In a landmark report on the *Mission of the Church*, we concluded officially, out of reverence for that Christ Spirit which has clothed the world since time's beginning (Colossians 1:16), that "God is redemptively at work in all the religious life of [hu]mankind." We became the first church anywhere to have a staff person for Interfaith Relations—whose task is not to convert but to listen to people of other faiths and help us hear news God has for us that, apart from them, we might have missed.

I love this inclusivity before the inclusive love of God.

I love the United Church for its consistent social witness, regardless of popularity or advice from church sociologists. The measure of a church, we know in our hearts (regardless of what annual statistical forms may demand) is not that the budget has been balanced or that more people attended than last year. As I read the Bible, the measure that counts emerges when we ask in our Sessions, our Presbyteries, our General Councils whether, if our churches and our church were lifted off the ground and disappeared, the streets around and the world beyond would sag noticeably for lack of love.

After seventy-five years in the United Church, the answer is, "Yes, they would." Disadvantaged children would be left uncared for, older people left unhoused. AA groups would have no place to meet. Ill people in remote areas would have no hospitals. Church partners across the broken world would be left with no well-diggers, teachers, doctors requested and required and sent from this rich land.

Long Before It Was Popular

Justice issues in God's family would be left unaddressed. Decades before it was commonplace we welcomed Russian church partners to this country—and were branded communist for that. In the 1960s Evangelism and Social Service Secretary Ray Hord was a lone North American voice naming the dirty Vietnam War for what it was. We have supported refugees, opposed military flying on Innu land in Labrador, condemned apartheid before it was fashionable to do so, challenged rich corporations to be socially responsible, and stood solidly beside mothers left to beg for bread beneath Caesar's golden domes and towers.

We haven't always been right. We've been blinded by the blindness of our culture, and for that we have apologized to our Aboriginal brothers and sisters. "In our zeal to tell you of the good news of Jesus Christ," we said, "we were blind to the value of your spirituality. We imposed our civilization as a condition for accepting the gospel." We asked for their forgiveness, set up a multimillion dollar Healing Fund to address wounds that are still left raw. Just saying "Sorry" is not enough. As current Moderator Bill Phipps says, "We repent of our role in the spiritual and cultural abuse inflicted upon First Nations over many generations." We are appalled at what happened in residential schools of which we were a part, and are trying to make whatever recompense is compassionate and just.

We get involved in these social concerns not to leave the gospel and forward some political agenda, but to run to the side of One who, the Bible teaches, loves the world, not the church, and who waits in broken places for those who use Christ's name to come.

Beyond Three Score and Ten

And now we're seventy-five years old. According to Psalm 90, "The years of our life are three score years and ten, or maybe, by reason of strength, four score." Have we lived long enough? Is it time for the United Church to do some intentional dying?

Certainly some deaths must happen for life ahead to be secured. Death to ingrownness, backward looking, duplication, and narrow thinking. Jesus said unless a seed falls into the ground and dies no new life can come (John 12:24). But we're not good at dying; we prefer keeping everything as it was. It's as though we live on the shell of an egg. When cracks appear, we lament the passing of all things familiar and exhaust ourselves trying to glue the old bits of shell together. But there's another way to look at cracks. They could be signs of new birth.

And new birth always lies forward.

In 1970 another younger minister and I travelled with then Moderator Bob McClure on a hectic three-week journey through five countries in the Middle East, meeting cabinet ministers, guerrilla fighters, aid workers, and refugees. Nobody believed this amazing man was seventy years old. We were exhausted trying to keep up to him. One hot morning in Jerusalem, ostensibly out of concern for our older companion, we suggested taking a taxi to the next appointment. "Whatsa matter, you paralyzed?" snapped Bob, striding forward into the noonday sun.

The straight furrow runs forward, this year, every year. At the end is an open gate through which the whole world, not just the church, will finally come home. In the meantime, in our beloved United Church, we plough on in Christ's beckoning name, listening, like that Saskatchewan farmer, for the echo of God's laughter from the high white following birds.

Bruce McLeod was moderator of the United Church from 1972 to 1974.

Roller Coaster History

by John Shearman

For over seventy-five years, the United Church has been in the forefront of change—internally, nationally, and internationally.

On the spur of the moment, William Patrick, principal of Manitoba College and fraternal delegate from the Presbyterian Church in Canada, made a dramatic proposal to the Methodist General Conference meeting in Winnipeg in the summer of 1902. This relative newcomer to the prairies voiced a concern much in his thoughts: "The time is opportune for a definite, practical movement concentrating attention and aiming at the practical organic union."

The idea of union was far from new. Various branches of Presbyterians had already united back in 1875. The Methodists had done the same in 1884. Now several Protestant church leaders urged working towards a wider union.

Immigrants from eastern Canada and from the British Isles and Europe had swelled the population of the prairies. The need for co-operation on the vast mission fields in the west pushed the churches to respond creatively. Limited co-operation had gone well in recent years. These impulses had a notable effect in the formation of many "union churches" on the prairies once official union negotiations got under way.

Church Union Gets Started

Principal Patrick's proposal did not fall on deaf ears. The Methodists, Presbyterians, and Congregationalists formally established church union committees. The Joint Committee on Church Union gathered in Toronto in April 1904, and quickly agreed to press ahead. Within seven years they had drafted and approved the main doctrinal consensus, organizational framework, and legal requirements according to the constitutional systems of the three churches.

Codified as *The Basis of Union*, the constitution set forth the doctrine and the polity of the proposed United Church of Canada in two sections. The first contained an amalgam of traditional Christian doctrine common to all three denominations. The Joint Committee as a whole averaged well over fifty years of age, had an individualistic, conservative viewpoint, and had no desire to write a systematic theology or a new creed for the twentieth century. In an age when theology was less emphasized than mission, the *Twenty Articles of the Doctrinal Basis of Union* contained very little original thought. In fact, it depended primarily on *A Brief Statement of the Reformed Faith* issued by the Presbyterian Church U.S.A. in 1905 and on *The Articles of the Faith of the Presbyterian Church in England* adopted in 1890.

The second section of the *Basis of Union* set forth the administrative system by which the church would be governed. It melded the three denominational systems giving particular responsibilities and authority to congregations, presbyteries, and conferences, with a national governing body, the General Council. Believing that everyone must be open to the leading of the Spirit in search of new truth, the Congregationalists resisted subscription by ministers to any statement of faith as a condition of ordination. They convinced everyone that nothing more than "essential agreement" with the *Doctrinal Basis of Union* would be required.

Opposition to Union

Despite the fact that the structure of the union was primarily Presbyterian, the Presbyterian Church mounted the strongest opposition. Denominational and Scottish identity, theological conservatism, and the appropriate procedures for making decisions appear to have been the anti-unionists' chief concerns. A majority of the 1910 General Assembly approved the *Basis of Union* and forwarded their decision to the presbyteries, sessions, and congregations. Everywhere the proposed union was accepted by a two-thirds majority.

Fierce debates led to a second vote in congregations in 1915, and in presbyteries and the General Assembly in 1916. Soon after losing all of these votes the minority formed a Presbyterian Church Association to continue their tradition. Inevitably this led to the formation of two new churches, The United Church of Canada and a smaller continuing Presbyterian Church.

When necessary legislation came before the House of Commons, Prime Minister Mackenzie King, an elder in St. Andrews Presbyterian Church close to Parliament Hill, opposed it. An ardent Methodist unionist from Québec's Eastern Townships skilfully negotiated enough votes from French Roman Catholic backbenchers to pass the bill despite their leader's opposition.

A New Church Is Born

On June 10, 1925, a congregation of ten thousand assembled in Mutual Street Arena, Toronto, to witness the solemn covenant bringing the new denomination into being.

The new church established headquarters in the Wesley Buildings at 299 Queen Street, Toronto. The United Church Publishing House consolidated the publishing enterprises of the uniting churches, and the national journals amalgamated in *The New Outlook*. A new hymn book appeared in 1930 and a new book of services in 1932.

A surplus of ministers and church buildings created some critical problems. One congregation got a court order evicting their unionist minister, his pregnant wife, and five children from the manse. The family spent the winter of 1925–26 in a chicken house lent by a compassionate farmer. Civil lawsuits or local exchanges settled some property disputes. A lawsuit about the use of the name of the Presbyterian Church in Canada lasted fourteen years before being abandoned.

The Socialist Movement Flowers in the Thirties

The privation of the Depression caused many ministers, led by J. S. Woodsworth and Stanley Knowles, to participate in the fledgling socialist movement, the Canadian Commonwealth Federation. A-cent-a-meal mite boxes appeared on many family tables to support the Missionary and Maintenance Fund. Many congregations in central Canada sent bales of clothing to prairie congregations. Continuing political and economic domination from central Canada, however, were a festering irritant, causing many recipients in western Canada to reject these acts of charity. Despite that the church's advocacy of social justice gained new momentum.

The Second World War emptied many congregations of young people and their ministers. At the height of the war, 206 ministers had enlisted as chaplains. One chaplain, Captain Uriah Laite, won the Military Cross for exceptional courage during the capture of Hong Kong and as a prisoner of war. Wilna Thomas, a diaconal minister, served as an assistant to chaplains because she could not be appointed to a full chaplaincy. In Ottawa, Jessie Clugston, wife of the minister of First United Church, gathered many young female civil servants in the manse on Sunday afternoons to give them a home away from home.

A pacifist movement had existed in the church since the First World War. On October 15, 1939, *The United Church Observer*, which earlier that year had

Act of Self-renunciation
by Alfred Alexander Radley

Although I had been greatly gratified from time to time at being appointed to the General Conference of the Methodist Church [prior to Church Union], I looked forward with ardent longing to having a place in the first great gathering of the General Council of The United Church of Canada.

The initial gathering was held in the Mutual Street Arena, the largest available building in Toronto, on the 10th day of June, 1925. So many applications had been made for tickets for this occasion that no other place was possible.

Promptly at half past ten, the orchestra and choir under the leadership of Dr. Fricker rose to sing the processional hymn, "The Church's One Foundation" as the doors in the rear of the building were thrown open and the 350 delegates led by Dr. S. D. Chown and Dr. G. C. Pidgeon marched in and took their places in the seats reserved for them in the centre of the building. The service opened with the time-honoured "Old Hundredth," liturgical prayers, the singing of the great Methodist hymn "O For a Thousand Tongues to Sing," and the reading of John 17.

After this, the leaders of the uniting churches made a declaration of the special contribution that each denomination made into the life and work of the United Church. Then Dr. Chown read the formula proclaiming the consummation of Church Union and the establishment of The United Church of Canada. The declaratory act was duly signed by the heads of the uniting bodies and the whole body of delegates.

A brief but exquisitely beautiful address by Dr. S. P. Rose was followed by the Communion Service. One thinks with amazement of the skill with which this part of the service had been organized so that, without the slightest confusion or delay and in the most orderly and reverent manner, some 12,000 people were served with the bread and wine.

The subsequent sessions of the Council…were characterized with a quiet enthusiasm and a spirit of brotherly love. One incident, however, deserves to be written in letters of gold. When the time came for the election of the first moderator of The United Church of Canada, there was an almost universal expectation that Rev. S. D. Chown, the former General Superintendent of the Methodist Church, would be chosen. As leader of the largest group entering the United Church, as one of the foremost advocates of Church Union, and as the senior in years of the heads of the uniting churches, it seemed altogether fitting that he should be honoured with this position. But before any action was taken, Dr. Chown rose to ask that no ballots be cast for his election. In a carefully prepared statement, he gave his reasons for doing so and moved that a single ballot be cast for the election of Dr. George C. Pidgeon.

The Council seemed bewildered by this unexpected action, until Dr. Pidgeon assumed the chair. Then, after making his acknowledgement of the dignity conferred upon him, he described Dr. Chown's "fine act of self-renunciation—the finest act of its kind in the history of Canadian Christianity." The Council burst into a whirlwind of applause that gave some expression to its pent-up feelings.

An excerpt from the memoirs of Alfred Alexander Radley.

replaced *The New Outlook* as the national magazine, published a manifesto from seventy-five ministers declaring their continued pacifism and recalling the General Council's 1938 statement that "war is contrary to the mind of Christ" and that "we positively reject war because war rejects love, defies the will of Christ, and denies the worth of man." The Sub-Executive of General Council immediately repudiated this manifesto.

The Post-war Boom Years

Returning from war service, veterans began making homes for their growing families in burgeoning suburbs. At the height of a decade of unprecedented church building, the United Church opened one new church, church hall, or manse every week. Fundraising became a dominant theme of congregational life. Men and women undertook leadership they had never dreamed of giving in church schools, youth groups, and adult fellowship groups. In 1959 another phase of this growth spurt saw church headquarters move from the venerable Wesley Building on Queen Street to the new nine-storey United Church House at 85 St. Clair Avenue East, Toronto.

Aware of the need for new church school resources applicable to adults and children, the church launched a curriculum research and publishing project. Hailed in Canada and abroad as the best biblically based curriculum ever produced, the *New Curriculum* succeeded in some of its goals of preparing teachers and parents for the task, especially for younger age groups. But the demanding student resources and teachers' guides for older classes did not meet with the same success. Many congregations tried them but gave them up after a few years.

In the 1960s, as the Cold War against communism became a bloody conflict in Vietnam, thousands of American draft dodgers fled to Canada. The radical fringe of society experimented with unorthodox lifestyles and attitudes towards sexuality and marriage. Television broadcast scenes of war and of rapid social change into every household.

Standing Up for Justice

For twenty-five years James R. Mutchmor, secretary of the Board of Evangelism and Social Service, had sounded warnings against the moral evils of teenage sex, excessive alcohol consumption, working mothers, and corporate monopolies. His successor, Ray Hord, encountered fierce opposition to his even more controversial comments. Hord openly welcomed the draft dodgers, comparing them to the United Empire Loyalists but with "better motives." When he called Prime Minister Lester Pearson "a puppy dog on (U.S. President) LBJ's leash," Moderator Wilfrid Lockhart sent a letter extending "sincere apologies…in the name of the United Church." Yet within five years the Canadian government had gone on record against American policies in Vietnam.

Global justice and peace initiatives became a major concern in the 1970s. The editor of *The United Church Observer*, Al Forrest, outraged the Jewish community by supporting the Palestinian cause against Israel. Many congregations became involved in sponsoring refugees from Vietnam. Inner-city and suburban congregations began to share their facilities with immigrants from Korea and the West Indies. Because not all new immigrants were Christian, modest initiatives in interfaith dialogue began. Overseas missions, no longer foreign, had long been in partnerships with indigenous churches. Missionaries [now called overseas personnel] still went out, but only where invited to meet a need for which no indigenous leadership was available.

Institutional Concerns

A new generation of lay leaders pushed for institutional restructuring. The Woman's Missionary Society and the Woman's Association amalgamated to form the United Church Women. Five divisions replaced the many boards and departments of the General Council. Conferences appointed executive secretaries, personnel and program officers, and support personnel. Challenged by radical new issues in theological and biblical studies, theological colleges struggled to educate an older student body that included many women and men seeking second careers in ministry. Co-operative arrangements among theological colleges of several mainline denominations, a reality in Montréal since 1912, became the vogue across the country when church-sponsored universities were required to become independent in order to receive government grants.

Negotiations for an organic union of the Evangelical United Brethren and The United Church of Canada came to a successful conclusion in 1968.

The Fourth Denomination
by Marguerite Miller

Church Union marked the coming together of *four* strands of Christian churches: the Methodist, the Congregational, the Presbyterian, and the Local Union Churches of western Canada.

In western Canada, many small congregations entered into local unions as early as 1912, and a General Council of Local Union Churches had been formed. The "Formation of The United Church of Canada" in the front of *The United Church Manual* says, "From 1921 representatives of this [Local Union] Council were welcomed to the yearly meetings of the Joint Union Committee."

And it goes on: "By 1924 there were various forms of Church Union, with approval of parent churches, more than 1,200 pastoral charges, including not less than 3,000 congregations or worshipping groups."

Here in Manitoba, the Macgregor United Church (just west of Portage La Prairie) came into being in 1912, thirteen years before Church Union. Similarly, the Methodist and Presbyterian churches in Lauder became Lauder United Church in 1917.

The story of the Local Union Churches in the western provinces needs to be given the place it deserves. Yet *The Manual* says, "On June 10th, the union of the three churches was solemnly consummated…" That is not true. There were *four* churches, for, as is recorded later in the same paragraph, "The Council was composed of 350 commissioners—the General Conference of the Methodist Church and the General Assembly of the Presbyterian Church each having appointed 150; the Congregational Union 40, and 10 appointed by the General Council of Local Union Churches…" And it continues, "The approximate strength at the time of Union was 8,000 congregations…"

If there were 8,000 United congregations after June 10, and if there were 3,000 Local Union congregations in 1924, that's a very strong group. It should be recognized.

However, a plan for a merger with the Anglican Church of Canada—which had dragged on for more than twenty-five years—came to an abrupt end when the Anglican House of Bishops and General Synod turned down a formal plan of union in 1975. A more recent party to the negotiations, the Disciples of Christ, also rejected the plan.

Trends Take Other Directions

On the local front the signs of change proved less than optimistic. Membership peaked in 1965 at 1,064,033 and then slowly declined. Subscriptions to *The United Church Observer* fell from 330,000 in the late 1960s to 104,000 in 1998. Baptisms, Sunday school attendance, and confirmation of new members fell as the birth rate declined. Inner-city churches closed as population shifted. Some urban congregations built residences for seniors where their sanctuaries had stood. New congregations in the still growing suburbs undertook similar projects to help pay off burdensome mortgages.

Other evidence of a different witness reinforced these signs of change. The United Church had ordained women since 1936, but never before in the numbers who now came forward to be trained and called to pastorates. Long-excluded Native peoples raised voices of protest, particularly in western Canada where large numbers had attended church residential schools funded by government-sponsored assimilation programs.

At one time the United Church had proclaimed the gospel in Canada in at least seventeen different languages. Now it revealed its increasing diversity in its choice of moderators. For some forty years, all the moderators were White, male, ordained clergy. Then in 1968, the General Council elected Robert McClure, a missionary doctor, as the first lay moderator. In 1974 Wilbur Howard, a Black minister, became moderator. In 1980 Lois Wilson became the first woman minister to hold the same office. Since then Sang Chul Lee, a Korean immigrant; Stan McKay, a Native Indian; and two laywomen, Anne Squire and Marion Best, have also been elected to lead the church.

Plunging into Controversy

Responding to social change, the church engaged in a decade-long study of sexuality during which three different reports were produced. Although the first two reports of 1978 and 1984 gave the issue of homosexuality only minor emphasis, strident conflict erupted immediately. When an openly lesbian woman, Susan Mabey, sought ordination, Hamilton Conference banned the ordination of self-declared homosexuals. In 1992, Tim Stevenson of British Columbia became the first openly gay candidate for ordination. Finally in 1988, the Thirty-second General Council had decided that all persons regardless of their sexual orientation were eligible to become members of the church on profession of faith in Jesus Christ, and that all members could offer themselves as candidates for the order of ministry. Candidacy, however, did not guarantee ordination or commissioning as diaconal ministers. After this decision, a few people already in the order of ministry declared their homosexual orientation publicly.

The fallout was substantial nevertheless. Some congregations suffered a significant loss of members who were convinced that homosexual practices were immoral and contrary to scripture. A number of ministers resigned. A few congregations left the church. To their surprise they had to leave without their property. A loyal opposition remained dedicated to reversing the 1988 decision and returning the church to a strict interpretation of scripture and the doctrines of the *Basis of Union*. Through all this distress, disciplinary procedures increased significantly against clergy who disrupted pastoral relationships.

Tough Times

Opinion polls and statistical data record declining church membership and participation in all denominations over the past several decades. As we prepare to celebrate our seventy-fifth anniversary, church membership has dropped to the level it was in 1942—about 720,000. Once more there is a surplus of ordained and diaconal ministers. Many congregations struggle with a sense of instability and anxiety about further decline. Scarce financial resources have forced severe staff reductions in the General Council and conference offices. Theological debate has a new intensity as the public media publicize challenges to traditional biblical interpretations and dogmas. The United Church of Canada has become embroiled with other denominations and the federal government in lawsuits over terrible abuse of Native children in the former residential schools.

For some time prophetic voices have been saying that The United Church of Canada will enter the twenty-first century smaller, poorer, but more vibrant. Some historians hail the general marginalization of the churches as the end of ecclesiastical power that has grown unchecked since the time of the Roman emperor Constantine in the fourth century.

It remains to be seen whether all or only part of these prophecies will come true. In the past, the Christian church generally has thrived when its faith has been most severely tested. These are again such times.

John Shearman is a church historian and a retired minister of the United Church who lives in Mississauga, Ontario.

The View from Outside

Expressions of
appreciation from
others

Your Adopted Son

by John Shelby Spong

"No community of faith has been more welcoming and receptive to me in my own theological and justice struggles than The United Church of Canada."

It is a pleasure to write a personal salute to The United Church of Canada on the occasion of its seventy-fifth anniversary. This faith community has been so powerfully important to me and such a force in the national life of Canada, that one could hardly be silent on such an occasion. The United Church of Canada has been a faith community marked with courage, vision, and a willingness to risk. Those are nothing less than the marks of life for which the whole Christian world should give thanks.

The United Church actually began its existence in the heartland of Canada, when Presbyterians and Methodists in small rural communities began to wonder why they were competing with each other. It seemed to make little sense, given their common commitment to one Lord, one faith, and one baptism. Someone is quoted as saying, "They forgot at headquarters to tell us we were supposed to hate each other." Whether that statement is historically accurate or not is almost beside the point. It expresses the experience of people who seemed to sense that there must be a distinction between that which is essential and that which is peripheral in one's faith tradition. Perhaps this action of separating the essential from the peripheral was the factor that built openness and sensitivity into the very fabric of The United Church of Canada, for those are qualities visibly present in this church of this very day.

This church recognized the equality of women long before any other faith community was ready even to discuss the issue. The United Church of Canada did it in a way that seemed always to characterize its life. This Church declared that there was no barrier to the ordination of women ministers as pastors, fully a decade before any woman even applied to test the process! When one compares this with the tortuous internal battles and continuous tension that have marked so many other parts of the Body of Christ as they wrestled with their own patriarchal prejudices, one catches a glimpse of the United Church's character and integrity.

When the issue of homosexuality emerged to challenge our ancient prejudices, The United Church of Canada once again acted with courage and resoluteness. Declaring that sexual orientation was not, in and of itself, a barrier to ordination, this Church became the first mainline Christian body to forge a new vision. It was not easy, and the negative reaction of its conservative elements was powerful. The United Church of Canada stood firm, absorbed its losses, kept its integrity, and issued bumper stickers that read, "Proud to be United." That battle is now all but over in the United

Church, while the more timid churches of the world that have tried to compromise on this issue are still torn up internally by the debate.

No community of faith has been more welcoming and receptive to me in my own theological and justice struggles as a Christian bishop than The United Church of Canada. I am pleased to be your adopted son, and I am pleased to bear witness to the fact that you have inspired me, strengthened me, and called me into new frontiers again and again. I am much in your debt.

Much Will Not Survive

As we survey the future of the Christian church, we discover sometimes to our fear and displeasure that much of the framework of classical Christianity is not going to survive. That it not because it is wrong, but because the earthen vessel in which it has been carried is breaking apart. We will have to learn anew the distinction between the *experience* of God and the *explanation* of the experience of God. The experience of God is timeless and eternal, but the explanation of the experience is always cast in the words, concepts, and world view of the person doing the explaining. That means that the explanation is always bound to its own time. In the words of the old hymn, "Time makes ancient good uncouth."

God was in Christ—that is the eternal experience that lies at the heart of the Christian enterprise. But how God entered the Christ—in the story of the virgin birth, for example—is a time-warped and today inconceivable human explanation of that original reality. The discovery in 1724 that every woman contributes an egg cell with a full genetic content to every newborn person removed forever the notion prevalent in the ancient world that to prove divine origin, one had only to remove the male from the reproductive act and substitute a divine agent. In that era, people thought the whole life of the newborn person was the gift of the male. They did not know that the woman contributed half of the genetic makeup. So virgin birth stories died, literally, and can no longer serve as an adequate explanation of how God was experienced as present in Christ.

The ancient world also had to explain how the God met in Christ had been able to return to the divine abode beyond the sky when the redemptive work was complete. The story of the cosmic ascension of Jesus accomplished this purpose inside the frame of reference of that particular time. But after Copernicus and Galileo shattered the three-tiered world view of antiquity, the story of the cosmic ascension became nonsensical to modern ears. It was an explanation that was not able to abide the knowledge revolution that marked the passage of time.

A Profound Witness
by Maitland Evans

I have come to know and value The United Church of Canada as one that appreciates, affirms, and strives to maintain "principled partnerships." In the south, we encounter daily the dispiriting ravages of counterfeit partnerships, drained of character and maintained as hypocritical form. Genuine partnership is as difficult for the people of the north as for the people of the south. Yet its *koinonial* potency empowers us to rise above instincts of self-preservation, that make an idol out of individualism, and that encourage us to live as adversaries and competitors. *Koinonia* calls us to share without boundaries and to love without conditions. That is indeed radical.

You have had no choice but to learn from each other, to learn with each other, and to learn from your mistakes. As a consequence, you have been able to open windows to a continuing healing ministry. I have experienced on many occasions your humility, your openness, and your willingness to be vulnerable. When vulnerability is rooted in Christian principles and beliefs, prayer and care become resources always at hand. Your history has bequeathed to you an experience that provides real keys to healing and wholeness.

My prayer is that The United Church of Canada will own and keep alive this liberating legacy and history.

The Rev. Maitland Evans is General Secretary of the UCC partner, The United Church in Jamaica and Cayman Islands.

The Theological Revolution That Is upon Us

I could illustrate this theme with many narratives. I use these, however, just to point to the necessity of keeping a faith community open to changing concepts, new ways of thinking, and different theological content. The United Church of Canada seems uniquely prepared not just to allow, but to encourage, the theological revolution that is upon us. For this reason, this church stands ready to assist Christians in the necessary transition from the theological formulas of yesterday, which are passing away, to the theological formulas of tomorrow, which are just being born. That is a major achievement for which members of the United Church ought to feel genuine pride.

In a world where the Vatican announces that every controversial subject before the church today is not to be debated; where the Southern Baptists declare in convention that for the Bible to be obeyed, women must be subject to men; and where Anglican bishops at Lambeth interpreted the scriptures to condemn and prohibit homosexuality, I rejoice that there is one body of Christians, The United Church of Canada, willing to live into the storms of modernity, to feel the tensions of conflict, and to acknowledge that they are led by the Holy Spirit who promised to guide them into all truth. That truth, this church does not arrogantly claim that it already possesses in some infallible and inerrant form—which in and of itself constitutes a refreshing reality in ecclesiastical circles.

All Christians need to note this witness and to salute these achievements. That is why sending congratulations to The United Church of Canada on the occasion of its seventy-fifth anniversary is such a distinct pleasure.

The Rt. Rev. John Shelby Spong is Bishop of Newark, the Episcopal Church in the USA, and author of numerous books including Why Christianity Must Change or Die.

Among Friends

by Remi J. De Roo

A Roman Catholic bishop looks back at a life of rich ecumenical partnerships with The United Church of Canada.

The congregation of St. Aidan's United Church in Victoria celebrated their 125th anniversary on November 15, 1998 and invited me to be guest preacher.

Even after thirty-six years, I still experience apprehension when I face a new challenge. It came as a great relief, therefore, when the host couple greeting people at the door recognized me. Ibbs Avery, now retired, had been the United Church minister at Ahousat, on the west coast of Vancouver Island. He and Min had made their home on a hill overlooking the Ahousat harbour. Min asked if I remembered visiting their home there.

Their friend, Rev. Bill Howie, used to dock his boat below their home. Bill Howie and I had walked up from the dock, looking for a cup of coffee and a shower after one of our forays up and down the coast.

Memories of Co-operation

A flood of memories came back. Bill Howie served for fourteen years (1982–1996) as a United Church Conference officer for British Columbia. He and I became fast friends. On more than one occasion I sailed with him in the seventy-foot mission boat, the *Melvin Swartout*, named after a minister who drowned in 1904 while ministering to the people at Ucluelet, on the west coast of Vancouver Island.

Ibbs introduced me to St. Aidan's two ministers, Paul Taylor and Karen Dickey. We joined the assembled community for a half hour of hymn singing and prayer before the formal service. To my delight, many of their favourite pieces were already familiar to me.

As we moved to the back of the church to join the choir for the opening procession, a surprise awaited me. There sat Bill Howie and his wife June, all smiles. After a quick greeting, I scanned the rest of the congregation, glimpsing several more familiar faces. Suddenly, I had no more worries about what I would say. I realized that I was among friends.

The ceremony was truly a moving experience. Paul introduced me by a vivid recalling of the Roman Catholic Second Vatican Council held in Rome from 1962 to 1965. He noted that I had personally participated in this historic event. He indicated how some of its teachings continue to influence members of the United Church.

My sermon focused on the theme selected for St. Aidan's anniversary: "New Heavens and New Earth." The selected readings were from Isaiah 12 and 65—plenty of material to link with the role of the Holy Spirit over the 125 years of the congregation's history.

Symbols of Improved Relations

As I reflect back on these matters, my mind and heart focus particularly on my years of association with June and Bill Howie. They have become dear friends—one example of how relations between members of different Christian churches have improved over the years.

During my early years I had no meaningful contact with other churches. Had I been asked to describe the United Church when I was first a student in theology, I might have hesitated to say more than that the United Church was not very demanding doctrinally. As a young priest, most of my experiences with other Christian denominations were over controversial issues, where I found myself on the other side of a wall of misunderstanding.

All of that changed for the better after the Second Vatican Council. Christians learned to appreciate better how much we have in common, instead of focusing on our differences. Other churches were now recognized as agents of salvation for their members and as partners in a global struggle to transform the world according to the divine plan revealed to us by Jesus.

Spiritual bridge-building, collaboration with a variety of agencies— religious, cultural, social, academic, political, economic—practically every dimension of human experience is being affected by the partnerships Christian churches are sharing. Under varying circumstances, believers around the globe are developing compassionate and supportive relationships. A new sense of unity and solidarity is emerging on our frail planet. Will it grow strong enough to save us from further humanly caused catastrophes like war, famine, and nuclear devastation?

Today, I perceive the United Church as a major partner in this ecumenical era. We share a period in history when all religious forces need to coalesce and to work together to overcome some of the massive threats that endanger the future of this planet. In many issues of social concern I have found members of the United Church struggling side by side with Catholics in local groups and national coalitions. This is a time of *kairos*, a graced moment when the Good News of our salvation by Jesus Christ, and of our ongoing call to transform the world through the power of the Holy Spirit, the Spirit of the Risen Lord, needs to be clearly heard by a world desperately searching for meaning. Never before has the need for a common profession of faith and for joint action to facilitate the coming of the reign of God been more obvious.

Taking the Risk of Joint Ventures

Two illustrations come to mind. In both, I believe my pastoral work with Bill Howie illustrates what this spiritual partnership means in the nitty-gritty of daily existence.

Bill and I first met in 1982, at ecumenical chaplaincy meetings at the University of Victoria involving leaders of the Anglican, Roman Catholic, and United churches. Bill Howie and I helped to shape the terms of reference and the mission statement for an interfaith chaplaincy. Gradually, ministers from other world faiths joined the initial group until today eight world faiths are represented. They minister to all who desire their services, regardless of religious affiliation. A splendid spirit of solidarity and collaboration prevails. Proselytizing is carefully avoided. The chaplaincy has already proven itself and is increasingly recognized as an international leader in its field.

To guarantee the survival of this demanding spiritual work, Bill and I worked closely to establish a broad support group known today as the "Friends of the Chaplaincy."

The second example was similar. Bill and I collaborated in the establishment on the campus of the University of Victoria of an institute for interdisciplinary academic research and dialogue between the sciences and world religions. Now known as the Centre for Studies in Religion and Society, (CSRS) it enriches the university and the community at large. It is gaining international status as well, serving as a model for dialogue between science and religion. A major book could be written about this endeavour.

Drawing Together Science and Religion

Bill and I had many conversations during which we shared our insights into this new pastoral sphere. It is one of the most important challenges that organized religion faces today. Our impact on the rising generations will be greatly conditioned by it. We cannot afford the costly mutual ignorance and even animosity that has prevailed until now.

Religion without science can deteriorate into superstition. Science without religion is prone to ideology. Religion and science need one another as partners in the search for the fullness of truth. Faith and reason are like the two wings of a bird, equally essential to raise it to lofty heights and to maintain its flight.

The CSRS is now well established. The full-time director Dr. Harold Coward continues to make an outstanding contribution to a better understanding between the various disciplines. Seminars have been held on topics of interest to the city and the university. Renowned international scholars give lectures dealing with the broad topic of spirituality as it affects matters of science and religious concerns.

As before, Bill and I started "Friends of the Centre," and are currently its co-chairs. Since he retired before me, he has borne most of the burden, a fraternal service I hope to share when my own term of office comes to a close.

Learning from Each Other

We have also worked together on political issues. Our Anglican bishop partner, Ronald Shepherd, joined us for informal discussions with the then Premier of British Columbia, Bill Vander Zalm. We worked smoothly together on a fuller understanding of the status and concerns of Native peoples, the appointment of chaplains in hospitals, subsidies for housing for the disadvantaged....In these areas, we felt we attained some limited objectives. Several other issues produced less apparent results from a political perspective, but we developed a constantly increasing respect for one another and appreciation for the benefits of ecumenical partnership and strengthening bonds of friendship.

The Catholic Diocese of Victoria celebrated an extended Synod at intervals from 1986 to 1991. That Synod, built as it were from the grassroots up, developed its own agenda on the basis of the lived experience of the people of God. It formulated eight new directions for the future. The United Church experience of local community involvement provided valuable reference points. Again, Bill and I had ongoing conversations about these developments as they occurred. Having another Christian church leader with whom to share such experiences was a gratifying ecumenical experience.

Pastoral work need not always be heavy duty. We have gone sailing together on several occasions, sometimes accompanied by the incumbent Anglican bishop. Our current companion is Bishop Barry Jenks.

Communion with Nature and with Friends

The most memorable example of this companionship was a trip along the west coast of Vancouver Island in June 1989. On the return run from Friendly Cove, we sailed around Estevan Point into Hot Springs Cove. Night had fallen. The stars shone brilliantly. June was on deck watching for logs, the dreaded "deadheads" that have spelled doom for many an unheeding craft. Bill manoeuvred deftly between the small islands and the sharp reefs that slipped by silently in the deepening darkness. I was in the forward cabin preparing my next speech, to be delivered in a few days "somewhere down East," as Bill put it. But I came up in time to watch the luminous, phosphorescent-like forms of large fish swimming alongside. It was truly awesome to find myself so close to living nature, floating on the dark bosom of the ocean, feeling the silent power of the eternal waves, in communion with good friends.

I could formulate a long list of United Church members whose friendship I value. It would start with names like Lois Wilson and Bob Smith, both former moderators. But perhaps recounting these few treasured experiences will provide some idea of how my relationship to the United Church has enriched my pastoral and personal life. My hope and my prayer is that more people will continue to benefit in many ways from the deepening understanding of our unity in the faith of Sarah and Abraham, revealed in its fullness by Jesus. God grant that we may more effectively promote the spiritual growth made possible by the ecumenical renewal, a special grace of our times.

When Remi De Roo retired in 1999 as bishop of the Roman Catholic Diocese of Victoria, British Columbia, he was the last Canadian bishop to have participated in Vatican II.

The United Church and Jews

by Dow Marmur

Dialogue has improved greatly over the years. Genuine understanding of the other's viewpoint may not have—yet.

Holy Blossom Temple, at the west end of what once was Forest Hill Village and is now part of the City of Toronto, is a kind of counterpart to Timothy Eaton Memorial Church on the southern edge of the area. Though the former is a Reform synagogue and the latter a United church, they have a similar sociology. Both congregations are largely made up of middle-class professional and business people who live in similar homes and have similar incomes. Most espouse the same mixture of values and politics. The worshippers in both places include members of the Toronto "establishment." Even the architecture of the two buildings is similar.

The church and the synagogue have developed close ties over the years. When I came to serve the Temple in 1983, I found an established annual exchange of pulpits. Members of the two congregations had travelled to Israel together. There were ties of friendship between the ministers and the rabbis.

Reconciling the Hostilities

This was particularly salutary in view of the uneasy relationship existing between The United Church of Canada and the Canadian Jewish community around the issue of Israel. Not many years earlier, editorials in *The United Church Observer* had been perceived by members of my congregation to be not just sharp attacks on the policies of the government of Israel but tirades against the Jewish state as such. Since, whatever the intention, attacks on Israel are seen by Jews as attacks on the Jewish people, Jews found in these editorials echoes of traditional Christian anti-Semitism, now in the name of justice and in the guise of defending hapless Palestinians.

The spirit of neighbourly co-operation between the congregations was a way of saying that Christian–Jewish relations were desirable despite the tensions, and that the views of an editor did not necessarily reflect the opinions of all readers. If Israel was an issue, specific projects, including joint visits to Israel, could bring the two congregations closer to each other.

I benefited greatly from this spirit. Among all my new professional colleagues, rabbis included, none was more helpful to me when I first arrived than the then senior minister at Timothy Eaton, Stanford Lucyk. He taught me how to be a team leader. He showed me how to combine the written and the spoken word so that those who could not attend services would nevertheless know what I had to say from the pulpit. He helped me to understand the ways of the Toronto bourgeoisie. We have remained close friends.

Travelling to Israel together cemented our friendship. In 1986 Stan Lucyk asked me to be the "Jewish resource person" for a group of members of his church he was taking to Israel. It was a marvellous experience. The piece I wrote upon my return for my Temple bulletin was reprinted in the magazine of his church. I have travelled to Israel with Stan Lucyk on two other, equally memorable occasions, the last in a mixed group of Christians and Jews.

Joint Pilgrimage in Jerusalem

Israel brought me also close to Lois Wilson, former moderator of The United Church of Canada and now a senator. We attended an interfaith conference in Jerusalem. With two other participants from Canada, we spent a day walking in the holy city. It was a true pilgrimage. Theological and political differences dissolved, at least temporarily, through the shared experience.

I had first met Lois Wilson in 1984 when the Pope came to Canada. CBC-TV had asked her, the distinguished Roman Catholic writer Dr. Mary Jo Leddy, and me to comment on the interfaith service the Pope was to address at St. Paul's Anglican Church in Toronto. He began his homily with "Dear brothers and sisters in Christ." The three of us had a lot to say about the hurtful confusion between interfaith relations and Christian ecumenism, and about the Pope's apparent insensitivity to Jews and Judaism, good intentions notwithstanding.

Liberal Christians and this liberal Jew understood each other and could challenge viewers to examine institutional divisions and perennial misunderstandings. We have remained friends and I was greatly honoured to be invited, some time later, to participate with Lois Wilson in the service when her husband Roy was installed as minister of another neighbouring church.

The Point of Getting Together

Liberal Jews and liberal Christians are at their best, not when they argue about politics or discuss theology, but when they share their religious insights and manifest their commitment to the teachings of their respective traditions by working together on specific projects. I was delighted when Bruce McLeod, another former moderator, invited me to co-chair with him the campaign against the re-introduction of capital punishment when the issue re-emerged in Canada a decade or so ago. We were part of a team of women and men committed to the service of God, each within his or her tradition all working closely together to preserve God's greatest gift—life.

Christians and Jews bring out the best in each other in such settings. In addition to the intrinsic merits of the project in hand, interfaith co-operation ultimately also influences the theology of the partners. Many of our theoretical divisions, today no less than in former times, are the results of ignorance and suspicion. Working together builds trust and prompts us to reconsider old prejudices. The result is often new thinking. Recognizing the other strengthens my own faith.

From Stilted Exchanges to Genuine Encounters

This is very much in evidence in *Bearing Faithful Witness*, the document about Christian-Jewish relations currently under discussion in the United Church. Indirectly, the document enabled me to get to know and admire one of its authors—the current moderator, Bill Phipps. *Bearing Faithful Witness* testifies to a deep understanding of Judaism. In its genuine attempt to address Jewish concerns and to elucidate Christian positions, the document has been rightly hailed as the most forward-looking and far-reaching statement by any Christian denomination in Canada.

Its wording is far removed from the Toronto of the early decades of this century when the "cathedral" liberal synagogue—Holy Blossom—had to seek acceptance, and perhaps even to imitate, the local "cathedral" liberal church, Timothy Eaton. The last five decades have turned the two institutions into true and equal neighbours, even though, in the process, special events such as the annual exchange of pulpits have disappeared. Symbolic acts no longer seem necessary.

The formal, at times slightly stilted, exchanges of former years have given way to direct encounters, usually for study and often under the auspices of Christian-Jewish Dialogue of Toronto. These are no longer conducted with one church only but with many churches of various denominations. In place of self-conscious, polite discussions about largely innocuous subjects, study sessions nowadays seek to address serious issues of pressing mutual concern. Instead of merely acknowledging each other, we are learning from each other and finding out what separates us and what unites us.

The Sticking Point Remains

But in spite of this progress, the radically different perceptions of the State of Israel by Jews and Christians remain a sticking point. In this respect, perhaps not enough has changed since the days of those editorials in *The Observer*. It has been said that Christians tend to view Israel through the prism of their theology of salvation, while Jews see it in the context of their quest for survival. The former will judge the Jewish state according to abstract theological principles, coupled with a genuine concern for the underdog; the latter experience modern Israel as the most potent tool for Jewish survival and the best guarantor that the Holocaust will not happen again.

As long as Jews are a small minority in any country in the world, their existence will be precarious, not only because of the risk of persecution but also because of the danger of assimilation. In Israel, on the other hand, Jews have learnt to defend themselves against attacks from without and to build institutions that counteract erosion from within.

They feel so strongly about Israel that they are tempted to suspect that Christians who find it difficult to accept Jewish sovereignty, however liberal and broad-minded on other issues, have not yet overcome the old prejudice that the destruction of Jerusalem in 70 CE should have put an end to Jewish aspirations once and for all, thus vindicating the "new" covenant/testament as a replacement for the "old." In other words, condemnation of Israel, as distinct from a critique of specific policies by its government, is in many Jewish eyes a manifestation of the doctrine of Christian supersessionism, which proclaims the church triumphant. Despite the best intentions, this makes genuine dialogue virtually impossible.

From a Jewish perspective, for all its vision, courage, and determination to remove offensive terminology, *Bearing Faithful Witness* has not adequately addressed this issue. Though supersessionism is abandoned and the kind of co-operation that initially brought me together with Stan Lucyk endorsed, there is little in the document of real understanding of what Israel means to the Jewish people today. Many members of the United Church still seem to find it difficult to fathom why Israel is so central to the very existence of Judaism. They fail to relate to the Christian theologian Walter Brueggemann's seminal distinction between "space" and "place." They do not seem to accept that, after the tragedy that befell the Jews of Europe during the Second World War, Jews could only emerge from the powerlessness that nearly destroyed them by having the option to come home to the land of Israel. They had to return to their own place.

Of course, Jews will continue to work together with members of the United Church on social issues. For me personally, some of my most satisfying interfaith encounters in recent years have taken place under the auspices of the Ontario Interfaith Social Action Reform Coalition (ISARC) where I have the privilege to interact with representatives of all Christian denominations. The United Church of Canada is one of the driving forces in the organization.

But the question of Israel cannot be indefinitely swept under the carpet for the sake of interfaith civility. As long as responsible Christians are tempted to view Jews in Israel as aggressors, true understanding between our faiths will not be possible. Existing contacts, however warm on a personal level, are bound to be shallow and ephemeral if the struggle for Jewish survival and continuity is ignored.

Recognizing Each Other's Tender Places

Because so much has been achieved in recent decades between The United Church of Canada and the Jewish community, the issue of Jewish sovereignty and statehood must also be addressed. Jews must learn to accept Christian criticism of specific policies and attitudes of the government of Israel by being less defensive. Christians must learn to appreciate the true significance of the State of Israel for contemporary Judaism. Together they must recognize the pain of the victims of the conflict and seek to alleviate it. The prospect of peace in the Middle East and the stability that we pray it will ensure should enable us to meet both demands and make it possible for us to walk together on holy ground.

In that hope, and in deep appreciation of what has already been achieved, it is a rare privilege for this Jew to pay tribute to past and present members and leaders of The United Church of Canada on its important anniversary and to pray for its continued strength to be a witness to the presence of God among us.

Dow Marmur is the senior rabbi at Holy Blossom Temple in Toronto.

Reaching Out

Mission changes; so does the way we fund it and the risks we're willing to take

Where Have All the Missionaries Gone?

by Rebekah Chevalier

In 1927 the United Church had 602 missionaries serving overseas. In 1998, it had thirty-five. Here's why things are different today.

I don't remember much about India. After all, I was just four when my missionary parents returned to Canada. My memories are few and dramatic—the time I fell in our well, the time my brother and I were chased by an angry mother baboon. But in a fundamental way, my time in India and the upbringing of my parents, Al and Pearl Connor, shaped the way I look at the world and the person I have become.

Missionaries and mission. In many peoples' minds, the two are inextricably connected. But that connection has changed dramatically over the thirty years since my parents left India and, indeed, in the seventy-five-year life of the United Church.

One of the most quantifiable changes involves numbers. According to the *Year Book*, in 1927 there were 602 United Church missionaries serving under the Board of Foreign Missions and the Woman's Missionary Society. In 1964 a total of 261 missionaries were serving worldwide under the Board of World Missions, as the amalgamated mission agency was then called. By 1998, there were thirty-five United Church overseas personnel, as they are now called. Beyond the numbers are fundamental shifts in understanding about the very concept of mission, and the role of mission personnel.

Lifetime Commitments

The modern missionary movement dates back to the eighteenth century, and had its zenith at the turn of the twentieth century. The pioneers of this movement took the gospel to people who had never heard it. In the early 1900s many Canadians, like Arthur and Lily Hockin, were inspired by American evangelist John R. Mott, whose rallying cry was "the evangelization of the world in this generation." When the United Church was born in 1925, most of its missionaries were evangelists and church planters.

Authors Mary Rose Donnelly and Heather Dau described the way things used to be in *Katharine*, the biography of Katharine Hockin*:

> When preparing for the Orient, all missionaries had to anticipate their needs for seven years, the length of their assignment. Young couples…who expected to start a family in that time, had to calculate the likely number of babies, multiply that by average yards of diaper cotton, bottles broken, and all the clothes a child might wear and wear

out…Since this was a lifetime career choice for most, some
even took tuxedos and long gowns for the weddings of their
yet unborn children.

Gradually this role changed as the church overseas grew. What had been
small Christian communities grew and became national churches that
developed their own national leadership. As authority and leadership shifted to
local churches, another role began to emerge for the missionary. The early
Christian missions had established a vital network of hospitals and schools,
and these institutions needed large numbers of technical and professional
personnel. The functions of missionaries shifted to specialists and
development workers. My father, an agriculturalist working with poor farmers
in India, was one of these missionaries.

Donna Sinclair described the role of another missionary, Frances
Walbridge, in her book *Crossing Worlds*, the story of the Woman's Missionary
Society†:

> Frances Walbridge was in Angola [during the 1940s and
> 1950s] teaching literacy.…In a letter to friends in Canada,
> Walbridge explains the system. "The girls begin with an
> illustrated Laubach primer, progress to fifteen easy-to-read
> stories about Jesus, and then read Mark in a special big-
> print edition just published by the Bible Society. Emi
> Hama, an African teacher, and I are writing stories for the
> girls with a 400-word vocabulary.…"

Gradually countries began to train their own doctors, teachers, and
agricultural workers. The United Church's understanding of mission was
changing and so was its understanding of the role of the people we send
overseas.

Responding to Requests

Patti Talbot is the United Church's global mission personnel secretary. She
describes mission personnel serving overseas today as seconded workers. "We
send overseas personnel to respond to the request of an overseas partner," says
Talbot. A seconded worker works collegially, she explains, not with special
status. "[In the past] there was a different understanding of missionary—they
came from a place that had lots of resources to places that had few resources,
and resources were defined in terms of finances. Missionaries were often a
kind of a channel of more resources. Today our overseas personnel don't go
with the proverbial loaf of bread and basket of money under their arm."

But the role of seconded worker has its own challenges. Garth Legge and his wife Joyce were United Church missionaries in Zambia from 1959 until 1964, a time when the country was struggling for independence and coming apart on racial issues. "It was drummed into us that once we got overseas we were to be obedient to the church to which we were sent, not to the United Church in Toronto," recalls Legge.

One of the Zambian presbyteries needed a moderator. Legge recommended a full-time position and said this person needed to be Black. His recommendation was accepted, but he was told there was no potential Black candidate and was asked to fill the position himself. "I was in a dilemma!" Legge recalls. He agreed, with the condition that an African deputy moderator would work with him and eventually take over the role.

The Dual Mandate

Legge later served as General Secretary of the Division of World Outreach, as the Board of World Mission became. In 1977, he was instrumental in creating the document *Mission with Justice: The Dual Mandate of World Outreach*. This dual mandate—"doing mission" and "doing justice"—captured a shift in understanding in mission. "To be faithful to mission you had to be involved in justice issues," says Legge. Justice worker became another role for overseas personnel. The dual mandate led the church to take human rights stands on issues such as apartheid in South Africa.

In the late 1980s, two documents were developed that undergird the substance and style of the United Church's global relationships today. The first, known as the El Escorial guidelines after the city in Spain where a world consultation was held in 1986, were internationally developed guidelines on resource sharing. They include a commitment to shared decision making with global partners, promoting mutual accountability in the use of resources, recognizing the resources those without money can share with us, and standing in solidarity with those who suffer from unjust systems.

The second document, *Seeking to Understand "Partnership" for God's Mission Today*, articulated partnership as a fundamental way of understanding mission. "[Our] partnership is...a partnership with them in God's mission," says the 1988 document. "We and our partners are called to work together in God's mission." The partnership document posed an interesting question: "If we have some role in God's mission with our partners overseas, then is it not a natural corollary that they must have some role in partnership with us in God's mission in this country?"

In 1972, the Rev. Elijah Lumbama became the embodiment of that corollary—the first missionary sent from an overseas partner to the United Church. Elijah and his wife Elizabeth came from the United Church of Zambia to Hamilton, Ontario. Since then, nine others have come to Canada to serve for up to three years as Mutuality in Mission partners.

Short-term Exchanges

In addition, overseas partners enrich the life of the United Church in other, shorter-term programs: the Partner in Residence program, where they come to theological colleges; the Face to Face program, where they spend time with a congregation for one or two weeks; the Internship program for theological students; and, most recently, the Twinning program, which pairs United Church congregations or groups with an overseas partner. This emphasis on receiving as well as sending people is an important shift, says Talbot.

Another shift is the way we refer to the people we send overseas. A 1989 Division of World Outreach motion changed the term used from "missionary" to "overseas personnel." For overseas partners in some parts of the world, such as Africa, the term "missionary" had become too loaded with connotations of power and authority to be useful any longer.

Other changes relate to the number and role of Canadians the church sends overseas:

Requests from partners are more focused. Instead of requests for ministers or doctors, partners may need a human rights worker or someone experienced in electronic communication.

People are going overseas for shorter periods of time. These days, a three-year term with openness to a second term, when language study is involved, is considered long.

It's harder to find people willing to go overseas. One reason for that is Canadians' fear about their future security. This reality has led to another:

More and more overseas personnel are retired people. They bring a great deal of experience, says Talbot, but normally they aren't prepared to spend a year in language study and then three years of service after that. Requests from overseas partners looking for longer-term staff are hard to fill.

Sharing Our Wealth

All of these factors mean fewer United Church people are going overseas. "In 1925, sending of Canadians to work abroad was by far the dominant part of being in global relationship. That's no longer true," says Rhea Whitehead, Division of World Outreach General Secretary. "The exchange of personnel is still very important, but it's only one aspect."

Other aspects include sending money instead of people. "Particularly in Africa, what our partners told us during the 1970s and 1980s was that their needs were to develop and train people within their own structures," notes Talbot. This led to a system of grants, still in place today, where the division sends financial support that overseas churches use according to their priorities.

Does all this mean there will come a time when the United Church will stop sending overseas personnel? No, say both Talbot and Whitehead. "Overseas personnel continue to be central to our living out of partnership and the reduction in numbers is not meant to be a diminishment to zero," Talbot states.

Allen and Betty Darby can testify to the continuing need to send United Church personnel overseas. The Darbys served, from 1971 to 1984 and again from 1994 to 1998, in community development, Christian development, and pastoral work with the Methodist Church of Haiti. In many countries where the United Church has partners, the community development work instituted by Christian missions in education, health care, and agriculture has been taken over by government. Not in devastatingly impoverished Haiti, where the government provides only 20 percent of these services. The other 80 percent comes privately, through churches or individuals.

The desperate situation in Haiti has prompted a crippling loss of qualified leadership in all professions, including ordered ministry, as people leave to work in other countries. During their second stint, the Darbys went to Haiti expecting to work as part of a team. "We became the team," recalls Allen. "There just weren't enough people." For many Haitians, the Darbys became an embodiment of solidarity amid difficult times. "I feel in Haiti that one of the biggest roles we played is the role of being present," Betty says.

"The role of overseas personnel varies," says Allen. "There are times when we're partners. There are times we're companions."

And there are times when it's difficult being in partnership. The Darbys were uncomfortable with some of the things they saw in the Haitian church, including sexism and a hierarchical system that allowed people to exert power over others. Allen says that when people come from overseas to Canada, we expect them to speak out, to share their understandings, but there is a different expectation for Canadian mission personnel. "They don't expect us to make waves," he says.

Talbot says she knows there are times overseas personnel question the structures within which they are sent to work. "We don't, in fact, send them to change those structures," she says. Overseas personnel have the same right to raise concerns as their co-workers, but they don't have any special rights.

Walking, We Make the Way

Over the history of the United Church, the need to respond to changing mission realities has continually pushed the church to think in new ways. One current reality is the desire of congregations and individuals to be more engaged in global mission in a hands-on way. More people want to have some kind of lived experience of partners, says Talbot, and for most, that means three months, not three years. Meeting this desire is hard because most of our overseas partners don't have the capacity to receive these people, she notes. But the division has realized it needs to work harder to engage the United Church constituency, and has re-deployed staff and dollars to do this. The twinning initiative is one way the division is trying to help Canadians connect in a personal way with overseas partners. Increasing volunteer opportunities for serving overseas is another.

Looking to future milestones, Whitehead wants the church to think of solidarity as something beyond giving money. "It's taking a risk to say that, because I'm not saying that financial resources from our church aren't very, very important," she says. "But if we think in terms of solidarity, then we're thinking in terms of *all* the ways we can work together."

The division has found a Latin American saying helpful: "Walking, we make the way." It's a useful concept as the United Church discerns its way in mission into a new millennium. It means we don't walk ahead of our overseas partners by leading the way or setting the pace. Nor do we walk behind— pushing or being led. We want to walk with one another, deciding together where to go and why. And as we walk, we learn about ourselves, our partners' lives, and God's mission in the world.

Rebekah Chevalier edits the United Church's mission magazine Mandate.

*Wood Lake Books, 1992, used with permission.
†United Church Publishing House, 1992, used with permission.

Moderators in the Dog Team
by F. Marguerite Nicolson

Shortly after the United Church came into existence, my Dad, the Rev. Joseph Jones, designed and built a cariole. Its sides were tanned moosehide; the lettering was hand-painted by an Indian artist. It was pulled by dad's magnificent team of five dogs, named Arnup, Endicott, Chown, Pidgeon, and Barner!

The cariole proudly proclaimed the United Church presence in the hundreds of miles that dad covered each winter.

Two years earlier—the year before Church Union—dad had been posted to this mission at Cross Lake, Manitoba. Two weeks after the birth of their youngest child, he moved his family (wife Florence; Philip, eight; Bruce, six; Marguerite, four; and Dorene, two weeks) some 60 miles (100 km) down the Nelson River by canoe. The trip took about three days.

Joseph Jones' mobile billboard for the United Church. Behind the cariole and team are the church, manse, and storehouse. Just behind the church is a meeting hall Mr. Jones built with the help of his congregation, for social gatherings.

In the cariole is Mrs. Florence Jones with her youngest daughter Dorene, about three years old at the time of these pictures, 1926.

Cold Feet

by Lois Wilson

The history of our ecumenical relations is cause both for pride and for hanging our heads. When did we lose our nerve?

At a meeting of the Canadian Council of Churches in the early 1970s, delegates were asked to share with each other their first ecumenical experience. A colleague told about living on the same street as the Schacter kids. He and his friends used to tie the Schacter kids to a telephone pole and not release them until they called out the name, "Jesus."

I told of growing up in Thunder Bay, knowing that kids very different from me lived across the street. They attended a big red brick school attached to the largest steeple-topped church in town. They went to worship services, even during the week, and sometimes after school as well, while the rest of us played marbles. Mind you, they had to—they were Roman Catholics. I knew, without being explicitly told, that I was forbidden to enter their church to find out what really went on there, though I heard all sorts of horror stories in my early years. Not until I was eleven did I enter a Catholic church in Winnipeg, pick up a missal, and try to make sense of the mass. Secretly, though I looked down on those Catholic kids for their casual Sunday practices, I also envied them. They were free to do whatever they wanted on Sunday, provided they had first gone to mass. So in the winter, I joined my friends in making icy snowballs and aiming for the whites of their eyes.

Mixed Results

We've come a long way since then, in most of our churches. The United Church of Canada was a founding member of both the Canadian and the World Councils of Churches. We actively shaped their constitutions; we contributed heavily to their budgets. We took the lead in developing their policies. We appointed our most able people to their boards and committees.

On the surface, at least, the old hostilities have passed away. Currently, the Canadian Conference of Catholic Bishops is a full member of the Canadian Council of Churches (CCC). A Roman Catholic, Janet Somerville, is its General Secretary.

Yet we still have a long way to go, I'm afraid. In the 1990s, when the United Church had to reconsider its priorities in the face of shrinking budgets, ecumenism ended up at the bottom of the lists. In 1996–97, the United Church reduced its financial contributions. At the same time the United Church made office space available to the CCC at reduced rates, but the financial contribution has never been restored. During the same period, we drastically cut the number of delegates we were entitled to send to the CCC's Triennial Assembly. Some called this gesture a way "to show our displeasure and teach them a lesson." That "them" is instructive—we started to see the Council as not "ours" but "theirs." It had taken a new form—out of necessity, as its budget was slashed—becoming a forum for deliberation among churches, including Roman Catholics. It was no longer an action-packed ecumenical body (if it ever was).

In cutting financial support, the United Church used the same tactics that it condemned when dissident members reduced their givings during the debate over the ordination of gay/lesbian clergy during the late 1980s and early 1990s. Withhold the cash, until "they" come to their senses.

Questions about Our Commitment

The United Church's reduced participation in the CCC's 1997 Triennial Assembly forces us to ask questions about our ecumenical commitment. How serious are we? Are ecumenical relations only a means to an end? Are we in danger of defining ecumenism in our terms, and of withdrawing if others won't play along with us? I have heard many a United Church member say with exasperation: "We can't get the other church to move, so we'll have to go it alone." But, as couples in relationships know well, relatedness sometimes means simply *being present* to another.

Here's another example where we risked, and pulled back. For years, the Student Christian Movement (SCM) was recognized by Canadian churches as the "agency of the churches on campus." It was a risk to trust a small ecumenical movement with such awesome responsibility. But it was failure when the churches decided to put their own denominational resources and personnel into university chaplaincies instead. Chaplaincies are a far cry from what many—including myself—experienced as the prophetic work of the SCM.

The SCM was foundational in confirming my life posture as ecumenical. It involved students of various denominations. It brought us interaction with Roman Catholic students when there was still a great divide between our churches and interfaith connections with Jewish students through B'nai Brith Hillel. It included believers and non-believers. It introduced students to international leaders. Those leaders had a profound influence on my fledgling faith. I met K. H. Ting, later Chairman of the China Christian Council and a key figure in the renewal of Christianity in China after the cultural revolution, and John R. Mott, one of the architects of the ecumenical movement for students. Suzanne De Dietrich taught me that it was possible for women to be serious scholars. Ted Scott, later Primate of the Anglican Church of Canada, taught me that authentic faith is not so much belief as risk. Much of the leadership of the World Council of Churches (WCC) sprang from this movement.

Since the early 1990s, our national church has been reducing financial support to denominational chaplaincies in universities. This means that much of the support, encouragement, and accountability for raising money for this ministry now lies in local hands. Not only does this policy fail to give priority to mission among university students (young, bright, and the future), but it lays the burden of supporting that work on the university community and a few adjacent churches.

Theological schools have tried to develop an ecumenical stance. Some have been more successful than others. However, few theological schools have courses on ecumenism as a subject on its own. What is even more serious than a lack of ecumenical history and memory is the lack of any vehicle to nurture young people in ecumenism, and to sustain the growth of those few who have experienced the dynamic reality of the ecumenical community.

Pulling Back Our Purse Strings

Consider work with children and youth. The driving force behind the formation of the CCC in the 1940s was booming ecumenical work among young people. Abandoning this focus seems to me to signal a failure of nerve. Long ago, ecumenical young people's groups such as the Canadian Girls in Training (CGIT) began to falter—but nothing has been put together to replace them.

My growing up years in the United Church gave me positive ecumenical experiences. Annually, some five hundred teenage CGIT girls drawn from Baptist, Presbyterian, and United Churches sat down to one of my mother's famous "mob dinners" served in Westminster Church, Winnipeg. That dinner was the climax of a year of reading and studying the work of Christian churches around the world. These ecumenical friendships were deepened by CGIT summer camps, usually with an international guest, who gave me my first inkling that the Christian community had an international dimension.

When did our reluctance to risk begin? I'm not sure. A former mayor of Winnipeg, a United Church member in good standing, told me once that he used to be invited to gatherings of every church and denomination in the city except the United Church. There seems to be a wide gap between the church and the elected officials of our wider society.

In 1998 the United Church presented briefs to politicians about proposed extensions of gambling in our provinces. We received little or no notice. Have

Tribute from China
by K. H. Ting

My wife Siu May and I came to Canada with the Student Christian Movement for a year in the summer of 1946. The United Church of Canada had much to do with bringing us.

My year in Canada, as missionary secretary of the SCM, gave me education on at least two important matters:

1. The question of church union. I was deeply interested in the theory and practice in the process of the formation of The United Church of Canada and in why some other churches found it difficult to join.

2. The missiological thinking that was evolving. It was consonant with the "Three Self" emphasis the churches in China began to advocate in a big way some years later.

After coming back to China, as I participate in the Three Self Movement and promote the cause of post-denominationalism, I often recall my experiences in my Canadian days. It has always been a joy to me to return to Canada on a number of occasions. The friendships formed have proved to be precious and long-lasting.

we simply become one more lobby group? Why has communication with our legislators failed, even at a courtesy level? Some in our church, I suspect, see government as an enemy. They would think it collusion with the powers-that-be even to listen to greetings brought by the premier of a province. Little wonder that some elected officials no longer respond affirmatively to our invitations.

Some of these trends, I believe, contradict our goals as a church. The ethos of our church is ecumenical. The *Basis of Union* states, "It shall be the policy of the United Church to foster the spirit of unity" in Canada. Have we abandoned this ethos? Is unity to be only on *our* terms?

A Unique Gift of Canadian Churches

There are still some significant accomplishments.

Among the strongest ecumenical commitments of our church has been the work of thirteen ecumenical coalitions in Canada. Most of these came into being in the early 1970s in response to international crises. Needs arose that had to be addressed quickly, effectively, and ecumenically, but that the institutional churches did not hold high on their internal agendas. So together we created the Inter-Church Committee for Human Rights in Latin America, the Canada Asia Working Group, the Task Force on Corporate Responsibility, the Inter Church Africa Coalition, the Ecumenical Coalition for Economic Justice, and so on. These coalitions are staffed by a very few people, they run more or less on a shoe string, and they have developed strong credibility both with partners in other continents and with some Canadian government agencies. When I was moderator, I visited Brazil. I remember being told by the Canadian Ambassador that he respected the work of the Canadian ecumenical coalitions, even if he disagreed with their conclusions! These coalitions are viewed internationally as a unique gift of the Canadian churches to ecumenism.

Recently, the WCC's Ecumenical Decade of Churches in Solidarity with Women drew to a close. It turned out to be more a Decade of *Women* in Solidarity with Women—but even that is a feat not to dismiss lightly. The Decade raised consciousness around the world about the situation of women in church and society, and prepared churches for what must happen in the next decade to make necessary changes. In Canada, the Decade was plagued by the disproportionate size of the United Church in relation to other churches—a factor that has always been a problem in ecumenical affairs in this country. Our church ran freely with the Decade. But typically, we did it in our style and culture, which is not always that of Anglican or Catholic women.

Omens for the Future

Recently, the United Church has launched some initiatives that may assist us in reclaiming our original ethos as a church. They are omens for the future.

The document *Bearing Faithful Witness* calls for a more informed dialogue between Jewish and Christian faith communities. It is a significant step forward. Among other things, it invites congregations to study scripture to ascertain whether anti-Semitism has been rampant in our teaching. It captures again our capacity to risk theologically, when others seem unwilling to do so. It responds to the changing religious landscape in Canada.

Interfaith concerns will land us in difficult theological waters. One doesn't have to travel to India to meet Hindus and Muslims. We mingle with them in the grocery line-up. Our children study in the same classroom. I am proud that the United Church is responding to the changed picture. But there is risk involved. Interfaith encounters do not simply involve making common cause with other faith communities on societal concerns. We need to ensure that dialogue is truly "religious" in the sense of probing each faith community's theological convictions—including our own.

For most of us, the thorniest questions will deal with the nature of Jesus Christ, and the witness of scripture in this regard. To risk interfaith encounter is to risk our most precious theological insights.

Another significant document, called *Mending the World*, was presented to the 1997 General Council. It invited the church to a broad interfaith and world-focused agenda, as a church priority. After vigorous discussion, General Council re-affirmed the United Church's commitment to interchurch relations within a renewed understanding of ecumenism; it refused to downgrade those relationships in favour of an extended discussion of interfaith matters. The official action of Council clearly linked the church's historic and ongoing commitment to be both a united and a uniting church with "God's work of healing, sharing the good news of the Gospel of Jesus Christ, and making common cause with all people of goodwill, whether they be of faith or not, for the creation of a world that is just, participatory, and sustainable."

Hallelujah! Our church came through again! It was a notable exception to the ecumenical winter that threatens to freeze us.

Still Plagued with Cold Feet

At the same time, I have to admit that the Council rejected the recommendation of the Inter-Church Inter-Faith Relations Committee to reshape the budget so that more dollars would be directed to interfaith work in Canada. That did not mean abandoning our relations with other faiths. It meant that the church decided there needed to be a new balance between our historic interchurch connections and our relatively new interfaith thrusts. So we are still willing to risk whether we can achieve that balance. Yet because ecumenism remains at the bottom of our list of priorities, we are in danger of failing to reshape our original vision of 1925.

What about ecumenism in its original meaning—*oikoumene* being the whole inhabited world? In the heady days of Vatican II, my husband Roy and I were ministers in Thunder Bay, Ontario. There we initiated "Town Talk," a community-wide ecumenical program to involve the citizens of a city of one hundred thousand in conversations about our common future. We invited people to use every means of communication to focus on issues the community itself had identified—television, radio, phone-in, university convocation, Toastmasters' Club, unions, churches, Pee Wee Hockey League, the newspaper….In the sense that it involved the *entire* community and dealt with issues common to all, the program was truly ecumenical. It invited informed opinion and authentic faith. It dealt with our "whole inhabited world."

How we Christians have narrowed the original meaning of that word *oikoumene*! How little of the church's energy goes into healing the whole inhabited world! Yet that work must be informed by faith, or it will be nothing more than good works that could be done by any other current agency.

If "Town Talk" was my conversion to community, a trip to Crete gave me a new set of glasses. I saw Canada with new eyes. I had been invited to Crete for a consultation with the World Council of Churches, about applying "Town Talk" in a different context. That visit transformed my parochial perspective to a global one. It marked my conversion to giving priority to the concerns of the world church and to the ecumenical movement. It was a veritable Pentecost. The more I saw of the world, the smaller it became. The more I experienced love and justice in the worldwide Christian community, the more I recognized the need for love and justice in my local community. I began to understand how one can "take the ecumenical movement home." I coveted the vitality and wholeness of *oikoumene* for my own church. I realized that no one national church could express the fullness of the gospel. We need each other.

It wasn't until I became moderator and began travelling widely on behalf of the United Church that I recognized other rich ecumenical dimensions of my church. Because we are a national church, existing only in Canada, we work in partnership with other churches that have historic ties with us. So in 1998, we celebrated one hundred years of partnership with the Methodist Church of Argentina, the United Church of Zambia, and so on. Not many churches in the world can say this. It is not a virtue of our own—it happened because we are a united church, melding several traditions out of a variety of historic roots.

We are part of the world family of United Churches. But that body decided some time ago not to install staff and programs. Rather, it asked the World Council of Churches to convene all the United Churches of the world every five years, for consultation. Thus we were spared having to support another layer of ecumenism in the traditional model. We do retain membership in the World Alliance of Reformed Churches and the World Methodist Council, in a cousin-to-cousin relationship.

Loss Of Vision with Increasing Age?

If this article sounds like a complaint, it isn't. It's more a lament, for the partial loss of our original vision, and our seeming inability to express that vision in current contemporary forms—with a few notable exceptions. Let's celebrate those exceptions! Let's multiply them!

Church Union in 1925 represented a great risk. We have had some successes and a few failures in our short history. My hope and prayer for the new millennium is that we continue to risk boldly, even though risk always has implicit in it the possibility of failure. That is the nature of faith.

Lois Wilson was the first woman to be elected moderator of the United Church, in 1980. She was recently appointed to the federal Senate, and is the author of a number of books retelling stories of biblical women for women and children today.

The Essential Beliefs

Does anyone really know what the United Church believes?

What Do United Church People Believe?

by Michael McAteer

If the United Church were to tack a statement of its faith to a post in the middle of a meadow, could we agree about what should go on the post?

Back in the early 1960s, the Department of Sunday School Publications in Toronto received a telephone call from a woman who wanted to tell the editor-in-chief a thing or two about "that new curriculum." She was told the editor, the Rev. Peter Gordon White, was at home resting after an accident.

"That," said the caller, "was no accident," and hung up. It was obvious from her tone that the caller was not a happy camper.

She was not alone. Publication of the *New Curriculum* unleashed one of those bouts of controversy that rocks the United Church from time to time. Evangelicals—inside and outside the church—lambasted the church, accusing it of abandoning basic Christian tenets and of downgrading the Bible. There were calls for firing all connected with the program's production.

The Media Fan the Flames

Like wasps to a picnic, the national media were attracted to the church tempest. Headline writers vied to produce the snappiest headline. Canada's largest circulation daily *The Toronto Star* topped a front-page article with: "New teaching says Bible is a myth."

A reference in the program's introductory book to the "creation myths" in Genesis sparked that particular headline. A small thing perhaps, but enough for those who took the Bible literally to go on the offensive. Accusations that a coterie of church liberals was out to undermine the very foundations of Christianity flew fast and furious.

Despite the chorus of angry, accusatory voices, the *New Curriculum* was a runaway publishing success and was widely accepted in the United Church.

The strength of the negative reaction surprised Peter White, the man at the centre of the storm. "What we were offering was being taught in all our theological schools so all our ministers were familiar with it," he says. It may have been old hat for scholars and for ministers in the pulpit, but for some people, especially those in the pews, it was all a little too avant-garde. It represented a major crisis of faith.

Much the same reaction—and much the same media attention—greeted the Rt. Rev. Bill Phipps after an interview with the *Ottawa Citizen*'s editorial board in 1997. Grilled by the board on his Christian orthodoxy, Phipps said, among other things, that he did not believe that Jesus is God or that Jesus is the only way to God. In a later statement, Phipps said he believed that nothing he had said was outside the broad mainstream of United Church belief. And, while his faith is well rooted in scripture and Christian tradition, "it is not frozen in the language of early creeds."

Responding to cries of "heresy" from church conservatives and calls for Phipps' removal from office, the executive of the church's highest court, General Council, defended his right to express personal points of view. At the same time, the executive acknowledged that the personal views of church spokespersons must be tempered by "the need for congruence" with stated United Church policies and statements.

Tacked to a Post in a Meadow

Seventy-five years after Methodists, Presbyterians, and Congregationalists hammered out a *Basis of Union* and brought forth The United Church of Canada, there is still heated debate—inside and outside the church—about what it is the church believes, or should believe and proclaim.

So, how does the United Church handle doctrine?

The Rev. Peter Wyatt, the United Church's General Secretary for Theology, Faith, and Ecumenism, offers a wry parable.

> Some churches herd people into corrals and tell them they must believe everything they've been told. If they don't, they are out of the corral—out of the fold, so to speak. Other churches handle it differently. Anglicans, for instance, rather than building a corral, drive a post in the middle of a meadow, attach their articles of faith to it, and invite people to get as close to the post as possible. United Church people do something similar. Of course, in all likelihood, they would disagree on what precisely is tacked onto that post.

> The difference between us and other churches is evident in that we are prepared to allow a greater degree of

Maybe
by Jim Taylor

Maybe the United Church tries too hard to define what it believes. Maybe.

My friends and I sat on their patio, enjoying the late autumn sunshine. We talked, as friends do, of many things. But in the end, as friends do, we always talk about the things that matter most to us.

And they wanted to know about the state of the church. They had stuck with their church through good times and bad, through controversies and doldrums. But fewer people now attended Sunday services. The Sunday school staggered along with a few old faithfuls as teachers. Yet down the road, a conservative chapel had an overflowing Sunday school and parking lot.

"Why are they successful, and we aren't?" he demanded.

I hedged: "It depends on what you mean by 'successful.'"

"Is it their music?" she demanded. "They have guitars and drums and amplifiers."

"Maybe," I said.

"Is it their theology?" he pursued. "They seem to have all the answers. Do people want absolute answers, so that they can park their brains at the door?"

"Maybe," I said.

"That's ridiculous," she snorted. "Those people have been to school. They know the world wasn't made in seven days! Their kids are all nuts about dinosaurs!"

"Are we the only church that acknowledges science at all?" he demanded.

I squirmed. "Maybe," I said.

"What about the Unitarians?" she asked. "I know they believe in evolution. But do they believe in Jesus?"

"Maybe," I said lamely. "Some do. Some aren't even sure there's a God."

"More to the point," he interrupted, "Do we believe in Jesus?"

I winced. Our church had just been through the feeding frenzy of sharks that passes for media coverage over the moderator's comments on the divinity of Jesus. "Maybe," I said.

"Oh, come on, Jim!" they both stormed. "Is that the true creed of the United Church? 'Maybe'?"

And all three of us burst into laughter. "Maybe," we all said at once.

We laughed, because it's not a bad creed at all. "Maybe" says that we don't reject an idea without considering it. It doesn't commit anyone to accepting a view, but neither does it put on blinders. It allows an openness to possibilities, including the possibility that God's spirit may speak to us in new and unfamiliar ways.

I think that's why I have found a home within the United Church all these years. I have been allowed to dream dreams and have visions. Many have been wrong, or short-sighted, or slightly off the mark. But the mistakes have shaped who I am, and how I got here, just as much as the times I was right.

No one told me I mustn't dream those dreams, or have those visions, or ask those questions. No one told me I couldn't colour outside the lines. They said, "Maybe."

Simply saying "No" closes doors. And minds.

Maybe "maybe" is what the United Church believes, after all.

Jim Taylor is the author of ten books, all dealing with religion in everyday life.

importance to the question of what people actually believe in the pew than other denominations may.

So, what does the United Church believe? What do the people in the pews believe?

Everything and nothing, is one cynical response. It has been said that almost every theological position you might think of can be found in the church. In fact, it is said that the diversity of beliefs, attitudes, and preaching of United Church people is so wide that it is nigh impossible to pinpoint what they believe.

Just what is tacked on to that post in the meadow? There is, of course, the *Basis of Union* and its twenty *Articles of Faith* that form the constitutionally accepted beliefs of the United Church. Among other things, these articles proclaim Jesus Christ, the Eternal Son of God, as the only mediator between God and Man. They declare that the Bible contains the only infallible rule of faith and life.

A Slide Away from Authority?

For the church conservatives such beliefs, and other traditional articles of faith spelled out in black and white, are immutable and non-negotiable. They argue that actions taken by the church over the years point to a radical, ongoing shift by the United Church away from the authority of scripture and from clearly held beliefs outlined in the *Articles of Faith*.

In their view, these actions have included:

- The introduction of a contemporary *New Creed*.
- Changes to the hymn book including the elimination of traditional, well-loved hymns.
- The "feminization" of God and the use of inclusive language in church documents and services.
- The position that sexual orientation should not be a barrier to ordination.
- The ongoing re-examination of the nature and person of Jesus Christ.

Other church people counter that, coming as they did from different theological viewpoints, the people who put the doctrinal articles together were conscious that they were doing the best they could at a particular time in history. Consequently, the founders of the church produced a document of "pragmatic compromise." Their document, says Phyllis Airhart, who teaches the history of Christianity at Emmanuel College and the Toronto School of Theology, outlines what they thought they had in common, what they could affirm together, and what they could carry forward into Church Union. They believed that the document, the statement of faith, had to be rewritten in each generation.

Fifteen years after the *Basis of Union*, the United Church issued a *Statement of Faith*. While it affirmed that the church's faith is "the unchanging Gospel of God's holy redeeming love in Jesus Christ," it also declared that each new generation is called to state this gospel afresh, "in terms of thought of their own age and with the emphasis on their needs."

Church Statements vs. People's Beliefs

A *New Creed* ecumenical in scope and summarizing "the main message of Scripture as the church understands it" was issued in 1968. It has been amended twice to remove exclusively masculine language and to stress respect for the environment. This creed, together with later doctrinal documents, recognized the "diversity of interpretation" of official statements and documents within the United Church's membership.

Over the years, General Council has approved numerous official church statements on such wide-ranging subjects as immigration, refugees, the economy, Native issues, capital punishment, and human sexuality. Agonizing moral issues such as abortion, genetic engineering, and euthanasia have all prompted official church positions. However, these statements on contemporary issues are considered to deal with pastoral, not doctrinal, matters. They are issued to help people make decisions in complicated and usually tense situations. And "help" is the key word. Underlying all is the recognition that what General Council says the church believes is not necessarily what every individual church member believes.

The Rev. Gordon Nodwell of Toronto puts it this way: "We have always cherished the right and responsibility of each individual Christian to come to, and formulate, his or her own understanding of faith. Our religious beliefs are in constant tension with changing information, knowledge, perceptions, language, and ways of thinking. That means that while our trust in and loyalty to God may remain constant, the ways in which we understand and express that faith will change."

Who's in Charge Here?

All of which allows for a lot of theological latitude. And, at times, confusion. Who's in charge? Officially, the elected General Council, the church's highest court, legislates on "matters respecting the doctrine, worship, membership, and government of the Church."

If there is an official position on just who is in charge, it is that the Bible is the "primary source and ultimate standard of Christian faith and life," and that Jesus Christ is the "chief cornerstone," says Ralph Milton, author of the perennial best-seller *This United Church of Ours*. "It means that no one person in the church can claim to have the last word." It also means there is no creed you have to say or sign before you can become a member of the United Church. Membership is based on a profession of faith in the triune God—Father, Son, and Holy Spirit—and a commitment to faithful conduct in church and world. Nor is there a demand that you use a certain set of religious words, or pray in a certain way, or believe in a particular interpretation of the Bible.

Ask United Church people what they believe, where they go for authority, where they find their faith source, what's important to them and what's not, and you will get a variety of answers.

Unitrends, a report based on a 1994 survey of United Church members—active, marginal, and inactive—showed that those highly involved in the church tend to hold traditional beliefs. God, the divinity of Jesus, life after death, were all soundly endorsed. Close to 90 percent recognized the authority of scripture. But only a small minority—led by active members—interpreted it literally.

However, for the church's conservative wing, the survey produced other disturbing, even shocking, statistics suggesting that the good ship United Church is foundering in a sea of liberalism. While a high proportion of pastors and church workers described themselves as "committed Christians," only 40 percent of active members did so. More than a third of ministers responding to the survey did not consider "confessing Jesus Christ as Saviour and Lord" very important; and more than three-quarters of United Church faculty did not consider it very important.

It all points, says the Rev. Donald Faris of Vancouver, to a "deep faith crisis" within the United Church. "What future does our denomination have?" he asks. "More importantly, what kind of future does it deserve?"

To Leave or to Stay

The experiences of two long-time members of the United Church highlight the diverging views.

Gladys Young, an unabashed conservative, also wonders and worries about what the future holds for her church. A widow who lives in the Toronto suburb of Etobicoke, she grew up Presbyterian. She joined the United Church in 1952 when she married, and found it a reasonably comfortable spiritual home until "the United Church head office began to go off the rails."

Church leaders driven by a liberal agenda, Young says, used the homosexual ordination issue as a smokescreen to steer the church away from its traditional moorings. "Behind our backs they were trying to get Christ out of the centre of the church and harassing ministers who didn't toe the line on inclusive language," she charges.

After twenty-eight years at a local church, Young left to join Streetsville United, led by a conservative theologian, the Rev. Victor Shepherd. Her new congregation is a member of the National Alliance of Covenanting Congregations, a caucus of traditional churches within the United Church. "It suits my temperament," she says of her new spiritual home.

Hilda Craig, of St. Andrew's United in Matheson, Ontario, was ten years old in 1925 when the United Church was born. She has been a president of Manitou Conference (in northern Ontario). She's seen a few changes, a few upheavals, in her time. But nothing has made her even think of leaving her church.

Lay people, she says, have come into their own: "We are not the followers that earlier generations were." And she continues:

> The United Church has not demanded that people believe certain tenets of faith. That has made room for people with doubts and uncertainties, and many people have found a home within the church because they were allowed to explore their thinking in many ways. The church welcomes seekers who have questions and doubts.

Craig turns to the *New Creed* for inspiration and authority. She's comfortable with its contemporary language. It's not cast in stone like the more ancient creeds. It's a "living" thing: "There's room for growth and learning. We don't have to take all those old statements as absolute truth." Many people her age find change frightening, she admits. She finds it challenging, even stimulating.

Still, not everything fits snugly. Despite her liberal bent, she clings to a few things she started with. For example, a former minister at her church never used the Trinitarian formula at baptism. "It hit me a little that he did not use it," she recalls. "I would be reluctant to write that off completely, to throw it out." But if she was shocked at the omission, she was even more shocked that others did not seem to notice. Or, if they did notice, they didn't mention it.

Does Doctrine Develop?

As it enters the new millennium, the United Church struggles to come up with a new understanding of its faith in a fast-changing world. Ecumenical consideration is at a premium. In the process, the belief that Christianity offers the only path to salvation may be further challenged.

Conservatives warn that any further dilution of traditional Christian beliefs will have dire consequences for the United Church and for the broader Christian community. It will result, they say, in an even more confused, liberal, middle-class church that lacks a clear theological foundation.

Born to a background of theological dispute, the United Church appears destined to continue its discussions, its arguments, its disagreements on what it means to be Christian in a society that now pretty much ignores its Christian origins. Just what does the church tack on to that pole in the middle of the meadow?

Much depends, Peter Wyatt suggests, on how one responds to a rhetorical question: Is there such a thing as development of doctrine? "If you say 'No' to that question, then you can sit with the 1925 *Articles of Faith* and say 'That's it, full stop!' But if you answer 'Yes,' then you cannot treat those articles as if they have usurped every generation's right to encounter the Bible afresh."

In 1925, a third of Presbyterians refused to join the United Church, largely on theological grounds. The Very Rev. George Pidgeon, the pro-union Presbyterian who became the first moderator of The United Church of Canada, said of the *Basis of Union*: "This is not all we believe; these are the truths on which we agree, and they are the life-giving message of the Gospel of Christ."

Michael McAteer is a freelance writer and journalist, and a former religion-page editor of The Toronto Star.

Hospitality to Difference

by Christopher Levan

The unique mark of the United Church is not just openness—which can turn into its own straitjacket—but genuine hospitality to ideas that may differ from our own.

As church budgets buckle and break, there is an increasing interest in schemes designed to generate alternate sources of revenue from existing congregational assets. Parking lots, day cares, and even art galleries are now seen as money trees, whose harvest supports the local community of faith.

In my dreams, I fantasize about transforming our national denominational gifts into big bucks. For instance, could we rent out our four-layered model of governance? How often have other Christians from a broad spectrum of contexts praised our logical, collegial style? Business-like believers from other churches extol the United Church way and pine for something so clear and directive for themselves. "I know just who to call in head office when I want help," they gush. So we have a desirable product. Why not lease it to others? It's an idea. (We won't tell our potential customers how often we have commissioned task forces on restructuring.)

In another direction, maybe our predilection for prophetic pronouncements is worth something on the open market. Could we sell ourselves as consultants? We could call ourselves, "Trouble R Us." No matter where people live, we can make an apathetic public sit up and take notice. We'll turn your indifferent image into one that cracks open the stoniest secular heart.

Dreams are great fun!

More Homogenous Than We Think

But, alas, the genius of The United Church of Canada could never be exported. It would wither in the hot passion of Texan religious zeal, freeze in the cold propriety of Swiss reformationism, and I doubt if our worship of polite order would garner many adherents in politically passionate Chile.

We're a peculiarly Canadian invention: the open and inviting company of Jesus that holds its faith lightly, believes in ecumenical inclusivity almost as much as it believes in God, and springs into surprisingly quick action to protect the rights of minorities in our midst and around the globe. Canada shaped us as a church and vice versa. You couldn't replicate our peculiar mixture of social responsibility and spiritual devotion in any other context. If I had to put the unique gift of United Church doctrine and polity into a few words they would be: "We are hospitable to difference and open to justice."

Of course, each sector of the denomination looks over its small fence and talks about "those people" over there. But the United Church is much more homogeneous than we might suspect. Geographic and cultural mosaics do affect the tone of our gospel and our liturgical flexibility, but at its core, the United Church embodies similar levels of hospitality and openness across the country.

The Patron Church of Doubters

Jack proves my point. He had been a Christian as a child—came, as he puts it, "from one of those grimy gospel halls down the block." As often happens, when he became a teenager, Jack grew restive and left God-talk behind. After a few years in college, religion didn't seem to be all that important anyway. His sales work took him out of town frequently, making regular attendance at Sunday service problematic. And what his travelling started, the bottle finished. His drinking problem made spiritual contacts both unlikely and unwelcome. Each morning he woke from a bender, he knew he was a lost soul. No one could reach him or help him. Least of all, God!

When Jack hit rock bottom, he was saved by the Alcoholics Anonymous group that met in a United Church basement. The church within the church. In that community, he came to know his need for a faith, to trust his spirit to a Higher Power, to forgive himself, and to reach out to others with compassion.

The minister of the local congregation where Jack found his salvation asked him each week, "Why don't you attend worship?" But Jack, the skeptic, took his time. After five years of invitations, he finally accepted, came up from the cellar and found, to his delight, a space where there was "lots of elbow room for my doubts," as he put it. Bingo! Whatever people might call us, the United Church is the patron church of doubters.

I celebrate the spirit of openness that has marked our communion from its inception. Whether it was the place of women or homosexual persons in positions of leadership, the respect of Aboriginal people or ethnic groups as full members, or the inclusion of the vulnerable of all kinds in our deliberations, the United Church has consistently tried to be hospitable to difference. Of course, we have made mistakes, ignored the demands of just relationships, and been slow to act with mercy. Our history has not been all sweetness and light. But over time, God has given us the humility to admit our errors, the courage to call for better ethical standards, and the wisdom to know when our faith should remain silent, acting rather than speaking the gospel.

Hallowed Be Our Differences

I believe this is not just an ideological orientation, as if the United Church were the NDP at prayer, as many journalists and political pundits have argued. In the congregation of my childhood, Sam a stalwart conservative, Arthur a determined liberal, and Victor a dyed-in-the-wool social democrat were the best of friends. Come election time, they disagreed vehemently on their respective political platforms. But in the sanctuary there was no division, only a common front. This building would be a house where doubts were honoured, questions welcomed, and differences hallowed.

In a real sense, therefore, the United Church has functioned like a door on Christianity through which skeptics have entered and cynics have exited. How many pilgrims from fundamentalist religions made their way to our chancels, delighted to find the freedom for their suspicions? An equal number of convinced atheists will claim to have arrived at their enlightened dis-association with Jesus from their roots in the United Church.

And why not? Surely, the religious world needs a gate, be it the inviting door that stands open or the fire escape available for a hasty exit.

This openness has not simply been a technique, like a hollow evangelical gimmick. It is also substantive. We are hospitable to difference because it is in this posture that we speak and act out our commitment to justice, which was, after all, the primary goal of the ministry of Jesus—to create a circle where all were welcome, all were fed and forgiven. You don't have to twist yourself inside out to join the United Church. As with the carpenter of Galilee, a trusting heart and expectant soul were the necessary tools to receive God's love. No creedal restrictions, no dogmatic prerequisites. Know yourself as a beloved child of God and you're on the way. The United Church replicates this grace when we welcome the new gifts, unique experiences, and special talents that insiders and outsiders both bring to our tradition.

At Ease with the Secular World

I rejoice that we play that hospitable role in our world. And it is precisely because the United Church has easy commerce with the secular world that we have exerted considerable influence on political affairs. Medicare, unemployment insurance, universal pensions have their origins, in no small part, in the social gospel movement whose heartbeat in Canada has been the United Church.

Those who are troubled by what appears to be the United Church's faddish preoccupation with "justice issues" must recognize the history of our

Our Minister Resigned
by Marion D. Christie

I was eighteen in December 1924, when I voted for Church Union. I had been brought up a staunch Presbyterian, but my family had missionary relatives who described the difficulty of explaining denominationalism to new Korean Christians.

The possibility of such a union caused great excitement and many heated arguments in the little village congregation in Bedford, Nova Scotia. Our two ministers in the years preceding 1925 had both been fervent anti-unionists. However, in the months preceding the vote, we had visiting ministers present both sides of the question.

In our church, there were sixty-eight communicant members who could vote. The voting took place between December 22, 1924 and January 8, 1925. The decision was thirty-five for Union, twenty-four against.

Our minister resigned. Twenty-six members withdrew their membership. Our communicant roll was reduced to forty-two.

The continuing Presbyterians in Halifax sent out a bus on Sundays to transport the loyal Bedford Presbyterians to church "in town."

The few Methodists in Bedford before 1925 had attended the Presbyterian Church anyway, so they noticed little difference. The order of service and liturgy remained the same.

A new minister, kindly and gentle, was called. He was able to pour oil on troubled waters. Services continued and bitterness abated.

denomination. We have consistently pushed the envelope of individual compassion and social reconstruction. Consequently, we have always been embroiled in crisis. But as past-moderator Clark MacDonald once said, "I'm glad to be in a church that's in trouble, and if we ever weren't in trouble, I'd go out and join a church that was."

Now, there has also been a very helpful counterbalance within the United Church community that calls the church back to its roots and reminds us of our doctrinal imperatives. Contrary to our public image, United Church disciples do believe in God as revealed in Jesus, the Christ. We do have some codes of faith, adhere to reformed theological positions, and live out a spirituality based largely in Methodist evangelicalism.

True, our Christological pronouncements have been on the "low" side, accentuating the humanity of Jesus. But the concern to retain a full richness of the humanity of our Saviour is well within the tradition of our faith, finding its source in such apostles as Paul and Martin Luther and establishing itself in such saints of our denomination as J. S. Woodsworth, Nellie McClung, Bruce McLeod, and Lois Wilson. Unable either to abandon the world or to see salvation simply as an other-worldly event, the United Church has remained faithful to the God we encounter in the Jesus of history and to the love the Creator manifests for this world.

Enough praise.

Four Potential Pitfalls

Every ecclesiastical position has implicit temptations or dangers. The danger of our hospitality to difference is at least fourfold.

First, in the perverse manner in which human virtue turns to vice, our openness can become an obligation. Rather than being refreshed by openness, inclusivity can become imperative. It can become a duty—"you must be open" to be part of our circle. It's a subtle and very damaging reversal. The very posture that we hope will open the door, slams it shut, creating a boundary within our happy clan.

There is no question that, once having been welcomed into a tolerant community, we desire new or older initiates into our community to have the similar open spirit. But surely, when inclusivity becomes a sine qua non of our gatherings, then we lose its great benefit. An imposed openness to all things translates into theological acid tests. When you *must* use certain language for the god-head, when you *must* be willing to accept any kind of leadership—and the more minority, the better—then we have fallen prey to the same dangers of absolutism that haunt all Christian traditions.

Instead of inclusivity, it would be more appropriate, as Douglas Hall suggests, to employ the biblical concept of "hospitality." Hospitality does not assume that all people can be made part of a single community—at least not easily and without changes of certain hearts. Hospitality is an open gesture. It holds arms wide open, but it does not seek the conversion of the other.

Second, we must differentiate between openness and abandonment. All too often, we claim to be a welcoming community and use as examples of our welcoming nature the low standards we set. We'll baptize anyone, marry you even if you never come back, and bury you. While this hospitality is laudable, it is less than honest if we do not work hard at providing tools for discipleship that individuals might use if they, having been so warmly welcomed, desired to go further in their faith journey. It's one thing to allow space for everyone's questions; it's quite another to make no attempt to provide some answers and exercise to these same questions. To be blunt, all too often, our hospitality has been an excuse for sloppy leadership.

Third, as is the case in many human institutions, form becomes confused with substance. How regularly have I been hugged in church, as was the fashion for a time, and felt at that very moment both alone and manipulated. Openness is not the end of the story. Getting people to wear visitor's tags, passing the peace—these are just tools for hospitality, a beginning. They are not the end of the story. Our openness is a function of our hospitality to justice. If we are unable to move beyond the hug to acts of compassion for this world, all gestures of openness will be fruitless.

Here is the primary challenge for the future. There is little question that the turn of the millennium is generating a tremendous resurgence in spiritual and ethical passion. People want to care for their souls and the earth. But they are not turning to the institutional church for guidance in this quest because we lack integrity. We can't walk our talk; we can't move our professions of faith into prophetic action. Liturgically we have difficulty adapting our worship to a more individualized piety, and theologically we are too cautious in making contact with secular expressions of faith.

Fourth, the openness that shaped us as communion assumes a high degree of biblical and doctrinal literacy. We were able to begin as a uniting church in 1925 because we knew very well the roots from which we had grown. *Sola scriptura*. My grandmother's generation was able to defend a hospitable church because difference did not threaten them. Grandma Mabe knew her Bible, and from its pages she learned to trust in the common bond that joined humanity. She knew the codes and creeds as well and had memorized paragraphs from the catechism. So she was able to dialogue with strangers from a position of knowledge.

Alas, as our biblical literacy thins, we have less security from which to speak. Witness the erratic debates of the last two decades. The titles of our reports are still strong: *The Lordship of Jesus*, *The Authority and Interpretation of Scripture*. But the average lay person's ability to fill in the background content has dramatically weakened. All too often, the United Church has cashed in its loyalty chips, asking members to trust the opinions of commissions or committees who supposedly know what is right and good. But this is unacceptable as a common practice. Without stronger teaching leadership and more theologically inspired membership, our denomination will eventually wither into a slogan-rich and content-poor church.

Continuing the Journey

As we move from the first seventy-five years into the next millennium, surely we can be proud of our heritage as a hospitable, courageous institution. But without attention to our ideas of openness and inclusivity, leadership, integrity, and biblical literacy, I fear we may arrive at our 150th anniversary decidedly weaker.

Christopher Levan is principal of St. Stephen's Theological College in Edmonton, Alberta.

When We Gather

The context of
Sunday morning
worship

Born in Controversy and Divisiveness

by Robert A. Wallace

From its beginnings, the United Church has been bathed in the spotlight of controversy. But the church has rarely turned its back on difficult issues.

The United Church of Canada was birthed in both hope and controversy. There are still many who, on its seventy-fifth anniversary, recall tales of communities, even families, split by the decision either to unite or to resist in 1925.

When I first began to travel to international meetings I'd be asked two questions. "What were you before Union?" Rather than reply, "An embryo," I confessed that The United Church of Canada was born before I was. "How is the Union going?" I was tempted to reply, "And how's your marriage doing?"

I entered the United Church at nineteen, an apostate from agnosticism. I found little evidence of the early denominational differences—other than some communities having two United Churches within hearing distance of each other's anthems. Differences seemed to relate more to preferences in hymnody than to doctrine or even liturgy.

There were tensions, but at that time they had more to do with social issues than doctrinal ones. While some of us were picketing "Arms to China" ships in the Vancouver harbour, others touted John Foster Dulles and Dwight Eisenhower as prototypes of post-war Christianity. As the Cold War escalated, clergy from some affluent communities voted against ordaining any candidates who had strayed in from the peace movement, perhaps carrying in their back pockets well-thumbed copies of Lex Miller's *The Christian Significance of Karl Marx*.

Continual Controversy

Issues change, but tensions remain. In recent years some well-heeled church members have been more infuriated by the United Church's stand on free trade than by its policies on ordination of self-professed homosexual persons.

This insensitivity to an opposing position is epitomized, for me, in the story of two New England intellectuals, each unable to imagine the stance taken by a fellow Christian. Ralph Waldo Emerson visited his friend Henry Thoreau, who was in prison for protesting a hot justice issue of the time, the poll tax. "What are you doing in there, Henry?" Emerson demanded.

To which Thoreau replied, "And what are you, Waldo, doing out there?"

The tensions in our church have been often divisive. Though there have been dropouts with each issue, somehow our church has managed to keep the two extremes in communication with one another. This has been made possible by two God-given traits of this particular branch of God's church: the genius of the United Church for encompassing wide divergences of opinion, and its unique capacity for relating creatively to the secular world. Most of its members seem able to tolerate a wide range of political/social/economic stances without tearing the fabric of the church.

The Bible Drives a Wedge

The authority of scripture seems to create deeper, sometimes irreparable, rifts. The United Church contains both ultra-conservative and ultra-liberal members, when it comes to interpreting the Bible. But when biblical interpretation is linked with moral issues, rifts become splits.

The differing attitudes to the authority of scripture has smouldered beneath the surface since Union. It surfaced with the publication of the *Revised Standard Version* of the Bible in 1952. A few in the church sided with conservative groups who saw any version other than the *King James* as a work of the devil. One pastor in Vancouver, a Reverend Busch, burned a copy of the RSV in the pulpit—and was henceforth known as "Burning Busch."

Open flame flared, however, with the publication of the *New Curriculum* in 1961. It was seen by many as an insidious plot to undermine the authority of Holy Writ. Opposition members within were helped considerably by inflammatory public statements from leaders of other communions. Though many saw it as a liberating movement that made faith possible, rather than destroying faith, the church retreated. The project soared for a short time then nose-dived into oblivion. Had the curriculum survived its critics, the United Church might never have had to face its 1988 crisis over ordination of homosexual persons. The "proof-texting" that replaced a holistic approach to scripture would have been more widely recognized as an invalid exercise.

Making a New Music

By the late 1960s, as controversy over the *New Curriculum* faded, a quieter diversity began taking shape. The musical revolution in the secular world that produced rock and roll and the Beatles on one hand and folk festivals on the other, had its ecclesiastical counterpart. The surge of new music was typified by the Medical Mission Sisters. Their hit album, *Joy Is Like the Rain*, was as much an anthem of renewal as Luther's hymn "A Mighty Fortress" was the anthem of the Reformation. Folk masses followed and were enthusiastically received. An army of songsters ignored the standard question of would-be authorities on church music: "But will it last?" Ice sculptures are lovely, but no one asks if they last. This was disposable art.

The revolution spread from music to other forms, and led to a new tension—the traditional worship service vs. the innovative, experimental, or contemporary service. The organ lost sole possession of first place in church

An Example of Success
by Henry and Christine Hansen

The first religious services in the Vulcan, Alberta, district were conducted by student ministers. Later, church services were organized by a Mr. Fletcher of the Presbyterian Church, Mr. MacKenzie of the Methodist Church, and Mr. Melrose of the Anglican Church.

When the movement towards union of the Methodist, Presbyterian, and Congregational Churches was in progress, Vulcan Community Church was presented throughout Canada as an example of success in union.

music. Groups got together to stitch banners. Bulletin covers were fair game for local artists. New forms of liturgy sprang out of the congregation itself. After all, the word "liturgy" means "the people's work."

Not everyone was happy with the changes. In some congregations, worshippers were polarized by the practice of setting the "traditional" service in one time slot vs. the "contemporary" in another. Parishioners had to make choices that they should probably never have had to make. A few left their church for other denominations that would avoid facing the same issue for another twenty years.

The new approach to worship re-opened the doors of the church to the world of the arts. The stark interiors bred by the Puritan strain in the Reformation yielded to grace and colour. Christians once again worshipped with their eyes as well as with their ears. Geneva gowns gave way to off-white; United Church clergy rivalled their Catholic colleagues in colourful costume.

The Genius of Compromise

For the most part the United Church, true to its genius, moved towards compromise. The enthusiasm of the reformers was tempered by time. Those who preferred forms familiar to their grandparents learned to at least tolerate guitars—as long as they didn't have to hear them every Sunday!

The most lasting effect on the United Church was in its music. The stunning successes first of *Songs for a Gospel People* and then of *Voices United* are evidence of the willingness to embrace good changes that has always typified the United Church's approach to divergence.

Another lasting result has been the increased participation of the laity in the Sunday worship, particularly as "lectors." Inevitably, as more lay persons became involved in leading worship, the question arose as to the uniqueness, the authority, of ordination. The question became sharply focused with the election of the first lay moderator in 1968. While moderator, Dr. Bob McClure was expected to perform acts normally limited to ordained persons. The repercussions led to extensive studies of ministry—most of which the vast body of the United Church blithely ignored. Most of the church began to enjoy a far broader participation of lay persons in church ceremonial.

Thorny Issues for Ecumenical Relations

That too had unexpected consequences. Some felt that this "cheapened" the traditional conviction of a "calling" to ordained ministry. Added to this, the United Church's ecumenical partners found these practices confusing. A major stumbling block to the proposed union of the United Church and the Anglican Church of Canada may have been an Anglican perception that the United Church failed to give due authority to ordination. It seems to have caused little tension within the United Church itself, but did add to the difficulty of relating to sister communions.

Another thorny issue in the ecumenical movement has long been the ordination of women. The United Church tends to assume a superior air in this matter. It was, after all, the first major denomination to ordain a woman— Lydia Gruchy in 1936. But that acceptance was certainly not universal from the beginning. A sizable minority fought Lydia Gruchy's ordination for almost a decade, claiming ordination as a masculine preserve.

Echoes of that argument still linger. At the church's seventy-fifth anniversary, many still object to changes in hymns and prayers in order to avoid sexist language. Still, the United Church has often led the way in recognizing the feminist viewpoint.

Freedom Fighters or Terrorists

There has always been, within the United Church, a debate between personal piety and social activism. The United Church had strongly supported the World Council of Churches (WCC) from its inception in Amsterdam in 1948. It might be expected that a church born of union would look towards unity, if not actual union. So there was very little division of opinion when the United Church became a founding member of what William Temple called "the great new fact of our age."

The World Council had begun as a solidly "Western World" product. However, when the Orthodox Church of Russia entered the Council, along with other churches from the Eastern Bloc and when it appeared that some of the African delegates were leaning rather far to the left, conservative church folk in North America became uneasy. When the Uppsala Assembly in 1968 created its controversial Program to Combat Racism, the *Reader's Digest* joined the fray. It drew a number of conservative media personnel in its wake. The issue became hot. The Program to Combat Racism made grants to groups that were labelled either "freedom fighters" or "terrorists," according to one's political persuasion. A well orchestrated anti-WCC campaign, with a "guns for guerrillas" theme, upset many church persons—especially those in the private commercial sector. A few congregations actually withheld their money from the Mission and Service Fund, mistakenly believing that United Church contributions to the fund for the Program to Combat Racism came from that source.

The controversy died down somewhat when Vancouver hosted the sixth WCC Assembly in 1983. Thanks to outstanding television coverage by the church's Division of Communication, Canadians could see for themselves the responsible nature of debate and decision making on the floor of the assembly. The issue dissolved as some of the "terrorist organizations" became the recognized governments of African nations.

Once More into the Limelight

As the United Church reaches its seventy-fifth year, it is again the subject of critical media attention. Countless legal complications surrounding abuse of Aboriginal children in United Church residential schools even threaten the future of the church. The church is having to learn not just humility but humiliation. Almost as a whole, the church experiences dismay, even horror, and moves to apology and repentance with few resisting.

Born in a maelstrom of controversy and divisiveness, rarely turning its back on difficult issues, plunging into decision making guaranteed to bring about discomfort, the United Church has held together because at its heart are two poles around which all else revolves.

1. The earliest creed of the Christian church—"Jesus Christ is Lord."

2. A profound conviction about the pastoral care of its people as a precious children of a loving God.

It is my conviction that so far we have not failed these two convictions. Yet both are under threat.

The first has always been threatened by the United Church's unique capacity for relating to a secular world. The danger is always the possibility of yielding to that secular spirit. So far, the United Church has dealt creatively with that spirit without being sucked in by it.

The second is threatened by a bureaucratic spirit within the church that values the institution, its procedures, and its decisions, more than the people it serves. The church could easily strangle itself in its own red tape. This appears to me the more serious threat.

So far, though, despite seventy-five years of splits and departures, unity prevails. The United Church holds together and presses on, guided by the conviction that, "God is with us. We are not alone. Thanks be to God."

Bob Wallace, a United Church minister now retired, has written a number of books on preaching and liturgy, and has a particular interest in the relationship of the arts to worship.

A Feast for More Than the Mind

by Carolyn Pogue

Worship can be "as engaging as an afternoon at the opera or the ball game." Religion can be brought alive by the arts.

On a sunny August morning, three hundred children and adults sat under a rich green canopy of trees at Naramata Beach, British Columbia. In the centre of the worship space a large wooden beam hung from ropes. The beam was off balance, weighted down on one end by large globs of clay.

The call to worship began when six young people moved forward, removed a handful of clay from the beam, and told of a way they found balance in the turmoil of their own lives. As the clay was removed, the beam slowly achieved a horizontal position.

What was dramatized was then spoken:

> *Come, people of God; come, as you are.*
> *Come, stressed and rested.*
> *Come, off balance and in balance.*
> *Come, in touch and out of touch. Come, healthy and healing.*
> *Come, connected and adrift.*
> *Come, people of God; Come, come as you are.*

Throughout worship, the beam remained a focus. It became a boat during the scripture story about Jesus sleeping through the storm while the disciples panic: one person held the end of the beam, moving it like a great wooden boat puppet while four others simulated waves on either side with lengths of blue silk. When people told their own stories of storm and unbalance in their lives, they rested a hand on the beam, as though reaching back to that moment when the disciples turned to Jesus out of their desperate fear.

Later, the beam was anchored and became the communion table.

A tree had become a beam, had become a scale, had become a boat, had become a table.

Tim Scorer, Director at Naramata Centre says,

> No amount of comparison in words could carry the power of seeing that simple object transformed into a succession of connected symbols. This is the artistry of worship and faith, transcending boundaries and limitations of age, education, and scholarship. We are visual, kinesthetic, and auditory meaning-makers. Our faith and worship spaces should hold an abundance of sight, sound, and sensuality. Our dependence on word has impoverished us. No wonder

This Goodly Heritage
by Mary Welch

An excerpt from the "Hallowing of Church Union" in the Inaugural Service of the United Church of Roland, Manitoba.

Representative from Knox Church

According to the grace given unto our fathers, as witnesses of the Apostolic Gospel and standard bearers of the Church commissioned to make disciples of all nations, more especially in the manifestation of the Spirit for Christ's Kirk and Covenant, in the care for the speak of education and devotion to sacred learning, receive ye our inheritance among them that are sanctified, and I hereby present and lay on the table the names of the members of Knox Church who are favourable to the consummation of this Union.

All: We glory in the grace given unto us in this goodly heritage.

Representative from Zion Church

According to the grace given unto our fathers, as witnesses of the Apostolic Gospel and standard bearers of the Church commissioned to make disciples of all nations, more especially in the manifestation of the Spirit in evangelical zeal and human redemption, the testimony of spiritual experience, and the ministry of sacred song, receive ye our inheritance among them that are sanctified, and I hereby present and lay on the table the list of the members of Zion Church.

All: We glory in the grace given unto us in this goodly heritage.

Minister: I hereby declare that by the regular action of the congregation of Knox Church and by the regular action of the Official Board of Zion Church, and having deposited the Roll of Membership of these two Churches, I declare they are united and constituted as one church, to be designated and known as The United Church of Roland and a Congregation of The United Church of Canada.

people turn from the sterile wordiness of our worship times to seek stimulation in other shrines.

It's my guess that most people in our churches, leaders and laity, are not aware of the potential for worship to be as engaging as an afternoon at the opera or the ball game.

Dancing Partners

Faith and art are not new dance partners; they've always danced with biblical people. Art, like faith, draws us to witness, interpret, and proclaim the truth with new ears, new eyes, new hearts. Is it any wonder, then, that Jesus used the art of storytelling in his ministry? Throughout the Bible, faith and art dance together in song, drama, poetry, movement, parable, fabric, clay, metal, and wood.

Saint Francis used drama centuries ago to narrate Christ's birth to illiterate worshippers. He has been credited with "inventing" the crèche. We still tell the story with costumes and props; sets and lights; movement, music, and words. The Passion story, performed by whole communities, dramatically portrays the life of the carpenter, the one who crafted wood with his hands and used his voice to explain, to mesmerize, to challenge audiences with fictions he created to illuminate his faith. He taught them many things with parables: "Listen! Once there was a man…"

When The United Church of Canada was created with fierce and tender imaginings just seventy-five years ago, we inherited stories in ink, stained glass, wood, song, and story. We have continued telling and showing, explaining and expanding. As our theology grows and changes and is invigorated, our expression through music reflects this.

An Abundance of Opportunities

The 1960s introduced new dance steps, both in and out of the sanctuary: *Joseph and the Amazing Technicolor Dreamcoat*, *Godspell*, *Jesus Christ Superstar*. Jesus really rocked during those years. Fabric banners splashed colour in our churches. Lenten study groups still watch *Jesus Christ Superstar* or explore newer films such as *Jesus of Montréal* or *Romero*.

In 1976 the controversial *Crucified Woman* sculpture by Almuth Lutkenaus appeared in the sanctuary of Bloor St. United Church in Toronto. Some applauded this artistic offering, others were appalled, but all who saw her were moved. Like no sermon, this symbol focused hope and despair and determination. Today the sculpture stands in a garden at Emmanuel College offering a gathering place, solace to the weary, and food for the soul. After the Montréal Massacre, many were drawn to the garden of the *Crucified Woman*.

Today, the invitation to join the dance with faith and art is heard more often throughout the United Church. Women's groups learn ancient sacred circle dances and offer them at Sunday morning worship. Scripture is presented as an exciting story through intergenerational gatherings, readers' theatre, poetry, and dramatic dramas that challenge complacency, boredom, and biblical illiteracy.

Storytellers like Fran Hare of Calgary and former moderator Lois Wilson enliven worship, meetings, and learning sessions with wit, wisdom, and new insights. United Church Book Rooms carry a rich variety of audiotapes, books, and videos. Training centres offer courses and workshops on personal writing and using *midrash*.

The current moderator, the Rt. Rev. Bill Phipps, is encouraging. "Artists are the prophets of any given age," he says. "Poets, novelists, painters, composers—artists of all kinds—reflect our world to us in all its beauty and ugliness, calling us into the future with new insights and passions. At their greatest depths, they touch the dream of God and connect it to our hearts. Prophets can be found in theatres, galleries, concert halls, and book stores in our neighbourhoods."

Changing Perceptions

Rev. Jeff Challoner of Red Deer, Alberta, has promoted the dance of faith and art during his ministry. "I believe strongly that the arts have a place in the church, as a means of presenting the gospel in an interesting manner. Theatre actually began in the church."

Clowning had its roots in the church, too; Jeff learned the art and has ministered through it. "I have led clowning ministry workshops and conducted clown worship, always being careful to prepare the congregations beforehand in understanding the place of humour, the Hebrew love of parable and storytelling, and 'picture language,' as well as the effectiveness of the visual, non-spoken word. I believe firmly that Jesus had a sense of humour, and that he used this gift in his teaching," he adds.

Jeff was concerned for years about the dull way in which scripture is often read in worship. Lately he has been involved with the Biblical Literacy Project of Alberta and Northwest Conference and helped create a Biblical Readers' Theatre Kit containing a manual and interactive video.

More Than Words Alone

The United Church of the 1990s celebrates faith and the arts in other ways, too. Author Keri Wehlander, of Nanaimo, B.C., has been described by the United Church Publishing House as one who "ministers through creativity—writing, liturgical dance, music, drama, and photography."

When people open the front door of Beaconsfield United Church in Québec, they enter an art gallery. "This is a transition place between the street and the sanctuary," says Rev. Peter Short. "It is where spirituality through the medium of art is permitted and enjoyed. It's a place of dialogue between the spirituality of the street as expressed by artists and the spirituality of the sanctuary." This is art to engage the viewer. Peter sees the church as a public building and the gallery as a place for public dialogue. Themes of exhibits change monthly. In the past, the gallery at Beaconsfield United has shown art from the church school; the local Catholic school; and from local painters, photographers, and sculptors. When the art reflected a Lenten theme, Peter said some comments were "provocative, even shocking." But then, so is crucifixion.

Peter believes art is important in our faith journeys. "It allows more than just articulate speakers to participate in the expression of faith…not only for those creating art, but for those receiving it, too."

Helen Hliaras Wood encourages the idea of art in the churches even further. Helen is a student minister at United Theological College in Montréal.

> An artist-in-residence in a church could challenge and en-
> courage a congregation. I've seen [visual] artists-in-resi-
> dence in schools….The students had an hour a week with
> the artist….I've also seen art therapy used with adolescents
> and youth groups. We don't use the resources we have for

young people. I think art in churches would draw other
youth from the community, too. Imagine!

Although many people in the church decry the number of young people
who leave during their teen years, one might also ask whether art in most
United Churches makes them feel welcome. Do they notice it? Care about it?
Do they contribute to it?

Broadening Our Horizons

Ava Kelly believes we need new art in our churches. Ava is a candidate for
ministry, also at United Theological College in Montréal. "There's a
disservice to keeping old art," she says. "One is the lack of inclusiveness.
When you continue to have 'White Jesus' art, it perpetuates the isolation of
WASP congregations. WASPs isolate themselves and others feel isolated."

Ava recalls a First Nations friend who told her about the huge framed
picture he'd grown up with. "All the people in heaven were White. He
learned through art that there was no place there for him."

"I am a fifth-generation Black Canadian," she says. "Union United
Church in Montréal began because Black people weren't welcome in other
churches." Ava muses further: "Where was the art for my grandparents'
generation? It's only in the last few years you can even buy a Christmas card
with Black people on it."

Both Old and New

Visual impressions pack power. New images or interpretations need not
replace art in our sanctuaries; it can be displayed alongside. In the sanctuary at
Emmanuel United Church in Englehart, northern Ontario, works of art
reflect different aspects of God's community: colourful fabric banners created
by member artist Dorothy Peverley, graced with butterflies; a traditional
Bruozetti print of *The Last Supper* (under which probably generations of babies
have been baptized); a breathtaking original acrylic painting by artist
Bebaminojmat, Leland Bell of the Anishnabek Nation, Manitoulin Island,
whose art links Emmanuel to other churches across northern Ontario. To
commemorate the United Church's Apology to First Nations peoples in 1986,
collector David Humphries donated one of Bell's paintings to each
congregation in Manitou Conference.

A Visual Feast

The 1997 General Council in Camrose, Alberta, featured an art gallery and
performance area. Displayed there were faith expressions by professional and

non-professional, young and old artists, from throughout Canada and from countries where we have partnerships. The art was haunting, jolly, profound, beautiful. The styles were as varied as is the church. Traditional and modern expressions created a visual feast through fabric, metal, clay paint, papier mâché, crayon, and pencil.

The performance area provided a place for drama, liturgical dance, poetry reading, storytelling, organ music. The gallery provided an oasis for council members who needed respite from long days of meetings. It was a sanctuary for recharging spiritual batteries.

Art opens new pathways for our thinking and thus for our deliberations. In 1998, the Daring Hope conference celebrated the Ecumenical Decade of Churches in Solidarity with Women. Crayons were part of each table group's centrepiece, and paper covered the tables. By the end of the conference, almost seven hundred people had drawn, doodled, and coloured their reactions and impressions and hopes on their table tops. Using large canvases, Regina Coupar, Nova Scotia poet and conference artist-in-residence, painted her impressions of the stories, music, worship, and discussion she was hearing. Her reflections surely opened new pathways for God to walk among us.

Samuel Johnson once said that "Language is the dress of thought." Might we say that "Art could be the dress of prayer"?

Today, youth, elders, and in-betweens are buying crayons, pens, drums, cameras, dancing shoes, paint brushes, and clay for themselves as well as for children. Some haven't touched these tools in years, but they are making surprising discoveries about the power of art—about themselves, their abilities, their faith communities, and their faith. They are learning that God speaks with many voices and is full of surprises. That play shouldn't end when childhood does. That the process of creating is more important than the result. That possibilities don't have straight lines. That imagination is a gift from God that needs exercise. And that creating and receiving art in community can be an astonishing, life-giving form of prayer.

May we enter the next seventy-five years in a joyful, courageous, and imaginative spirit. May our dance, paintings, banners, music, and drama enrich our worship, enliven our faith, and help us become living prayers for the world.

*Carolyn Pogue is a freelance author and
editor who lives in Calgary, Alberta.*

With Voices United

by David Kai

Both the content and the process of producing a new hymn book proved typically United Church.

Considering the diversity of worship styles, theological leanings, and congregational settings within The United Church of Canada, the title *Voices United* for a hymn and worship book might seem optimistic. And yet *Voices United* has received a warm reception across the country, providing a uniting voice in worship for hundreds of thousands each Sunday.

The title for this book was gleaned from the third verse of the hymn, "We Praise You, O God" by Julia Cory, which reads:

> *With voices united our praises we offer,*
> *and gladly our songs of thanksgiving we raise.*

Jeeva Sam, a member of the Hymn and Worship Resource Committee (HWRC) that produced *Voices United*, noticed this phrase after the hymn was sung by the committee during worship. He quipped that it might make a good title; the committee eventually agreed.

Appropriately enough, the whole process of producing *Voices United* reflected the United Church way of doing things. It involved committees and consensus, consultation and creativity, and, of course, controversy.

Prelude

It is often said, "A journey of a thousand miles begins with a single step." The production of a new worship resource is an enormous task, yet it is composed of a multitude of comparatively small steps.

By the time I joined the HWRC in 1993, many of these steps had already been taken. The 1990 General Council had decided to produce a new hymn and worship resource. Members had been sought for the HWRC who would reflect the diversity within The United Church of Canada. John Ambrose, a gifted leader and musician, had taken on the enormous responsibility of being the managing editor. The management of the project was lead by key staff such as Fred Graham, Consultant, Congregational Worship, Division of Mission in Canada, and Beth Parker, Director, Publishing and Graphics.

The HWRC, ably led by its co-chairs, Nancy Hardy and Len Lythgoe, had begun consultation with the wider church. It had divided itself into subcommittees to address areas such as Text, Tune, Psalter, Liturgy, World Music, Intergenerational Music, and Service Music. There would also be regional groupings to prepare proposals for different sections of *Voices United*.

Some committee members told me that I was joining them at an opportune time. Theological and language guidelines, already agreed upon, would result in the editing of some hymns and the laying aside of others. Stylistic and regional differences had been aired; the committee was functioning well as a team, working by consensus, agreeing on most issues while agreeing to disagree on others.

The task at hand was to rate the hymns of the three most widely used hymn resources in the United Church—the blue *Hymnary* (1930), the red *Hymn Book* (1971), and the green *Songs for a Gospel People* (1987)—and to determine which would be carried forward into *Voices United*. A national survey of congregations guided our deliberations.

In a sense we were being asked to assess the musical heritage of The United Church of Canada and to preserve it for future generations. To carry out this task would take the wisdom of Solomon, the political smarts of Esther, the searching spirit of Mary, and the industriousness of Martha.

Turning Pages Back

The importance of hymns in worship is no better expressed than in the preface to *The Hymnary*, published in 1930:

> Since the early days of Christianity a crowning glory of the Church of God has been the place and power of spiritual song in [its] worship and life. The Church "has come singing down through the ages." Through this gracious medium [its] people, generation after generation, have lifted up their hearts and voices in adoring praise; have poured out their aspirations in prayer; have proclaimed the verities of the faith; and have expressed the higher emotions of the soul.

The further we became involved in the work of preparing *Voices United*, the more we realized that we stood on holy ground. It was our task to honour the musical and liturgical heritage of the United Church, to add to that heritage, and to launch it into the next millennium. To do this we began by examining closely the hymn resources that had served the United Church in the past.

The so-called "blue book," the 1930 *Hymnary*, had captured the hearts and imaginations of United Church people for decades. *The Hymnary* succeeded in bringing together the musical heritage of the denominations that joined to form The United Church of Canada in 1925. It came to be cherished as the United Church's own hymn book; our surveys showed that many congregations continued to use it into the 1990s.

Although *The Hymnary* was the mainstay of United Church worship, it did not always stand alone. Even in past generations, many felt the need for different, more energetic music. The popular *Songs of the Gospel* (1948), containing many gospel and camp meeting songs, was a supplement found in many church pews.

By the 1960s the church was aware that the blue book had become dated in its language and theology. Many of *The Hymnary*'s hymns were considered too personal and sentimental; changes in the social fabric demanded hymns that were more "relevant," more linked to the everyday experience of worshippers.

As The United Church of Canada and the Anglican Church of Canada were discussing a possible union, it seemed appropriate that the two churches work together on a joint book. All of our churches were entering what is now known as the "hymn explosion," a time of great creativity and change in hymnody. The red *Hymn Book* captured some of that excitement in new hymns written by Fred Kaan and Sydney Carter, and by Canadians such as Walter Farquharson and Herbert O'Driscoll, many of them set to new arrangements by committee members F. R. C. Clarke and Stanley Osborne. *The Hymn Book* was also notable for its inclusion of spirituals and hymns from non-Western cultures.

While the *Hymn Book* was well accepted into the United Church, some mourned the loss of favourite gospel and children's hymns; others found some arrangements too pianistic for choirs and congregations more accustomed to traditional four-part writing. More important, changes within church and society continued to accelerate during the seventies and eighties. Contemporary and folk-style hymns accompanied by guitars and other instruments became increasingly popular. Developments in theologies of liberation, whether Third World or feminist, led to heightened awareness and concern about the theology and language of hymns.

The popular supplement, *Songs for a Gospel People* (1987), addressed many of these changes and concerns, incorporating contemporary folk-style hymns and hymns more modern and inclusive in language and theology. It presented a more global vision of the church, introducing hymns from different cultures and traditions from around the world. It also introduced many United Church congregations to service music, particularly that of the Taizé community.

As the HWRC carefully combed through these resources, we realized how rich a tradition had been handed down to us. We became aware of the breadth of the United Church: a hymn that was a favourite in one part of the country may have never been heard of in another. We agreed that the diversity within

A Musical Legacy
by Fred J. Thompson

Surely one of the most famous unpaid and tireless workers for the early United Church was Amy Ferguson—a musician of note.

During the Depression, in February 1931 (only six years after the United Church was born), Mrs. Ferguson started the Boys' Choir. Little did she know what a legacy she would create and leave. The beautiful boy-soprano voices she trained were only the beginning. Many became soprano soloists or sang in groups and choirs. They competed in festivals and competitions, and usually came away with the highest marks and favourable comments from adjudicators. As a result of the exceptionally well-trained voices of the Boys' Choir, St. Paul's United became very well known. On those Sunday mornings when we were in the choir loft or when we put on concerts, the church was overflowing.

As the boys reached adulthood, they naturally scattered to various parts of Canada or elsewhere. Many continued their musical education. Many became soloists in demand. Many joined the Armed Forces. Some lost their lives while serving during the Second World War. Many became career musicians, such as my brother Ray who taught music and passed on Mrs. Ferguson's teachings.

I think it was 1972 that Mrs. Ferguson passed away. That was the end of an era, as her beloved Boys' Choir also passed away. What a void that created in Nelson and the Kootenays.

the United Church should be reflected in *Voices United* so that all could find a home within the book. We sought to restore the best of what had been lost from the past, to maintain that which was treasured in the present, and to add what we thought to be of value for the future.

Turning Pages Ahead

As well as sensing that we stood on holy ground, we also came to realize how much we stood on shifting ground—how much had changed in the social context even in the years since the 1971 *Hymn Book*. It was up to us to find fresh ways to express the gospel in turbulent times. And so we looked for new and "new-to-us" hymns that would reflect this reality, and hymns that would challenge our culture, not simply mirror it. Our search would take us literally to the ends of the earth.

As the HWRC sought to strike a balance between the old and the new, it could fall back on some wise advice:

Young people especially wish to sing hymns cast in the style of the twentieth century. Despite the difficulties involved, the church must be hospitable to all creative energies for it to live as Christ's body in these times, and seek to adapt contemporary modes of poetic and musical expression for use in public worship.

Surprisingly, these comments come not from some current publication, but from the preface to the 1971 *Hymn Book*!

In search of fresh ways of expressing the Christian faith in song, the members of the HWRC and other consultants pored through thousands of hymns and hundreds of resources: recent hymn books and hymnal supplements; compilations by hymn writers such as Sylvia Dunstan, Brian Wren, Shirley Erena Murray, and Ruth Duck; resources from different cultures around the world; independent publications by composers such as Linnea Good, Carolyn McDade, Ron Klusmeier, and the Iona community. Consultations were held with representatives from Ethnic Ministries, Francophone, and All Native Circle congregations to include resources with special meaning for them. In addition, thousands of new submissions from hymn writers across Canada were sifted to find undiscovered gems. New psalm settings were sought and written as the Psalter subcommittee endeavoured to include all the lectionary psalms.

The constant problem for the HWRC was which of these wonderful new resources we would have to leave out. Although it was impossible to include everything, we were grateful for the opportunity to sample the works of so many gifted authors and composers. Gradually, meeting by meeting, hymn by hymn, old and new began to blend into a collection as exciting and diverse as The United Church of Canada itself.

Accompaniment

At one gathering of the HWRC in 1994, John Ambrose passed around a fully bound mock-up version of *Voices United*. While duplicating the finished book's size, weight, colour, and cover design, all the pages were completely blank! As the book passed from hand to hand, each member had a vision of what those blank pages would contain and a growing sense of excitement for the completion of this project.

Naturally, there were bumps in the road along the way. The 1994 General Council decided to remove the liturgies from *Voices United*, thinking that they would create doctrinal issues that had not been officially addressed. While this was a setback, the work of the liturgy subcommittee continued in a service book sampler that eventually resulted in the production of a companion service book to *Voices United*. Controversies arose over decisions to edit some hymns and to exclude others, "Onward Christian Soldiers" in particular. After much deliberation, the committee decided to stand by their theological and language guidelines.

The sheer volume of work was a hurdle in and of itself. Even as the HWRC completed its role there were still months of frantic work ahead to meet the constant deadlines, to push *Voices United* to completion.

But equally, there were uplifting and inspiring moments: Fred Graham's spontaneous composition of the delightful tune for "A Woman and a Coin— the Coin is Lost" in the midst of an HWRC meeting; the growing sense of excitement as piece by piece, a truly Canadian and United worship resource began to take shape; our continuing good-natured disagreement over whether "A Part of the Family" should be a part of the family of hymns included in *Voices United*....

The development of *Voices United* demonstrated much that is vibrant and alive in The United Church of Canada—its spirit of inclusivity, its ability to embrace diversity, its willingness to risk and address its current social context.

Our Praises We Offered
by Beth Parker

As well as being a runaway best-seller, *Voices United* was a huge publishing achievement for The United Church of Canada. "Producing" the book involved years of planning, scheduling, budgeting, designing, and promoting. Every piece of music was input on an electronic synthesizer attached to a computer. Databases were created in order to collect the vast amount of information needed for the indexes. The information was sorted, cross-referenced, and then tied to page numbers. On-staff designers worked for several years, first to create the logo, then to design the pages and the layout. Editorial staff proofread along with volunteers; copyright and permissions staff contacted contributors from around the world in order to secure permissions or, in many instances, alter a phrase or a word, and collect contracts; production staff worked with numbers, budgets, and schedules to meet the publication date.

I will always remember those seemingly endless days of working on *Voices United*, not being able to see the end of the tunnel, but moving forward with confidence that this indeed would all come together in the end. We all worried constantly about every facet of its publication. Even when the books finally rolled off press in Québec one sunny day in spring, 1996, rather than feel a great weight of relief, all we could feel was the continued weight of responsibility. We all wanted to know that collectively we had put together a physical product that equalled the kind of care and time spent by the editor and the committee on its contents.

Beth Parker is Director of Publishing, Division of Communication.

The HWRC embodied these characteristics as well. We felt in many ways like a microcosm of the United Church, a small, United Christian community that, in spite of its diversity, enjoyed being together and working together towards a common goal. While we were not always unanimous in our thinking, we were respectful and open to the gifts of the other. All of us feel very blessed to have been a part of such a special undertaking. Equally gratifying has been the warm reception that *Voices United* has received, turning it into a runaway best-seller.*

Postlude

Even as *Voices United* establishes itself in the life of the church, it is inevitable that future generations of Christians will require new worship resources. Will even more modern styles of music be needed as many United Churches choose to become more "seeker-friendly"? Will there be more hymnal supplements or perhaps some more "high-tech" resources? Might *Voices United* be the last United Church hymn book in printed form? Will some committee in the future regard "In the bulb there is a flower" as "that old chestnut" or as a "heritage hymn"?

Whatever the future holds, we know that our praise of God will continue—whether in forms ancient or modern, in hymns written nearby or halfway around the globe, in chorale, calypso, and chant. For God will be with us to guide and to inspire, to challenge and to nurture, to comfort and to bless. To God the Word, the Singer and the Song, may the church forever raise its voice in songs of praise. Amen.

> *With voices united our praises we offer,*
> *and gladly our songs of thanksgiving we raise.*
> *Our sins now confessing, we pray for your blessing,*
> *To you, our great Redeemer, forever be praise!* (VU#218)

David Kai is diaconal minister at Orleans United Church, Ottawa.

* To date, more than 256,635 copies of the full-music edition have been sold!

Stewardship

The subject we don't like to talk about

Stewardship in the United Church

by Christopher White

Stewardship is to the United Church what a root canal is to dentistry.

O Lord, no matter what we say or what we do,
this (point to offering) *is what we think of You.*
— Stewardship Prayer of Hilbert Berger

Stewardship is not a subject that we in the United Church embrace with joy and enthusiasm. In fact, if you are clergy and wish to experience a root canal without anesthetic, I strongly encourage you to explore what is called a "Stewardship Campaign." I can testify to this personally, having just gone through one myself with my congregation.

While the results were excellent, the process left me limp with exhaustion and prone to screaming whenever the phone rang. My wonderful warm congregation was transformed into a group of people who acted as though they were on a bus tour whose destination had been changed without their consent. It was not a pretty sight. Some people stopped coming to church all together; others simply waited out the weeks until the program was over and then returned. Some didn't like the process we used, some were offended, some were mad. Some liked one part, but not another. All of them called me about it. The period from September to November 1998 was what I termed, with apologies to Queen Elizabeth, *Fallis Horriblis*.

And yet statistically the Stewardship Campaign was a tremendous success. Pledges raised givings more than 23 percent without an every member visitation. Our pledge rate was high on gifts of time and talent, while financial givings rose not simply among our core givers, but among those new people whose givings had been relatively quite low. Instead of ending the year with a deficit, we came through with a $5,000 surplus. Even more amazing, in January and February 1999—traditionally low giving months—we were up $7,500 over the previous year!

Always a Strong Reaction

So why did we get this hostile reaction? I know from other clergy and lay people that we were hardly unique. What is it about the United Church that causes people to react so strongly on issues of stewardship? Does this also explain the holding pattern and decline of the Mission and Service Fund? Or are there other issues that we need to urgently address for our denomination?

The reality is that we are totally confused about what the "stewardship" means. Is stewardship about money, about donating my time, or about how I live my life? The answer, of course, is "Yes" to all of the above. True stewardship is a radical repositioning of our lives to God and God's work. The Rev. Vince Alfano, formerly of the national Department of Stewardship Services, tells of a member of his congregation who came to him. "Vince," the member said, " I trust the church to spend the 10 percent I tithe, but I need your help with the other 90 percent." That is for me the living definition of stewardship.

Or as Janet Marshall Eibner from the Potentials Group put it: "God gives us everything, our work, our spouses, our children—and in return we give God pocket change." For too long we have encouraged the giving of the pocket change of our lives to God.

A Short-term View of History

Our problems around stewardship go back to the very beginning of our denomination. Our name says everything. First, we are a *united* church: four denominations spliced together under one structure. And we are quintessentially Canadian. Our traditions have been formed only since 1925. That is both our blessing and our curse. It is a blessing because we left interdenominational strife behind (although we quickly invented our own internal battles). It is our curse because we have a short-term view of history. Instead of seeing ourselves within a context that goes back two thousand years, we only look back seventy-five, and so we miss the big picture.

In fact, we understand ourselves mainly in terms of the period immediately following the Second World War. It was a period of unparalleled and almost unnatural growth caused by the combination of the Great Depression and the war. We had seen nothing like it before; we may never see anything like it again. In that period of time we became Canada's church, and we thought of ourselves as Canada's church. People flocked in. To use the line from *Field of Dreams*—"If you build it they will come"—we built and they came, in their thousands.

We became the church of our culture. The economy was more than stable; it was growing and the much feared return to Depression never materialized. Instead, the longest period of economic expansion our country ever experienced began to unfold. Jobs were secure. If the church's coffers were not exactly overflowing, we were at least solvent and viable. As the church of the culture we became experts at welcoming people into the building, but less good at integrating them into the faith. They came for stability and for their children, but instead of integrating them into a faith of commitment, we simply assumed that they would always be there.

Hay for the Parsonage Stable
by Evan Tonin

On February 8, 1998, two historic United Churches in Medicine Hat, Alberta, amalgamated. Fifth Avenue United Church had been the first Methodist Church in the city, started in 1883. Memorial Salem United Church had itself been the amalgamation of three previous churches: Knox Presbyterian, founded 1907; Washington Avenue Methodist, 1913; and Salem Congregational, about 1914. Some excerpts from the minutes reveal how times (and values) have changed.

29 September 1897: "The trustee board were instructed to fix up the parsonage with tar paper and siding, shingling and painting. The cost to be about $150, $68 of which was subscribed at the meeting. Sisters Porter and Sprague were appointed to collect the balance required."

Motion, 3 October 1900: "That brothers Cosens, Collier, Bridgman be appointed to sell the old church at a minimum of $350, without seating."

Motion, 20 November 1900: "That we contract with Mr. H. C. Cooper to supply the church with coal for the winter at $3 per ton."

24 July 1906: Brother Gordon introduced the question of more room for hay in the parsonage stable."

From Boom to Almost Bust

My own congregation's history is instructive here. Westminster United Church was founded in 1958. At its peak it had more than 250 children in its Sunday school; the place was packed. By the early seventies, though, the children were grown and gone. The church was in dire straits. At one famous congregational meeting, the plate was passed three times before sufficient pledges were gathered to keep the doors open. In less than twenty years we had gone from boom to almost bust. As our Sunday school approaches the 200 mark again, I see this as a cautionary tale.

This story was also mirrored in our national revenues. The Missionary and Maintenance Fund, the precursor to today's Mission and Service Fund, was the unified fund that arose out of church union. It moved us from a church of designated givers to a model of unified giving. The strengths of this model are obvious. It allows the church the flexibility to fund a wide variety of important ministries, whether they are popular in the eyes of the church or not. It is, in fact, the most apparently mundane projects that are the most critical.

This model allowed the church to expand its ministries both nationally and internationally all through the post-war decades. Until the 1980s. By 1986 the M&S fund target was $35 million. But well before the storms of 1988, the fund had reached a plateau. Expansion was over. The money was still there to meet demands, but the growth of the church's ministry had stopped.

Then in 1988 the storm hit.

Voting with Their Dollars

It is said that after the General Council decision money became a weapon in the political makeup of our denomination for the first time. People who disagreed with the denomination's policies "punished" the church by reducing their givings and, in some cases, boycotting the M&S Fund completely. Another argument was made that those who found themselves in opposition to the church's actions had no other way of expressing themselves in the present structures, and had only this way of sending a message.

I suggest something quite different. The decision of 1988 simply brought to a head tensions in the denomination that had been building for years. The results that we now have were inevitable, regardless of 1988. The decline in revenues had already begun. Why? Because we had become the church of the culture, the welcoming church, not a denomination of commitment. We were embarrassed to ask for money, for time, for talents. As Canadians we were diffident; we found the whole subject embarrassing. As one stewardship consultant said, "It is easier for the church to talk about sex than money." She was absolutely right. That inability is slowly strangling the church.

This was combined with a number of other factors that exacerbated the problem. First, denominational loyalties were loosening. We were becoming far more congregational. This was due in part to the changing nature of church people and the changes in our society as a whole.

As Reginald Bibby has pointed out, Canadians still identify with institutions far more than Americans do. Our "brand loyalty" remains quite high. But I believe that is changing. My congregation consists not just of United Church folk but also of Anglicans, Baptists, Catholics, Lutherans, and even a family with a Pentecostal background.

Some of our people have come from other congregations in the wider community, and some leave to go to other churches or denominations. In other words, our church is a fluid and ever changing environment. People go where they are comfortable. If it stops being a comfortable place for them, they simply leave. Whether we like it or not, that is our reality. Their primary focus is therefore the local congregation, not the denomination. Frankly, for many of them, the denominational identity is simply irrelevant.

The next important factor is economic. In the wonderful post-war world, jobs were secure. Today I don't know anyone with a truly secure job. Our unemployment rate stays in the 8 percent range. Both the federal and provincial governments now treat 8 percent as full employment. Full-time jobs with benefits are shrinking, while part-time and contract work continues to grow. People work long hours in uncertain times. And into that world comes the church asking them for a long-term financial commitment for both the local congregation and the denominational mission.

When you combine these factors with a steep decline in membership, what is surprising is not that our M&S dollars have shrunk, but that they haven't plummeted through the floor.

A People of Good Hearts

But there is another reality that comes to the fore as well. God created us to be a generous and a giving people. Church people have good hearts. They have faith, they want to heal our world, they want to be the hands of Christ. If

The Offering
by Ralph Milton

Liturgies may vary, but there's one element of every worship service that you don't dare forget.

I do a bit of what I euphemistically term "preaching around." That is, I preach in a variety of different pulpits, from time to time. I've discovered that no two churches across this great United Church of ours use exactly the same order of service.

Because I'm a visitor—and because the part of me that works better than any other part is my forgetter—I tend to get those orders of service mixed up occasionally. I put the reading before the hymn, or the prayer after the children's time. And everyone just smiles tolerantly.

One year, I filled in as pulpit supply at St. Paul's United Church in our city for eight whole months. During that time I forgot hymns, missed the anthem (the choir was miffed but nobody else), overlooked the children's time, etc. And I discovered you can forget any of those things, and forgiveness is not hard to find.

I discovered that there is only one inviolable element of the United Church's liturgy. (It's rather like former Moderator Lois Wilson's comment that the only question in clergy ordination vows to which candidates absolutely must answer with an unequivocal "Yes" is, "Will you subscribe to the Pension Plan?")

One day, as we were singing the closing hymn, I noticed some folks at the back of the church waving frantically at me. "Strange," I thought. "Why are they doing this?" There were some charismatic folks in the congregation who occasionally sang or prayed with their hands up, but I'd never seen them waving little white slips of paper in the air.

I was stepping out from behind the pulpit into the centre of the chancel, preparing to close the service with the benediction, when one of the elders walked up to the front. In the final lines of the hymn, he whispered to me: "You forgot the offering!"

I guess it's the one thing in the United Church that you don't dare forget.

Ralph Milton is a co-founder of Wood Lake Books, and author of the perennial best-seller This United Church of Ours.

the opportunities are given to them they will respond. They will give faithfully as they are able, but they want to know that their money is making a difference. They have less disposable income and more demands for it. It is therefore critical that they have a clearly accountable connection to what they give.

This is where the crunch between unified and designated giving becomes apparent. Unified givers believe that we give in faith; they trust the church to spread the money appropriately. Those who support designated giving argue that people have the right to give their money to God's work as they see fit.

Both are right. The trust level in our society for all institutions has dropped, not just for the church. So we need not take it personally—we need simply adapt to it. But today is not the first period that we have attempted to bridge the gap between the two views of giving.

The Program That Almost Worked

In 1969 a campaign was launched called "Live Love." The Live Love Campaign was designed to connect congregations to the recipients of Mission and Service dollars. A portion of your M&S contribution could be designated to a particular mission unit; the local church would send letters and enter into a relationship that would benefit both giver and receiver. You would experience your dollars in action.

The idea was sound, but it failed for a variety of reasons. First, all the attention was centred upon high-profile projects. I was told that the mission boat *Thomas Crosby* could have sunk under the weight of the mail that they received. Second, there was not adequate administrative support in place for the project. Live Love was considered to have failed. It was wrapped up in 1972.

I suggest that it is now time for us to revisit Live Love and come up with a modified program that will work. Indeed, we have no choice. While individual Mission and Service donations are higher, fewer are giving and the donors are ageing. The days when we can count on automatic support have ended. The time has come, I believe, to re-invent ourselves—not out of despair but out of realistic hope. We can no longer cling to what was. We can attempt to raise funds until we are blue in the face. But in an atmosphere of growing individualism and congregationalism, we are bound to fail unless we connect the people to the projects.

The Unified Budget Is Dead

The Mission and Service Fund is no longer the sole funding instrument of the United Church. We have so many individual funds that no one can make that claim any more with any seriousness. From *The Observer*, to the Native Healing Fund, the special appeals of the colleges, and various disaster relief funds that appear regularly, designated giving has already returned to the church.

So let us move forward based on reality, not nostalgia. The model I propose would work something like this. Presbyteries, in co-operation with the Conferences, would assign mission units to individual congregations. For a period of three to five years a congregation would have a relationship with that unit. They would be responsible for fostering communication. A portion (say 10 percent) of their M&S donation could be designated to them. Mission units would rotate among congregations, so that a balance of high- and low-profile projects would work their way through the churches.

This would become an educational opportunity as well. I am sure that those congregations who participated would increase their givings. It would also in concrete ways tell the story of our church. We know the stories of our congregations but the national links that hold us together are shrivelling faster and faster.

As a church, the time has come for us to proclaim boldly that the church and God's realm have first call upon the charitable dollars and gifts of time of those who participate in our congregational life. I advocate nothing less than a change in the very culture of the United Church. It is time for us to move from offering simply a Sunday welcome to becoming a way of life. It will not be easy, but it is the way of the next millennium.

We are, by and large a liberal church, but true stewardship means a requirement of commitment that is more closely connected to those churches we consider conservative. A liberal church with a conservative commitment—can such a church exist? Yes. It's already being born.

Christopher White is the minister of Westminster United Church in Whitby, Ontario, and a freelance author and broadcaster.

A Passion for Justice

How the
United Church
expresses its faith

Threatened with Resurrection

by Julie Graham

The United Church doesn't struggle with justice issues just because it thinks they're easier than building faith—God doesn't offer us any other choice.

Most people involved with the United Church have an opinion about its ceaseless meddling in the affairs of the world. This article, written as a present for a seventy-fifth birthday of a young church, reflects my own connections and opinions. But justice seeking and justice making belong to each individual and the entire community. As our friends in Latin America have taught us these past few decades, it is important to name your own story, see in it the connections to God's world, and then decide how best to take action on those parts that need changing, or renewing, or encouraging.

Chocolate Was My Downfall
It happened in the bulk food section of the grocery store, in front of the bin marked "20% OFF." The sign read "Real Smarties (Nestlé)." I broke my boycott. Five minutes later I sneaked out of the store, my favourite childhood treat tucked into my bag, the damning receipt tossed in the garbage.

The churches' boycott of the giant Swiss food company, Nestlé, began over marketing practices for its baby formula in Third World countries. The United Church supported the boycott from the beginning, as it had the pioneer of all such actions, the grape boycott led by César Chavez at the end of the 1960s. These early boycotts were the forerunners of today's consumer actions that chip away at the corporate walls of environmental destruction, union-busting, and child labour. It was also my first-ever boycott, thanks to the church members who explained how the issues fitted into my four-year-old world. Thanks to their influence, I keep that boycott to this day—with, as noted above, the odd lapse.

Pushed out of Places of Power
My generation is the first in Canadian history to have grown up largely without the influence of mainline Christianity. We have watched the end of "Christendom" in Canada. It hasn't been dramatic, this shift away from a power and authority held since Christianity became the official religion of the Roman Empire. It's been a slow decline, a silent drifting away in day-to-day life, culture, and thinking.

The older, mainline churches, including the United Church, no longer set the tone for our multicultural society. Many people now follow another path to God. Or they may see the formerly large churches of Canada as either unbearably liberal and lacking in a fiery faith, or mild hypocrites who long ago ceased to practise what they preach, and who tiredly drag around a great mound of baggage left over from the days when they had power.

Yet some of my friends tell me that, on principle, they will not walk into a church—except for the United Church. "Why?" I always ask, wondering how my church wound up with this reputation. And the answer is almost always the same: yours is the only church that has risked conflict and uproar within and without in order to include people. It takes risks; it doesn't simply sit back and preach, and it doesn't let disapproval deter it from doing the right thing.

Doing the "Right Thing"

Doing the "right thing" has been both blessing and occasional plague throughout the existence of The United Church of Canada. It sees itself as playing an active part in bringing to birth God's vision for a new Earth, a somewhat confused and clumsy midwife at a holy birth.

In so doing, the United Church treads a theological fine line, cautiously, and with the odd stumble. In a typical attempt at balance, this church community calls on the freely given grace of God to bring about change. At the same time, it labours mightily, often blindly, to do good work on God's behalf—just in case the Creator of Heaven and Earth doesn't get around to it soon enough to make a real difference.

What does our God require of you? To seek justice, and love kindness, and walk humbly with our God. The prophet Micah expresses in a few well-loved phrases (6:8) the essence of a church that tries to reflect God's wish for compassion and dignity and peace among all God's creatures.

It has been frequently suggested that the United Church should quit meddling in things that do not concern it. It's true that meddling takes up a lot of our collective time and energy. The United Church meddles in national policy (social programs, refugee law, trade laws); in provincial affairs (gambling, welfare, the environment); and in the community (economic development, food banks, women's shelters and violence prevention, hosting refugees). Justice-seeking, God forbid, even meddles in worship—getting into song and sermon, petition signing, and coffee talks.

Keeping Governments on Their Toes

The United Church has a uniquely Canadian approach to justice. Those United Church policies and statements show the church's vision of governments as mediators, institutions responsible for social good. Whether your concern is nuclear weapons, hunger, violence against women, or agricultural policy, the government has a role. Governments are obligated to make sure that everyone has enough resources and freedom to live with dignity and that only a few have too much. Yet during the past decade, government policies have helped the poor get poorer—or, at best, governments have seemed helplessly caught in a system that considers profits more important than basic human needs.

In the past, part of the United Church's power and strength of conviction flowed from its ability to address the government strongly, in the certainty that we would be listened to. Our present reality is a faded reflection of that time—thanks be to God!

We have been handed a wonderful opportunity to renew our relationship with One who was lynched for his challenge to the established order.

Longing for Lost Power and Privilege

At a time when the churches mourn lost power and privilege, it is tempting to long for the power to feed the world, set slaves free, be a powerful advocate for the myriad of wrongs that we see around us. That temptation confronted Jesus directly; it confronts today's United Church constantly. There is a risk in setting yourself up as the access to the corridors of power, even if you're trying to set injustices right and raise a cry for freedom. Soon you become someone's voice, rather than helping them find their own.

It is more difficult to admit to being broken and in pain ourselves. Harder to choose to set aside the power of walking ahead of the crowd, of leading it— and instead join the crowd and start walking *with*...sometimes dancing, sometimes limping, sometimes lying in the gutter or locked outside the corridors of power with everyone else.

We live in a lonely world. More and more members of our global village are discovering that it resembles a mall more than a village. In this global market, there is no room for those without money and the ability to make money by competing and winning. Bound by fibre optic cable and satellite links that carry the voices and money of the powerful, we are trapped in a world that relies on exclusion, rather than one that is bound together in a community of respect and nurture. How does, or should, this reality have an impact on our faith?

The United Church Creed begins with the words "We are not alone." As we reach the ripe old age of seventy-five, the assurance seems more important than ever. On top of declining numbers and money, the United Church seems to have lost its vision of a just world—just when we need it most. We seem to be fumbling to find a purpose and mandate in a changing world. Do we develop new policies, both prophetic and well-worded, so that we can tell the world what we're about? Do we take on local actions, and quit trying to tell the government how to behave? Do we practise justice first in the church, or do we reach out and find inspiration in connecting outside our walls?

The Church's Mid-life Crisis

We appear to be having a mid-life crisis. What should we do and how should we be?

A story and an idea:

> An ancient rabbi once asked his students how they could tell when the night had ended and the day was on its way back.
>
> "Could it be," asked one student, "when you can see an animal in the distance and tell whether it is a sheep or a dog?"
>
> "No," answered the rabbi.
>
> "Could it be," asked another, "when you can look at a tree in the distance and tell whether it is a fig tree or a peach tree?"
>
> "No," said the rabbi.
>
> "Well then, what is it?" his students demanded.
>
> "It is when you look on the face of any woman or man and see that she or he is your sister or brother. Because if you cannot do this, then, no matter what time it is, it is still night."

In the midst of complicated policies and endless meetings beneath fluorescent lights in basements, justice may be found in the simplest of forms. The seemingly simple act of looking on the stranger's face and seeing a sister and brother is the greatest of challenges in today's world, because it calls us to confront all the forces that keep us apart.

Overcoming a "Suicidal Coldness"

Jeanette Armstrong is a First Nations leader and member of the Okanagan Nation. Her homeland and identity are rooted in a corner of what is now called British Columbia. In a reflection that views our global economy as driven by a "suicidal coldness" that deliberately drives people apart, she speaks of community as a blanket "keeping out the frost." She explains.

> In a healthy whole community, the people interact with each other in shared emotional response. They move together emotionally to respond to crisis or celebration.

They "commune" in the everyday act of living. Being a part
of such a communing is to be fully alive, fully human. To be
without community in this way is to be alive only in the
flesh, to be alone, to be lost to being human. It is then possible to violate and destroy others and their property without remorse.

Before we can be in community, we must accept those times and places
where the church has appeared to act without remorse in the past. Two
current issues are the end of the Ecumenical Decade of the Churches in
Solidarity with Women and the controversy over the residential schools run
by the federal government and the United Church "on behalf" of Canada's
First Nations. Both shout at us to recognize the abuse, the wounding, the
twisted power that has silenced voices and denied worth over many
generations. Many women and First Nations people are strong but bruised
survivors in a church and a society that harasses and abuses and casts their gifts
aside—despite the apologies and progress the church has made.

These are but two wounds. Until we repent and accept our part in these
and other woundings, accompanying when needed and standing aside when
needed, we cannot be in community.

The Struggle Goes On

We will all need to own the struggle to heal, to quit asking the survivors to
solve the problem for us, to recognize that their struggle is our struggle, to
stop asking forgiveness without repenting first, and to accept that
transformation into wholeness requires upheaval and some pain.

Accepting struggle does not come easily for us. As a community and a
communion, the United Church focuses its theology on the resurrection
rather than the crucifixion. We are grounded in hope and promise, on a crazy
belief in bringing new life dancing in through closed and bolted doors. We
forget that rebirth comes out of death, that without the difficult end of the
old, the new cannot burst into flower.

When we face the death of the familiar and the convenient, we confront
our fear of the new form that our resurrected lives and church may take. Jean
Vanier writes that fear of change is the greatest block to our willingness to
move from exclusion to inclusion, from standing alone to standing in
community. We fear the process of coming to feel another's pain; we fear the
transformation into new life that will surely follow. As Guatemalan poet Julia
Esquivel writes, we are then "threatened with resurrection."

The Hard Labour of Giving Birth

Being resurrected to a new vision of community will be a hard labour, like any birth, and dogged by doubt. We will have to widen our crumbling walls, even pull some down in the process. We will open the circle to a stranger whose hand may be dirty, or scarred, or a colour different from our own. Community will be up close and very personal.

We will become different. We will widen the walls to think of justice as not necessarily relying on paper or policy or experts. And likewise, we will have to dare to accept justice as certain to provoke argument and dissent without and within—justice that topples tables in churches and banks, that questions the obvious and immediate wisdom of charity, that is occasionally very rude.

Maybe we will be called to break down walls between churches and faiths. Our circle might expand beyond the White, the older, and the Christian. Our theology and our living may come to respect the Earth in a new way. Maybe the local churches, the backbone of our church, will imagine themselves in a new way and offer a new vision of justice.

Can a church wounded by past conflicts stand yet another struggle, more uncertainty—and still be in holy community?

Fearful though we may be of challenge and change, let the questions pile up! Let us never dodge hard questions, questions that pinch and make us squirm, questions that whisper in a still small voice, questions that bellow "Let my people go!"

And so we dare to ask, "Where do we go from here?" lacking, as we do, map and compass. How do we be angry without hate, compassionate without fear, take stands and hold profound beliefs without hardening into a frozen and unresponsive posture that gives us all a major cramp?

Let us find our shared stories of community, learn about their inner workings, their struggles and successes, and, above all, the values and the spirit that form their bedrock. Let these become our commentary for today on the holy writings that map out our path. Let these be our markers on the path to community, to the challenge of being fully with a sister or brother in a world where differences are no longer suspect and isolation is banished.

We are not alone. Thanks be to God.

Julie Graham works in Toronto as an educator with the ecumenical coalition Ten Days for Global Justice.

The Heartbeat of the Church

by Ted Reeve

It's been called the "Social Passion." The United Church wove it into the fabric of this nation.

Social Christianity is the heart and soul of The United Church of Canada. In spite of feeling tentative about our identity, in spite of personnel and property squabbles, past injustices, and doctrinal wrangling, new members of the United Church tell me they joined because of the church's activist tradition seeking God's love and justice. They have come to this church because it represents more than "feel-good" religion.

Policies Shaped in Church Basements

Canada's international reputation for humanitarian social, economic, and international development policies did not just happen. A significant part of the public support that drove those public policies came from untold numbers of church-basement discussions that endorsed and prodded governments into responsibility for social well-being.

Joan Kuyek, a powerful community activist from Sudbury, was hired in the 1980s to be an "economic animator" for the United Church. She said, "You folks don't seem to realize how important those church-basement discussions are. They are the heart of community action and the political culture of this country."

The church's influence on social and economic decisions stretches back to the founding years of the United Church. Principal E. H. Oliver of St. Andrew's College, Saskatoon, and moderator of the United Church from 1930 to 1932, in the late 1920s wrote *The Social Achievements of the Christian Church*. He argued that the church's primary contribution to society was "blazing the trail in humanitarian and educational endeavours which it then leaves to the state or other organizations to further develop and manage."

Oliver saw his context, the early twentieth century, as a time of great change. According to Oliver, the industrial revolution pushed the church to act. Exploitative industrial developments and the state's incestuous relationship with capital provoked some Protestants to re-examine their social situation in light of their Christian theology and values. They began to propose new ways to organize society, which we now identify as social Christianity or the social gospel.

Combining Evangelism and Social Service

This social Christianity widely influenced the new denomination, The United Church of Canada. The church leaders who epitomized this perspective are most easily identified with the Boards of Evangelism and Social Service (BESS) of the founding denominations and subsequently of the United Church. These Boards integrated a Christian radical critique of the social order with work within established institutions.

The gospel values of democracy, mutuality, and the strong bearing the burdens of the weak (a redistributive ethic) were widely preached from pulpits across Canada. With the usual middle-class, liberal Protestant emphasis on incremental change and growth, congregational members were willing to entertain new ideas and show compassionate concern for the poor, but they wanted changes to happen in a democratic, visible manner.

Progressive leaders from the BESS became experts in using public forums, whether pulpit or town hall, to argue for concrete changes that would bring Canadian society closer to the kingdom of God on earth.

The efforts of progressive BESS staff and board members helped to institutionalize the social Christianity vision of church and society in the 1920s to 1940s. By emphasizing both evangelism and social service BESS secretaries gained wide constituency support. On the other hand, it was not an easy path—differing sides complained the BESS was not giving enough emphasis to their perspective. In their annual reports, board and secretaries struggled to appease different ends of the theological spectrum.

Treading a Fine Line

Using traditional notions of evangelization that involved telling the Christian story and seeking commitments to follow the tenets of the gospel, these reports emphasized that the direct outcome of conversion was to apply oneself in transforming society. In this social Christianity view of evangelism, equally high value was placed on individual faith and social transformation activities. A person was converted to being a follower of Jesus with a direct obligation to seek God's reign on earth.

Social Christianity evangelism did not involve a two-step logic of conversion and *then* doing good works. Rather, faith involved a dual responsibility of both personal and corporate ethical behaviour.

Richard Allen, in his book *The Social Passion*, credited the BESS and its staff for bringing a broad range of social reforms within the sanctions of Canadian Protestantism, and for bringing the multitude of social programs that make up the Canadian welfare state into the main channels of Canadian social attitudes. They were able to connect between faith and its concrete ramifications; in other words, to institutionalize their social passion in the structures of the church and society.

Church Union As a Common Cause

The institutionalization of this social passion became concrete in the movement towards Church Union. While union talks had begun as early as the 1880s, it was not until the three founding denominations saw the common cause of social betterment that they were able to overcome their doctrinal differences and come together.

Union set forth a vision of a national Protestant church engaged in the social developments of the Canadian context. The "social betterment" (social Christianity) objectives of Union marked a shift in theological thinking from nineteenth-century emphasis on predestination and Christian perfection, to a theology that put new emphasis on divine immanence, a more critical approach to the Bible, and realization of God's reign on earth through participation in social developments. As historian John Grant said (in *Past is Prologue*, p. 128):

> Union was...to embody the rising social gospel that understood the Kingdom of God not merely as the transformation of society through the conversion of individuals but as the inauguration of a new political and economic order. Above all, many unionists urged, the United Church should be rid of the shackles of the past and free to seek new solutions for emerging problems.

Utilizing Church Networks

In the 1930s, the United Church utilized its national network to build public acceptance for governments to take on social responsibility. When the United Church presented its case for welfare state developments in a brief to the Rowell-Sirois Royal Commission in 1938, details of the brief were sent to all ministers and pastoral charges. Groups were encouraged to discuss the implications of these policies and to feed back their views.

With nearly 3,000 ministers serving over 5,000 congregations all across Canada, as well as connections through foreign missions to many parts of the world, church leaders had a valuable means of sending and receiving information. Imagine a community organizer or political advocate today having front-line connections to almost every community across the country and in most corners of the world. Information could flow both ways, creating a strong voice in both local and national policy discussions.

As the church became more attuned to the use of this network, its flow of educational and policy materials increased to help local groups keep abreast of issues. Field secretaries and superintendents from regions across the country wrote annual reports that contained insightful analyses of both church and societal developments.

The Home Mission superintendents' annual reports from those years provide an excellent study of the socio-economic factors affecting life on the edges of Canadian society. For instance, the Rev. J. C. Cochrane's 1936 report followed mining operations from northern Ontario into northwestern Québec. Modern methods of prospecting and transporting freight, utilizing airplanes and trains, meant new mining communities. But while mining communities were expanding, logging communities were suffering a slow death.

Similarly, from Newfoundland, the Rev. Oliver Jackson's report analyzed the hardship facing fishers as wartime sanctions and political upheavals cut off their markets.

A key actor in heightening the church's research and public policy stances was the legendary General Secretary of the Board of Evangelism and Social Services, James Mutchmor. Mutchmor became a master of gathering press attention to build public awareness of the church's views. He also instructed ministers in how to gather public support for the church's positions. Annual gatherings gave ministers a sense of the larger mission of the church and of their part in achieving its social goals. Mutchmor even instructed ordinands in the art of public relations and how to gather media attention for their views.

Lessons to Be Learned

The significance of those many years of social Christian advocacy is increasingly evident in the 1990s as we witness the systematic dismantling of government policies that cared equally for all Canadians. Duncan Cameron, recent editor of the *Canadian Forum*, aptly described what is happening in a March 1995 article:

> The erosion of public services leads to mistrust of government. It opens the door ever wider to privatization where services are delivered on the basis of ability to pay, not on need. Citizenship becomes the ability to write a personal cheque.

While the United Church can no longer take for granted its formerly powerful role in a predominantly liberal Anglo-Protestant society, this is not an excuse to abandon concern for social developments. Smaller religious denominations (such as Mennonites and Quakers who have never had

Less Than the Cost of a Horse and Buggy
by Morton B. Stratton

In the early years, Methodist ministers came to Salt Spring Island from Nanaimo and later from Duncan, on Vancouver Island, as time permitted—in principle, monthly—to preach and teach. Meetings were held in homes or school houses and, for people at the south end of the island, in the Burgoyne church building erected in 1887. Not until 1905 was a church building erected at Central for families living in the north end.

In the early twentieth century, Ganges became the major population and commercial centre for Salt Spring Island. And in 1926, soon after the formation of The United Church of Canada, the church building at Central was moved to Ganges, where it could better serve the majority of its members.

Until the late 1920s, most ministers were non-resident and were assigned to Salt Spring for only a year or two. Many were student probationers or retirees. Before the First World War, the minister's stipend was sometimes less than the cost of the horse and buggy put at his disposal. But things began to change with the appointment of the Rev. William Allan in 1929, who was provided with a manse across the street from the church.

Although regular services ceased at Burgoyne in the 1930s, a loyal group of UCW members still cares for the little church in the valley, and occasional services are still held there. The other points of the charge, Beaver Point and Cranberry, all gradually dwindled in size and became inactive.

pretensions of being "mainstream") are able to present an admirable social witness to the values they hold for society. As quantum physics and chaos theory demonstrate, small actions can cause big reactions.

The opportunity before the United Church is not to long for its former status, but to examine the tremendous institutional capacity the church still has, and could effectively use, to help assert its social passions in Canadian and global society.

As the economy shifts towards knowledge-based structures—and ideally to sustainable, community-based developments—many of the social safeguards that have been part of the welfare state will also need to change. Programs of the post-war welfare state will need revitalization in creative formats meeting local and global needs.

Young people today are generally unaware of the United Church's long struggles to institutionalize its social programs. The survival-of-the-fittest attitudes that dominated Canadian society a hundred years ago—a classical belief in market economics, minimal government intervention, and traditional Victorian middle-class nuclear family values—have been reclaimed by a neo-conservative perspective.

While the shortfalls and inadequacies of existing welfare-state programs have been well documented, the period between 1945 and the early 1970s brought increased social and economic equality to Canada. We need to remember the role of church advocacy in creating these programs and their benefit for Canadians.

Addressing the Feeling of Powerlessness

Travelling across the country in my ecumenical and Division of Mission in Canada work, I have been heartened by many insightful church-basement discussions. The discouraging part is recognizing the limitations of the national church in supporting church-basement discussions and encouraging public witness on equitable and sustainable social and economic policies.

I know all the arguments about shrinking budgets. But when I consider the priorities that united our church, and the institutional commitment that built a national network of ministers and members engaged in changing their local social and economic realities, I have to say we suffer from a conviction that we have less political power than we actually do.

During our seventy-fifth anniversary activities, Moderator Bill Phipps activated a church-wide discussion on faith and the economy. Utilizing new communication technologies that our forebears would have loved, the church has the opportunity to consider current issues, debate them, and collectively respond to them (see www.faith-and-the-economy.org).

We no longer expect centre stage, unlike James Mutchmor who once threatened the Premier of Ontario that Protestants would rise up against him. Rather, in the political and communications climate of the new millennium, the multiplier effect of small creative actions of local congregations can send waves that can stir a whole community, a nation, or a world.

Ted Reeve is executive director of the Centre for Research in Religion: Emmanuel College, University of Toronto.

Seeds of Hope

by Alyson Huntly

"The frustrations, impatience, disappointments, as well as the hope I feel about our church are also feelings I have about myself as part of this imperfect body."

The United Church of Canada is both a human institution and the body of Christ. That's quite a mix—the divine and the secular. Somehow we manage to be both. We fail at our calling and often, in spite of our best efforts, we fail quite miserably and quite publicly. Yet throughout our history as a church we have also managed to nurture within this imperfect body the seeds of something else—seeds of hope for ourselves and our world, seeds of the church's own transformation, seeds of the reign of God.

The times when I have been most disillusioned by our failure to live up to our calling as a church have also been times when I have been most astounded by the signs of the Spirit's presence.

I don't know how or why this is. I only know it to be true. I know this, not as an outsider who can judge things impartially, but as an insider. I'm part of the mix. The frustrations, impatience, disappointments, as well as the hope I feel about our church are feelings I have about myself as part of this imperfect body. When I say "United Church of Canada," I include myself. I say "we." I say "us." And in those times when I catch glimpses of that other church—that church we are called to be and sometimes in fleeting moments are—those times I feel joy and pride that only a member of the family could experience. This, for better or worse, is my church, *our* church.

I Want Change; I Want It Now!

In my late teens and early twenties, I was passionate about transforming the world. Global disarmament, feminism, the environment, human rights in Latin America, apartheid—these were issues I cared about. I wanted change, and I wanted it now. And I expected our church to be doing more than it was. Fortunately I have lived a few more years, long enough to smile at the self-righteous zeal with which I expressed these commitments, though the commitments themselves remain strong.

I was very active in the church in those years. I was on church committees within congregation and Conference. I was often frustrated and critical. I remember when a committee I was on would make a presentation or hold a workshop on some important issue. Often the response was disappointing. I recall feeling impatient with those who thought the church had no business discussing issues of politics and injustice. I had a sense that, even if we did manage to convince people that action was needed, we as a church were able to do so little. Even when we could grasp the vision, we didn't know how to act in ways that would really make a difference in our world.

Sometimes we activists managed to get a resolution moved through presbytery or Conference, but even that wasn't enough. I remember feeling angry with church statements that seemed to speak only in generalities, with the slowness of change, with the inertia of this so-called Body of Christ.

Nurtured by the Same Imperfect Body

Ironically, along with my frustration and impatience was a deep sense of being nurtured in this struggle, by and within the church. The church, The United Church of Canada to be specific, kept me going and gave me hope. Within a local congregation I found kindred spirits—people who also cared passionately. Even amidst arguments and debates, at board meetings, presbytery, or Conference, I knew I was among friends. Even as I felt daunted by the immensity of what God called us to be and do, I found hope and inspiration in those who had been working at this for more decades than I had even been alive.

There were many people I looked up to—United Church people who for forty, fifty, or sixty years had been living out their commitment to justice and change, bit by bit, day by day. Mentors taught me how to plan a workshop, write a resolution, chair a meeting. Mentors taught me how to look at the world critically, to listen for the voices of those on the margins, to understand my own connectedness to and complicity in a world of injustice. The church introduced me to communities of other justice-seekers. It surrounded me by prophetic voices, and it planted me firmly in the soil of relationships that are still spiritual home for me.

The church that drove me crazy also kept me going. The church that seemed so slow to move was also, in many instances, the very institution that had introduced me to these issues and got me moving. It was in the United Church that I first heard the word "feminism." In the United Church I came to understand phrases like "social gospel," "solidarity," and "injustice."

A Faith Active in the World

But even before the Bible study groups, sermons, conferences, conversations that formed my adult faith and commitment to justice, the United Church nurtured within me a faith that was not "out of this world" but active in it. My days in Sunday school with the *New Curriculum* taught me about a Jesus who cared about people and about how they treated one another. Jesus stood with the poor and spoke up on behalf of the marginal. In a tiny rural church basement, with a local dairy farmer as our superintendent, we read *The Clue to the Mystery*, *The Mystery of the Rock* (my favourite), and other children's books. We talked about real-life issues, about loving God and loving others, about what was going on in the world around us. Biblical stories and characters came alive for me in ways that connected to my own life as a young child. As I look back on that curriculum, I am amazed by its solid biblical foundation, its profound and even radical connection between faith and acts of love and justice in the world.

The United Church continued to form and shape my faith and to keep that faith firmly grounded in a commitment to love and justice. In a United Church basement, many years later, I first watched scenes of the Sharpeville massacre roll across the screen and heard names like Biko, Mandela, Tutu....United Church people, prophetic witnesses to what was going on in South Africa, spurred me to action. I went, with other United Church friends, to change my bank accounts. I delivered a letter to my bank manager, protesting his bank's complicity in apartheid. That particular action was a small one. It took many more years, and many far greater actions on the part of thousands of others, before the mountain of apartheid began to crumble. But that action was important for me as a base of hope, a reminder through these many years since that small actions count, that small actions—mine, yours, ours—can indeed move mountains.

Tip-toeing into History

In the 1980s I watched in trepidation as the United Church moved a few steps forward, a few steps back, on an issue that may of us thought at least a decade overdue—the inclusion of gay and lesbian people. The church never did take a very large step. Even the historic 1988 decision was less an open embrace than a back-handed concession not to exclude. Even that came only after many deferrals and a thousand-and-one "studies"—with more apologies to those who were offended by these gestures of inclusion than to those who had for years been silenced or excluded.

There are today many places where gay, lesbian, and bisexual people are accepted in the life and ministry of the United Church. There are also many more places within our church where hatred, judgement, and exclusion still exist. It wasn't a very big step, that 1988 decision, and it continues to remind me of the imperfections of this institution I call my spiritual home. And yet, as I look back on that decision, my feelings of frustration and disappointment are mingled also with pride and amazement at what we have been able to do and be through those years.

The church struggled with the issue of homosexuality. It refused to back away from the discussion. When the church stuck its neck out and began this debate, thousands of faithful United Church people, most of whom probably wished we had never opened this can of worms, sat in United Church basements all across the country to study the issue. They dared to say out loud words like "homosexual" or "sex." They dared to meet and talk with lesbian or gay people. They risked being the church, right or wrong. And, when the 1988 General Council made its controversial decision, most of those people kept right on being the church, whatever their personal opinion.

Some claimed the decision might end The United Church of Canada. The church risked its future for an issue it believed to be just. It continues to be one of only a handful of denominations, worldwide, that has taken such an inclusive stance.

A History of Mixed Blessings

Years from now, we may look back at what we did in the 1980s on the issue of homosexuality. I suspect—I hope—that when we do, we will be appalled at our bigotry and lack of compassion. Perhaps we will wish we had moved faster and more justly. We may well lament, even apologize for, some of the things we felt so "right" about saying. That's because we will continue to be a church that changes and grows, a church that misses its calling even as it follows its vision.

The history of our church over seventy-five years has been a history of such mixed blessings—prophetic witness and misguided good-intentions, action and inertia, courage and complacency. From our early days as a denomination, it has been so. The onset of the Depression in Canada in the 1930s fueled fires of racism, especially anti-Semitism, across the country. The United Church, which had already been responding to immediate needs of food and shelter of the poor, began to speak up on issues of Christianity and race relations.

A national committee was formed, and educational programs were initiated in congregations, presbyteries, and conferences. Prophetic voices challenged the church to greater action. Reading back over those ancient minutes reminds me of many debates, resolutions, workshops that I have participated in. A few steps forward, a few back; amazing prophetic witness, appalling slowness to act.

With the outbreak of war, the church urged the government to respond to the growing refugee crisis. In the 1930s the United Church made some attempts to address anti-Semitism in Europe—a little bit of funding, a

Better to Have Waited Ten Years
by Fleming Holm

In the Maritime provinces, there were areas that had always been predominantly Presbyterian, where there were no Methodists and therefore no rivalry. Here there was no need for local union, as far as most Presbyterians could see. And since Methodists were largely unknown, they were sometimes suspect. It was feared that the new church would lose much that was valuable in the Presbyterian heritage. The Presbyterians had always been strong for doing things "decently and in order," and for high standards of education; the Methodists and Congregationalists depended more on evangelical fervour. Some false rumours grew concerning the new church, and in some places traditional breaches were widened and half-forgotten loyalties appealed to. Even politics was made a factor.

The West had been ready for union many years earlier; the East would have done well to have waited another ten years.

In our congregation, a preliminary vote had been taken in 1912, showing 217 for union, and twenty-one against.

On June 19, 1925, the Session decided that the final vote should be taken Tuesday, June 30. No outside speakers had been heard on the subject, and it was felt that none should be heard; the congregation was sufficiently intelligent to make up its own mind.

At New Mills, the vote was twenty-two in favour and nineteen against. At Jacquet River, it was thirty-eight in favour and thirty-eight against, and Mr. Millar [the minister] cast the deciding vote in favour. The vote at Charlo is not recorded in the minutes, but other sources indicate thirty-four to four in favour of union.

During the fall, eighty-seven members transferred out at their own request and formed a Presbyterian congregation: thirty-six of the 121 members at Jacquet River, thirty-seven out of ninety-four at New Mills, and fourteen out of eighty-five at Charlo.

From A History of the United Church: Charlo, New Mills and Jacquet River, *credited to Fleming Holm, 1961.*

conference or two, letters of support, a letter from the moderator, some collaborative work with Canadian Jewish groups to get Jewish children admitted as refugees. Some individuals were very outspoken but went largely unheard. It wasn't much. It certainly wasn't enough.

The church as a whole was largely silent on the Holocaust. In 1946 the United Church acknowledged its lack of action on behalf of Jews. In 1988 it reiterated that apology. In 1998 the church initiated another study program to continue to address the roots of anti-Semitism within our own Christian traditions, within our own church. We continue to speak out on issues of racism and anti-Semitism. We continue to work and dialogue with Jewish faith-partners. And it still isn't enough.

The same analysis could be made of any other issue which our church has addressed. We have acted, incompletely and often far too late, but we have also at times been prophetic and ahead of our time.

We Have Seen the Enemy…

Today, even as we seek to be the Body of Christ, we recognize ourselves to be fallible, infected by the very social evils we seek to redress. Racism, homophobia, economic inequalities, gender bias— we see them both outside and inside our own institution. We are a prophetic voice, and we sometimes silence or simply ignore our own prophetic voices. We initiate change and we are slow to change.

"Now that we have accomplished this extraordinary business of ridding the world of the spread of apartheid," says the Rev. Desmond Tutu, Archbishop Emeritus of South Africa, "the next moral campaign must be the international debt." Certainly one of the key moral issues facing the United Church as we enter the next millennium is economic disparity. We live in a world of appalling and increasing inequality, fuelled by an unconscionable international debt. We live in a rich country where there are thousands of hungry children and homeless families, where the life-expectancy of our poorest, many of them First Nations peoples, falls far below the national average. We watch helplessly as governments slash social programs and cut welfare or other services for the poor.

Once again we are struggling to be church, to live faithfully, to act for justice. We make resolutions and speak out. Grassroots people in United Church congregations all across the country give generously, form coalitions, attend vigils, appeal to their political representatives, speak out, stand in solidarity with the poor, take action.

It is not enough—it is never enough. Yet even as I say that, I feel hope stir within me. No acts of kindness, of justice, are ever wasted. All of those small actions can and will bear fruit in God's good time. They continue to give me hope—hope that change is possible, hope that our church, so profoundly human and so deeply flawed, continues to nurture within itself seeds of transformation, seeds of God's reign.

Alyson Huntly is a freelance writer and editor and diaconal minister currently attending First United Church in Ottawa.

The Struggle for Equality

We've come
a long way;
we've got a long way
yet to go

Equal? Since When?

by Sharon Davis

Women have fared better in the United Church than in most other denominations. But there's still some distance to go to make equality universal.

This happened in 1984—not long ago, in terms of history. I was in Liechtenstein, that tiny postage-stamp country tucked into the European Alps. It was a glorious August day, the kind of day I love to wrap myself in. Not too hot, not too cool. From my position on the street corner in a small town, the only things brighter and warmer than the day itself were the faces and greetings of people as they passed by. On this day, the course of their history had forever changed. Women in Liechtenstein had finally been granted (by men) the right to vote.

Let's back up a few years to October 18, 1929. Judge Emily Murphy, Nellie McClung, Louise McKinney, Henrietta Muir Edwards, and Dr. Irene Parlby had finally convinced the British Privy Council, then Canada's court of last resort, that "the word 'persons' includes members of the male and female sex." Finally we women were people. We could speak, we could have opinions, we were considered equal in rights and privileges....Or were we?

It took another seven years before the first woman was ordained. Lydia Gruchy was not only the first woman to be ordained in The United Church of Canada; she was the first in any major denomination anywhere in North America. It happened at St. Andrew's United Church in Moose Jaw, Saskatchewan in 1936. The proponents of her ordination had to be—of course—men. Dr. Oliver and President Murray, both of St. Andrew's College in Saskatoon were to achieve fame (or notoriety) for their strong and forceful insistence. After a great deal of struggle and debate—some of it ugly—the church agreed to ordain women.

Moving Quickly, Slowly

Fast forward to 1962. The Twentieth General Council heard the report of its Commission on Ordination. The report considered, in particular, the relationship of an ordained woman minister to her work following her marriage.

The Commission's recommendations included the following:

> Ordination for women is to be open only to those women who are unmarried or widows or at that time in life when they are no longer required in the home as mothers and if a suitable ministry can be arranged which does not interfere with the stability of the marriage and their positions as

wives and therefore able to fulfil the vows of ordination.

The ordained woman, if she marries, should enter then her special calling of wife and mother, and cease to be eligible for settlement as a minister of the Word and Sacraments. She may, however, during this time remain an ordained minister without Charge.

A married ordained woman minister of the Church who is without Pastoral Charge due to marriage, may seek a return to the pastoral ministry by application to her Conference under the following conditions:

a) If she should become the sole support of her family due to the illness of her husband or the loss of her husband through death.

b) At that time in life when she is no longer required in the home as a mother and if a suitable ministry can be arranged which does not interfere with the stability of her marriage and her position as a wife.

During the period that she is without a Pastoral Charge due to her married status, she may have the right of her ministry of the Word and Sacraments in any way which does not entail acting as an inducted minister of a Pastoral Charge or as Presbytery supply or as a full-time assistant minister.

The Executive of General Council appointed a committee of seventeen persons to study these restrictions. Their recommendations, to delete the provisions above, were accepted by the Twenty-first General Council. In 1964.

Persons in the Deaconess Order were not made official members of the Courts with full speaking and voting privileges until the General Council in Niagara Falls. In 1971. Also in the 1970s, women who were diaconal ministers were finally allowed to be married and retain their status in the order.

Lay women had, of course, been struggling for years before it occurred to anyone that women might enter the sacred halls of theological learning to be ordained, designated, commissioned, whatever. I do know that in my home town, in diapers, I was the youngest member that the Woman's Missionary Society and the Ladies Aid ever had. I remember that the anguish around becoming United Church Women was excruciating for many and incredibly freeing for others; they felt they had finally been "let into the church."

Equal? Really?

Reality Moves Even Slower Than Policy

It was one of those cold winter days that only those of us in the Midwest can brag about. The temperature was forty below. The wind raced around like a young pup looking for someone to play with. The only problem was that no one wanted to play. It was the kind of day you want to wrap yourself in a blanket, pull out a good book, light the fireplace, and settle in for a good read.

But that option was not open to me. I had to venture out through the wind and cold to meet with a committee in hopes of a call to a certain pastoral charge. It was a small rural pastoral charge with only one preaching point and relatively close to a city—an important point, for I am physically handicapped and need access to medical care. The discussion went quite well. I went home with a satisfied view of the future.

Later that night I received the phone call. "We're sorry," said a sympathetic male voice at the other end. "But we decided you are not the person we are looking for at this time." (Well, it happens. Sometimes we just misread the signs). "We've found a man. He is ordained. He is married and we are told that his wife will do some volunteer work. As well, we note that you are in F category which means more money."

Shame on me for being a woman. For not being ordained. For being single. And for being too old!

This was 1985.

Prejudices Persist

The headlines read, "United Church Elects First Lay Woman to its Highest Position." The woman was Anne Squire. The position was moderator. It was 1986.

We kid ourselves if we believe that women today find no barriers when it comes to receiving calls or jobs of many descriptions. And in many places, women are still paid less than men for exactly the same work. We still struggle with the belief in some congregations that a "real" minister is a man, and what's more, an ordained one. Prejudices persist, despite decisions and policies. In spite of the decision of the 1988 General Council, homosexual people still experience "gay bashing" and homophobic behaviour. In spite of the official stance of The United Church of Canada that women have a right to make decisions about their own bodies in consultation with their doctors, women who have acted in accordance with that policy are still put down, tortured, and in some cases killed. Although the United Church has issued an apology to the Aboriginal people of our country and continues to try to be a part of healing, there is still racism in abundance.

Making decisions and policy doesn't mean we change the attitudes of those who count themselves among the membership of The United Church of Canada or society in general.

But it's not all bad news. What if those decisions and policies hadn't been made? What if the women and men of the past and the present hadn't had the courage, the foresight, and the persistence to raise up those questions? What if we hadn't been made aware? What if we hadn't changed? Would we, in The United Church of Canada, be content to live with the beliefs and policies and systems that existed in 1925?

Changes All Around

Pre-1925 conditions would mean that we would not have telephones, cars, airplanes, dishwashers, clothes washers and dryers, electricity, the wisdom and achievements of medicine, modern heating, television, computers—and on and on. Last summer, I was in an antique store where they had one of the first wheelchairs in existence. It was wooden, and very rickety. There was no way for me, sitting in the chair, to push myself around. I would have been totally dependent on my "pusher." It was scary. I currently ride on a motorized scooter.

We really cannot comprehend life without what is now. So what of the Church? What of women in the Church?

It is the year 2000. Our community of faith known as The United Church of Canada calls this a milestone. We turn seventy-five beautiful years of age. One would like to think that we have long ago come of age. And, I believe, in many respects we have. We will always be a people on the edge, regardless of our number. A people who struggle to be prophetic and faithful to what we

Miles to Go Before We Rest
by Caryn Douglas and Ted Dodd

Throughout the history of The United Church of Canada, women have been involved in Bible study at weekly groups, WMS meetings, UCW gatherings, CGIT evenings, Sunday school teacher training sessions, and larger church workshops and events. These times for faith exploration and spiritual growth have been enriching experiences of intellectual challenge, community support, and lively discussion. Many women encountered the church most powerfully in these small groups.

In the last few decades, women have insisted that these studies reflect their understanding and perspective on the world. They asked:

- What does a twentieth-century woman do with the role of women prescribed in Paul?
- Why do the commandments assume women are property?
- What does a theology of sacrifice say to women in abusive relationships?

Clearly, not all women are asking these questions. But a significant number are. Facing the next millennium, will the church be defensive about such challenges? Will the church be threatened by attempts to reshape theology and to deconstruct traditional understandings of the practice of ministry and mission? Or will the church see this as an opportunity? Will we reconstruct ourselves in a more inclusive, more egalitarian, more faithful fashion?

In the last few decades women in the church, along with society, have begun to name the dynamics surrounding violence and sexual misconduct. Women, and those committed to justice, will no longer be silent about

- verbal, physical, sexual abuse
- abuse in the home or by a stranger
- harassment or professional misconduct.

The United Church has worked hard to put in place policies and structures that address these concerns. There have been many church court hearings, civil cases, and legal trials. An enormous amount of energy and time has attempted to right wrongs and seek justice. Numerous perpetrators have been charged, coercive actions stopped, and past abuses challenged. Huge strides have been made in naming systemic privilege and power violations.

The Ecumenical Decade of Churches in Solidarity with Women aimed towards a valuing of diversity, inclusive process, participatory access, building community, and developing leadership. The Decade offered opportunities for solidarity

- for women with other women around the world
- for men with women
- for affluent Canadians with those in poverty.

At special gatherings, conferences, events, and exchanges, they made connections—about racism, classism, sexism, and other forms of oppression. In these opportunities for face-to-face solidarity, the complacency of the church in systemic evils was named. New theologies and liberating structures were envisioned.

Many women in the United Church had their lives and faith deeply touched by these experiences. They are now committed to building new kinds of networks across the country and around the world. They want to develop new relationships with men, with children, and with other races and cultures.

"Who will roll away the stone?" was asked when the Decade was launched at Easter in 1988. The work of the Decade identified some of the stones, stones of both personal and systemic discrimination, injustice, sexism, exclusivity, and violence. It included strategies to chip, move, slide, roll, blast away at the stones. It included finding the support, encouragement, resources, and love of others to keep on with the struggle.

We have come a long way. There is still a distance to go.

Ted Dodd and Caryn Douglas are both on staff at the Centre for Christian Studies in Winnipeg.

believe and to who we are. I believe that is one of the special and unique gifts that our particular denomination offers to the world. We are constantly looking at what is just and what is unjust through the eyes of our beliefs. Through the grace of God, we make decisions accordingly. We will never be perfect, or arrive. But never to have tried—never to have pushed at the edges so that we are always growing, always on the move, always on that journey of faith—that would be the sin.

Dr. Jessie Saulteaux gave me a telling and meaningful quote, at the time when the United Church was making its apology to the Aboriginal people. She said, "Friends, all we want to say to you is that you made the mistakes for the first hundred years. Could you let us make them for the next hundred years?"

In her wisdom, she knew a vital truth that we often do not want to know. If we do not cry, we will not know the healing of laughter; if we do not fall down, we will never know the independence of getting up; if we do not dwell in the valleys, we will never know the beauty of the mountain tops. Of course we have made mistakes, and of course we will make more because not to make mistakes means we will not have opportunities to learn and grow and change.

We are women! We are The United Church of Canada! Together we will continue to make mistakes, to journey, to love, and to be the best that we can be for this moment in history.

Sharon Davis is a member of the ministry team of St. James United Church in Regina, Saskatchewan.

Revisiting Martha and Mary

by Fran Hare

In all the changing roles of women in the church over the last seventy-five years, the one constant factor has been the women themselves.

Whenever I think of the changing roles of women in The United Church of Canada, I always think of my grandmother, Martha McMaster.

By the time she was in her eighties (and no one would ever know from her just how far into her eighties) she had lavished almost sixty years of loving work, time, and presence on Melville United Church. She had participated in the conversations and voting that led to Church Union in 1925. Her spouse and five children had been "living stones" in the congregation.

One day a young woman from the church came around to visit her. Grandmother welcomed the woman with tea and one of her justly admired lemon buns. The visitor brought an invitation. To an event to honour the seniors of the congregation. To a special dinner with all the trimmings and with expressions of appreciation to the people whose care and wisdom had given so much to the community. Would Mrs. McMaster be able to attend?

"Of course I'll come," retorted Grandma. "You'll need me to help serve!"

Both Martha and Mary

Martha McMaster's commitment to service, to fine food and hospitality was firmly in place. And no one was going to apply the dreaded word "senior" to Mrs. M. if she could prevent it. She knew all too well how age, increasing physical fragility, sickness, and forgetfulness could steal away one's dignity, strip away one's strength, and drain away one's ability to participate fully in the life of church and community. In the biblical Mary-and-Martha story (Luke 10:38–42), Mrs. M. saw herself as Martha, always serving, always hospitable. As a member of the Woman's Association, she catered weddings and other events, made quilts, sewed, knitted, and constantly did the projects that helped keep the congregation functioning.

But there was more than that to Mrs. M. She was a Mary too, a devoted fan of Nellie McClung, committed to the Temperance Movement, committed to getting rid of the ridiculous notion that women were anything less than persons before the law and before God. When women were finally acknowledged in 1929 to be persons with the right to cast ballots, Mrs. M. sniffed and reflected that it was about time! From the moment women received the right to vote, she and her beloved partner attempted to vote for the same candidates, to avoid negating each other's vote. However, since one

124

of them favoured the Conservative party and the other was a Liberal, they debated the merits of the various candidates fairly vigorously in order to choose the best person as their representative. On occasion Grandpa would announce, "I'll vote with you this time, good wife," when the nominee of his preferred party was morally or intellectually unacceptable. Because she took her voting seriously, Mrs. M. pursued information about politics and politicians, the issues they faced, and the attitudes they brought.

She explained to a couple of her granddaughters that she liked women and liked talking to them, but too many thought only about recipes, managing children, dealing with husbands, and stretching their food money. "I talk to the menfolk," she said, "because they talk about politics, religion, the world, and what is going on in it."

As a Mary, Martha eagerly learned everything she could gather at the feet of any teacher with information to share. Mrs. M. wasted no time regretting that she had not obtained a formal education. She was much too busy reading, learning, and educating herself to spend energy on regret. She loved interviewing us, her grandchildren, about what we were learning in school, and she eagerly added any new bits of exciting knowledge to her store of information. When television became a reality, she was enthralled with the delight of stories, news, and documentaries to stretch her mind, heart, and soul.

The Mary in Mrs. M. never tired of teaching either. A new board game was an opportunity to teach the grandchildren about numbers, letters, and her own personal wisdom about winning and losing. It was also a way of instilling values: no cheating, no dishonesty of any kind, and lose or win with generosity and grace.

For a long time, the sermons I heard about Mary and Martha tended to take sides. Preachers who liked Mary affirmed her willingness for "the better part," sitting at the feet of a rabbi, a teacher, like Jesus. I sometimes suspected that these gentlemen of the pulpit wished more women would sit at their feet. Grandma shared this suspicion. She took pains to get to know the clergy who came and went through the congregation. She respected those who talked with her as an equal and who had wisdom to share. Clergy who talked down to her did not warrant further invitations to dinner. Her favourite was a sharp-minded man of the cloth with a wicked sense of humour. In an unguarded moment, this favourite clergy admitted to conflict with an influential woman in the congregation. Grandma was quick to defend her. "But Mr. G.," she exclaimed, "she's a good Christian woman."

"Not with that face," he snapped. And Mrs. M. laughed until her sides hurt, for the good Christian woman always seemed to be frowning and her mouth always curled towards her toes.

Both the Mary and the Martha in her found people endlessly interesting and hilariously peculiar beings, in need of great compassion well mixed with laughter.

Affection, Amusement, Awareness

The biblical story of the sisters who entertained Jesus in their home is one that has caught many women. It has often felt like judgement. If Mary with her lazy ways finds favour in Jesus' eyes, then that must mean that hardworking, long-suffering, endlessly care-ridden Martha is disdained. And many churchwomen identify with Martha.

Alternatively, if Martha's fussing and complaining is affirmed, then how can there be a place for the woman who yearns for learning, spiritual growth, a relationship with the holy and meaning in life?

There are two places in this story that squeeze my heart. When Martha has finally had it with being left to manage all the work, she says to Jesus, "Don't you care…?" Whatever else, she desperately wanted Jesus to care. It was easy to believe he cared about Mary. There she sat with him, absorbing every word, perhaps even arguing with him, obviously being treated as a beloved friend. And Martha worked alone, probably clattering the pots in her frustration and loneliness, feeling left out, invisible, forgotten. My grandmother and I both knew how that feels. It hurts to think that a beloved person does not care and the hurt goes to the soul's core if the beloved is also the holy.

But surely Martha should have spoken to Mary, asked her to bring her hands to the work and her mind to the meal-making. Why did she drag Jesus into her quarrel with her own sister? It seems to me that her distress was not that Mary was unhelpful so much as that Jesus didn't seem to have time or attention for her, for Martha, the woman of service.

The other place that stirs my heart is in Jesus' response: "Martha, Martha…." To say her name twice makes it impossible for those words to sound harsh or uncaring. "Martha, Martha…." The words convey profound affection, amusement, gentleness, and awareness. Jesus reassures her. She does not have to compete with Mary. In the repeating of her name there is an infinity of love. In my re-imagining of the scene, Mary scurries to set the table and Jesus picks up the tea towel to tidy the dishes.

Roles Institutionalized in Two Models

Some preachers through the years have held Martha up as a role model, to encourage women to continue their good works as housekeepers and homemakers. Women resist the term "housewife" because, as my mother says, none of us ever married a house. Preachers eager to praise Martha frequently suggest that she should read her Bible, pray, add some spiritual discipline to their already full lives, but not cease the labours of hospitality and service. Grandma and I suspected that those preachers were afraid women might give up washing their socks.

My grandmother was there when the United Church set out to combine the Woman's Association with the Woman's Missionary Society—to blend the Mary and Martha roles into a single institutional organization. In local congregations, the Marthas worked in the WA to raise money for the needs of the local church, for the salary of the clergy and any other paid personnel. The Marys joined the WMS; they developed funds for their overseas missionaries and kept themselves and the congregation in touch with the work those missionaries were doing. I grew up on stories of "Beulah and her babies" and the other heroic people who represented God and Church by feeding the hungry, caring for the orphaned, treating the sick, and telling the Good News.

At a meeting called by the minister to rally the women together and encourage them to combine the WA with the WMS, Mrs. M.'s voice was one of the few that raised questions.

"Just a minute," she said to the startled minister. "I think you are getting too many Yes's." I was at that preteen stage of being embarrassed by any apparent eccentricity in the adults of my family, but Grandma was allowed to be a bit different, so I listened with both distress and interest.

"Who is this change really for?" she asked. It seemed to her that if it truly served the best interests of church women, they would have thought of it themselves. She wondered if someone in Toronto was creating a job as administrator of all these new divisions and organizations, which had not needed such a person until then.

Of course, Mrs. M.'s opinion, while respected by other women, could not be allowed to contradict the opinion of the minister. She ended up voting against herself, voting for the United Church Women to come into existence, even though both the Mary and Martha in her were uneasy.

Both Workers and Thinkers

Mrs. M., like most of us, combined Martha and Mary in her person and her life. She worked hard; thought long and deep thoughts; treated family, friends, and strangers with warm hospitality and generous acceptance. She challenged her daughters, sons, and grandchildren to stretch minds and hearts, to be ambitious enough to make a contribution to society, and to take delight from whatever life offered.

What if Mary and Martha had been Terry and Matthew, two brothers entertaining the visiting rabbi? Would Matt have charged out of the kitchen to confront the guest with, "Don't you care?" Would Terry have brought out the good wine and seated himself and the guest comfortably to trade quips and puns? Would the honoured guest have hugged the distraught cook and said something like, "Matthew, Matthew, you worry so much! Come and enjoy some downtime with us." Would the dishes have been left in the sink until morning?

For Mrs. M. and her generation of women, the story of Jesus' visit to the sisters at Bethany was reassurance that the love of the Holy One embraces both workers and thinkers, both women and men. It was also warning against putting the accomplishing of tasks above reflection on life. It was permission for women to ponder things in their hearts, even in an era when the highest compliment paid to a woman during the eulogy at her funeral was that she had been a hard worker, faithful, modest, selflessly serving husband and children, active in church and community. Mrs. M. and her female friends were not expected to think; to be scholarly; to be interested in politics, economics, or religion.

Just One of Many Thousands

At the end of the book of Proverbs, the Good Wife is praised for good works, warned against the deceptiveness of charm and beauty, and given respect for all she does. I remember Mrs. M. very well, not merely for being a Good Wife, but for playing in the autumn leaves with us, entertaining us with her amazing ability to take out her teeth, insisting that as a special treat we could stay up until ten o'clock, and listening to every word of our chatter. I remember her critique of ideas and comments, her application of healthy skepticism to the pretentious claims that sometimes came her way. "Paper never refused ink," she told me one day, when I proclaimed as absolute truth something I had been reading.

Grandma McMaster is just one of many thousands of women who have served this United Church of ours loyally from 1925 to today, with all their heart and mind, all their soul and strength. People like her made it possible

To Lift Our Voices
by Florence Perry Shephard

In 1925, I was eighteen years old. I was a descendent of Robert Perry, a United Empire Loyalist who fled to Canada after Burgoyne's defeat at Sarasota in 1777.

Many of us from the church at Scarborough Junction, on St. Clair at Danforth Road, looked forward with anticipation and excitement to the big service at the Mutual Street Arena in Toronto. We practised so that we could lift our voices in praise and thanksgiving for our past, and in hope and prayer for the bright future we envisaged for the new United Church of Canada.

All that mass of people, in the choir and congregation, the band, all the church dignitaries in their gowns, all that pageantry and music and the speeches—it was thrilling!

for women to serve on church boards, to study the Bible, to be ordained, to be elected to the church's highest offices. When I see where women have come in the last seventy-five years, and when I see how the United Church has led society in encouraging women to be Marys as well as Marthas, I can't help personifying that progress in Mrs. M.

My grandmother McMaster combined Mary and Martha in her lifelong love affair with God, Church, family, community, and the world. She helps the strong sisters who befriended an itinerant rabbi live in all of us.

Fran Hare is an ordained minister and storyteller and co-ordinator of the MA program in Spirituality and Liturgy at the Calgary campus of St. Stephen's College.

Unfinished Injustice

Our treatment of Canada's first inhabitants

A First Nations Perspective

by Stan McKay

History, it is said, is usually written by the victors. In North America the people who wrote history have not been from its First Nations.

The first Methodist missionaries arrived in Norway House in 1840. By a "gentlemen's agreement," the north was carved up. Certain areas would be assigned to Roman Catholics, Church of England, Presbyterians, and Methodists.

There had been years of contact with explorers and traders before, but the arrival of the Methodists began a period of radical change for my people. The Cree language was put into syllabics; translation of scripture and hymns began. Historians are still sorting through this development to determine who was involved and what happened to enable them to succeed in this project.

The result of having worship resources in the language of the people was liberating. More than eighty years before the United Church was formed, the Cree were learning to read scripture and sing praises in our own language.

There were many small hymn books printed in Cree, but there were never many copies. These books usually contained just a few hymns and each edition was different. So people memorized their favourite hymns. It wasn't until 1971 that a large collection of Cree hymns was published by the Home Missions Committee of Manitoba Conference of the United Church. The Rev. Dr. A. Veldhuis did much of the co-ordination for this project. With the help of Elder Wesley Hart, many corrections and additions were made to the collection. The Cree hymn book is very much influenced by our Methodist history. The hymns most used are "gospel hymns." This book has been so popular, it has gone into its fifth printing with more than ten thousand sold. It is an important component in maintaining the health of our language.

Lay Leadership—Invoked and Ignored

The unique feature about Methodist missionary efforts was the development of lay leadership. As lay leaders travelled to their traplines and on trading expeditions, they shared Good News with all the people they encountered. Official church stories tell much about the wonderful dedicated missionary families who gave so much to the developing church, but little is known about the local Methodist class leaders who shared in that work.

In the early seventies I happened upon a booklet entitled *Commission to Study Indian Work*. The Commission was established by the Sixteenth General Council to report to the Seventeenth. Its work began in April 1955. Eleven men plus three women from the WMS were to consult with five males, all Home Mission Superintendents.

The Commission recognized that the "Indian population is increasing very rapidly." The Commission supported government policy to have Indian students attend non-Indian schools, since this will "assist in the more rapid integration of Indians."

The Commission to Study Indian Work made a powerful statement: "The story of the Native leaders and their faithful devotion to the cause of Christ is one that should be recorded in the Church's history."

Unfortunately, that insight was not reflected in the later recommendations. There was no recognition of these faithful "Native leaders" taking a part in the decision making processes or in "ministry." In fact, the very next section of the report states: "The Missionary is an indispensable man today." The Commission is so captivated by the image of a non-Indian male missionary that they further state: "His position of Christian leadership places him at the hub of community life—an indispensable person."

No Options Offered

The opening sentence about residential schools is obviously from another time (hindsight is 20/20): "There can be no doubt that the residential schools have, for more than a hundred years, made an incalculable contribution to the lives of Indian people in Canada."

My grandmother and grandfather both spent their entire childhood in the Brandon Residential School. My two eldest sisters went to Brandon, but when my parents visited them, they decided it would be better to have my sisters move from the United Church School to the Presbyterian School in Birtle. My other sister and I also attended Birtle Indian Residential School. We had no other options for an education.

The evolving church was structured to establish regional superintendents. The staff persons (missionaries) met in their professional gatherings and made decisions on behalf of their congregations. So it was that Church Union in 1925 did not involve consultation with Aboriginal peoples.

The missionary was, for generations, the authority figure in the church and community. Missionaries had power and influence in all areas—religion, law, medicine, and culture. An example is the missionary who worked in our isolated village for almost forty years: the Rev. Dr. Stevens. His final entry in local church records was my baptism in 1942.

The Indian Agent's Agent

From the large manse, Dr. Stevens, as he was known in the community, managed the dispensary supplied with medicines by the Department of Indian

Affairs. There are stories of him pulling teeth, without adequate equipment, and making "house calls" in the night. There were midwives practising in the community, but there was conflict if local medicine men and women were active and Dr. Stevens knew about it. He acted as judge in local disputes. He was the contact person for the Indian Agent or for RCMP officers when they visited.

The evolution of class leaders into church elders happened at some stage in the growth of the churches. In my reserve, Fisher River, there was a long history of strong elders. At one period during Dr. Stevens' time in the community, a power struggle developed and a number of elders left the church. What had been a Methodist community was divided. Soon after the dispute, a gospel chapel was built in the community.

My father tells of an experience with Dr. Stevens in this period. Some time in the early 1930s, Dr. Stevens had asked his son and my father to paint the floor of the church hall. Dr. Stevens came to the hall and started talking loudly to his son about all the trouble people in the community were causing him. My father was in the corner of the hall painting; Dr. Stevens did not know he was there. As he ended his rant, he said, "All the people on this reserve are crazy, except for me!" My father put down his brush, walked to the door, and said, "Thank you for the compliment," as he left.

My father continued to be very involved in the church. But it was disconcerting to experience the paternalism of the mission history.

The Image of Community

As a family, we regularly walked about a mile and a quarter (2 km) each way to share in worship. The most involved family member was my grandmother. She sang in the choir and was very active in the Woman's Association. The WA Hall was an important facility, a log building about 24 by 36 feet (7.5 by 11 m). It was the main community centre and the place for the community New Year's feasts, which often lasted two days and provided marvellous food for all who came.

I remember when I was about twelve and finally old enough to help with the United Church "wood bee." In early November, after the first good snowfall, people got organized. Families came on a Saturday morning with their horses and sleighs. The men went to the woods, the women to the hall. As many as forty men went out to get the wood for the next year. It was cut, hauled, and piled by early afternoon. Meanwhile, the women scrubbed and dusted the church and hall. The best part of the day was the wonderful home-cooked food covering the tables at noon. It was special to be able to work with the men for the first time. But it's the memory of the feasting that I carry as the image of a healthy church community.

The structures of the United Church shifted in the early seventies. For us, the dismantling of Home Missions was the major concern. The decision happened, once again, without consultation with Native churches. While a new approach was necessary, the process was not helpful. The history of mission and the Home Missions structures had made us increasingly dependent. The dismantling did not provide a transitional process; presbyteries were not able to respond to changes in the Native churches. Many felt abandoned, and recruiting for ministry was disorganized. Elders began to fill vacancies in leadership but there was insufficient support. Decisions by presbyteries were similar to the Home Missions Board, in that little consultation occurred.

These experiences have given me energy for cross-cultural conversation. They also indicate why I feel some frustration when I hear people say: "Well, we are all the same...."

The Courage to Continue

The journey through seventy-five years is indeed full of turns and challenges for Native peoples in the United Church. The 1986 apology in Sudbury was an exciting moment that we shared as a family. It was transforming and hopeful, because in many ways it addressed feelings we had carried all our lives. The sense for Native peoples that being different was negative was finally open for discussion. Sharing of spiritual insight might now be possible. Even as we began to explore the implications of the Sudbury apology, new issues began to emerge. The Oka crises in Québec and the growing awareness about residential schools made the nineties a period of stress for the United Church. The 1998 apology of the United Church for its part in residential schools has added a new level of recognition of the pain of our history.

The All Native Circle Conference (ANCC) is now the agency of self-government for Native United Churches. Along with four presbyteries, the ANCC attempts to shape the options that can be offered to the United Church as we seek a vision for the future. One thing has evolved: the identification and preparation of leaders. But the ongoing challenge to break the captivity of financial dependency remains. How can we function as partners in the United Church when financial policies and denial of access to resources make us so poor? The journey to justice and dignity is bound up with our spiritual quest.

The God who created us to have culture, language, philosophy, and faith

Our Own People Speaking
by Elinor N. Kent

I started on the road to the United Church at the age of three at Knox United in Winnipeg. I attended Sunday school and sang in the church choirs. As I grew, it was Young People's, and services morning and night. We enjoyed the company of other youth groups, and played all kinds of sports.

Later, I got married in the church.

As time went on, we moved to Windsor Park where there was no United Church. St. Boniface was mostly French and Catholic. A number of us canvassed the area. We saw that a church was needed. We approached the head office, and they sent a Dr. Freeman and his wife and a portable church. It was a wonderful experience—and there now stands a United Church that I helped to start. We had a choir, we did Christmas Nativity plays, we drove the children to Sunday school in car pools. During the building of the church, we had makeshift services at the school.

I have worked very hard to make every church where I have been involved a place of doing "God's ways." Sometimes I get into hot water, because some people do not like having me point out the errors of their ways.

Life dealt my girls and me a raw deal. We moved several times. Then our minister asked me if I would like to go with Gwen Axworthy (mother of Lloyd Axworthy, now in Ottawa) to Conference. We took my young daughter Patricia, as I had no babysitter for the weekend.

At the Conference, I spoke about how Native people should have their own people speaking for them, people who understood their ways and needs, rather than white people who did not understand.

brings us to this anniversary time with a deep sense of gratitude for the gift of life. We give thanks for the people of difference who have travelled with us and shared life from their culture and faith perspective. As we enter the next millennium there is a waiting for vision and courage to continue the journey of life, with hope that the God of love will continue the work of healing of the nations. "God so loved the world" is an inclusive statement—we offer this image of the power of love to our children and those who are not yet born.

Our Christology is founded on the call of Jesus to make room for children, the disempowered, the poor, the sick, and the despised. As the original people of "Turtle Island" we recognize the need for the four winds that will heal the peoples of the four directions. And when the people are healed, the earth will be healed.

In 1992 the Very Rev. Stan McKay became the first Native person elected moderator of The United Church of Canada.

Bring Many Names

by Robert Smith

The history of the United Church's relations with the First Nations people has moved from contempt to confession.

William Cockran

His name was William Cockran, Rev. William Cockran, and he had been sent from England by the Church Missionary Society in the 1820s to the Red River Colony to evangelize the Indians. In 1836, according to author and historian George van der Goes Ladd in *Shall We Gather at the River,** he reported to his superiors in London:

> I thought of making the Red Men Christians, and then Christians and Englishmen were so closely united in my imagination, that they appeared as one. Consequently I expected that when the Red Man became a Christian, we would see all the active virtues of English Christians immediately developed in his character. Here I endeavoured to make the Red Man not only a Christian but an Englishman; pressed the necessity of industry, economy, cleanliness, taste, good order, and all the other moral virtues....Every attempt, every invention…has failed.

Thirteen years later he wrote despondently,

> In whatever light you contemplate the Indian on earth, you behold him destined to suffer a large amount of misery. In his heathen erratick [sic] state, he is ignorant, brutish, vicious, and miserable; with a gloomy future of everlasting separation from God, the source of all good before him. In a Christian and civilized state, though his condition is ameliorated, he still continues poor, sickly, and miserable. It is only when you view him as heir of immortality that you are cheered, with his prospects under the gospel.

John

His name is—well, let's call him John. He sat across the circle from me in the basement of First United Church in Prince Rupert. All day long people had been arriving for the fall meeting of Prince Rupert Presbytery by car, float plane, and fishing boat. The presbytery covers an area the size of England, with a smaller population than an English market town. The members, long accustomed to isolation, clearly savoured the opportunity to get together, lingering over the wholesome supper that our hosts had provided. Now, following Aboriginal custom, we gathered in a "prayer circle" to speak to one another and to the Creator about the things that were on our hearts. For many of the presbyters the painful realities were economic: the collapse of the salmon fishery, the shutting down of the forest industry. For others the pain was rooted in the shattering revelations of abuse in residential schools, and the inability, or unwillingness, of the church to acknowledge its part in the abuse.

That was what John needed to talk about. For twelve years, from the time he was six until he was eighteen, the residential school had been his home, an experience so devastating that ten years earlier he had put a rifle in his mouth intending to blow his brains out.

The next day at lunch I went to sit beside him. "Was it the Alberni school that you attended?"

"No," he replied, "I was sent to Edmonton."

"Really?" said I. "I was a minister in Edmonton for a while. What years were you there?"

"From 1952 to 1964," he responded.

And I remembered. 1953. The yellow school bus pulling up at the curb outside Robertson United Church. The ranks of little brown children, all dressed alike, silently filing into the pews just before the organ prelude and, at the end of worship, silently filing out. 1962. Other yellow school buses disgorging Native teenagers at the door of the newly opened Jasper Place Composite High School where they attended classes with, but did not mix with, the teenagers who babysat for us on Saturday night. 1964. Driving out to the residential school on Sunday evenings to conduct worship there as part of my responsibilities as chaplain to the school.

As I remembered, I realized that he was still speaking—something about "the pen."

"What's that about?" I inquired.

"Oh," he said, "I had just done two years in the federal penitentiary when I tried to kill myself."

The same system that, under God, had been the source of unimagined blessing for me, bringing me honours and wealth and respect and privilege had, under God, been the purveyor of unimaginable suffering and oppression for him. I had travelled the world; he had come within a twitch of a finger of ending his life.

Bob Smith

My name is Bob Smith. I was moderator of The United Church of Canada in 1986, when the General Council of the United Church offered an apology to

Native congregations "for our denial of the value of their Native spirituality." Our apology did not cancel that suffering. We did no more than begin to acknowledge it.

It all started out simply enough—in Saskatchewan, source of so many visionary initiatives. In 1979 the Saskatchewan Conference of The United Church of Canada declared "a year of repentance" for the way the Church had contributed to racism both by what it did and what it failed to do. During that year presbyteries, congregations, and small groups spent time listening to members of Indian and Métis communities, hearing stories like the one John shared with me in Prince Rupert and, as a result of their listening, acquiring— at last—some awareness of the devastation wrought among Native peoples by those who, under the authority of the British monarch and in the name of Jesus, had set out to erase Indian language, culture, spirituality—"Indian-ness"—from the Canadian consciousness.

"Our objective," wrote Duncan Campbell Scott, Deputy Superintendent-General for Indian Affairs from 1913 to 1932, "is to continue until there is not a single Indian in Canada that has not been absorbed into the body politic." The result had been not assimilation but destruction; having force-fed the fathers and mothers with sour grapes, the children "unto the third and fourth generation" had not just their teeth but their whole lives set on edge (Jeremiah 31:29).

Alberta Billy

Her name is Alberta Billy, from Quadra Island, B.C. She wore the red and black button blanket of the Kwakiulth nation on the stage of the Great Hall of Laurentian University in Sudbury, Friday night, August 15, 1986. Beside her were Doreen Clellamin, from Bella Coola, similarly attired; Emily Oke of Kanesetake, Québec; Bernice Saulteaux, from Carry-the-Kettle reserve in Saskatchewan; and Floyd Steinhauer from Saddle Lake, Alberta, in buckskin with a magnificent feather headdress. For more than a half-hour, they told their stories to the commissioners to the Thirty-first General Council of The United Church of Canada. At a meeting of the Council's Executive some fifteen months before, Alberta had said, simply, "It's time for the United Church to apologize."

Now, with quiet strength she repeated her challenge. She said, "No longer can we live on the edge of society or of the church. We come to teach, because we must once again mend and keep the cycle flowing."

With that, she turned, and as the five of them filed from the stage the entire assembly spontaneously rose and stood silently. As they moved towards the exit, though, I became aware of a faint humming sound, from somewhere off to my right. A hymn tune. The right hymn tune—"Amazing Grace." More and more joined in. When they had left, the commissioners resumed their seats, again in silence. It was time to go to work.

At the beginning of the supper break the Rev. Ken Purdon had provided me with an excellent draft of an apology. Instead of eating supper, I had sequestered myself in a corner and, on a scrap of paper, revised it. I read the proposed apology to the commissioners and explained that, as we had agreed, we were going to eschew parliamentary forms of decision making and instead, as a sign of respect and of our new willingness to learn from Aboriginal people, we were going to try to come to consensus. Then, desperate for a break, I asked the music leader, Jo Sorrill, to find a song. Any song.

I made it to the washroom, where I was addressed by the person next to me: "What do you know about consensus building?"

"Not a thing," said I.

"Well," said Gary Webster, Professor of Political Studies at the University of Prince Edward Island, "I'd better teach you before they finish that song!"

Two minutes later, greatly relieved in more than one sense, I was confidently explaining to the assembly the process of building consensus. They were—I said—to place themselves provisionally in one of four categories: agreement without qualification; general agreement; questioning, or objecting. Then attempts would be made to respond to the concerns of the questioners so as to enable them to stand with the majority. Finally, those who still objected would be asked to indicate whether their objections were sufficient to prevent them from identifying with the community in its decision and, if that were the case, the process would begin again.

It wasn't a longhouse, and I was not a skilled and infinitely patient chief, so the exercise—for all its promise—ultimately failed. With the clock heading for 10:30 and two of the 370 commissioners indicating that they still could not join in the consensus, Vas Saklikar of Westminster Presbytery moved that an immediate vote be taken. I was charged with the responsibility of making the apology in the name of the Council.

All week long the national Native consultation had been meeting in a nearby retreat centre. Earlier in the day they had set up two teepees on a parking lot by the lake. About a hundred of them had spent the evening there, praying in a circle, led by traditional elder Jim Dumont.

A Circle of Elders

While the commissioners and observers sang a hymn I hurriedly donned my alb and a penitential stole. From here on—aside from the scribbled text of the apology—nothing was planned, or scripted. Our church had never done this before, so I had no precedents to follow. I opened my Bible to Psalm 51 and read it aloud. (It seemed perfect until I came to verse 7—"wash me, and I shall be whiter than snow." Wasn't that how we got into this mess in the first place?) Then, as I moved towards the door in silence, the humming started again. This time it was "Kumbayah."

Through the August night we walked, arm in arm, hand in hand, down the hill towards the flame of the council fire. We arrived in the clearing to the welcome of the drum as our hosts piled new wood on the fire and the flames leapt towards the stars. There was a long wait. No one seemed to be in charge. At last, I was ushered into the nearest teepee. Around its circumference sat the elders. The only light was cast by the fire smouldering in the centre. Murray Whetung, of the Curve Lake band in Ontario, invited me to say what I had to say. I knelt by the fire so as to see the words and read:

> Long before my people journeyed to this land your people
> were here, and you received from your elders an under-
> standing of creation, and of the Mystery that surrounds us
> all that was deep, and rich, and to be treasured. We did not
> hear you when you shared your vision. In our zeal to tell
> you of the good news of Jesus Christ we were closed to the
> value of your spirituality. We confused western ways and
> culture with the depth and breadth and length and height
> of the gospel of Christ. We imposed our civilization as a
> condition of accepting the Gospel. We tried to make you be
> like us, and in so doing we helped to destroy the vision that
> made you what you were. As a result you, and we, are
> poorer and the image of the Creator in us is twisted,
> blurred, and we are not what we are meant by God to be.
> We ask you to forgive us and to walk together with us in
> the spirit of Christ so that our people may be blessed and
> God's creation healed.

I stood up. Tears—only a few caused by the smoke from the fire—were streaming down my face. No one moved. Then an old woman—Edith Memnook, an elder from Saddle Lake in Alberta—struggled to her feet and came to stand in front of me. She said: "I have been waiting all my life to hear those words. Not just for my own sake, but for the sake of my children and my grandchildren." Then, opening her arms wide to embrace me, she said, "Of course I forgive you."

I left them there and returned to the waiting crowd. They listened, rapt, as I read for them the words. Donna Sinclair described in *The Observer* what followed. When I finished "there was the soft sound of a woman sobbing into the darkness, rising into a rhythmic wail of emotion overflowing into the crowd. The drums began, embraces, tears, dancing, the spoken wisdom of the elders until the place ceased to be the lower parking lot of Laurentian University in Sudbury and became what it had always been: Ojibway territory, with two peoples meeting on it, this time in a moment of grace."

Acting Our Way into a New Way of Thinking

His name was Erich Fromm. Long ago he said something like this: "No one ever thinks his way into new ways of acting; he always acts his way into new ways of thinking." In the years since Alberta Billy challenged The United Church of Canada to act we have been led into new, then-unimagined ways of thinking. The words that I spoke in the parking lot in Sudbury have new and fearsome resonance. The brokenness and pain of Native peoples, Native communities, is there in our face, day after day. And while Edith Memnook was willing, graciously, to forgive me—and through me, the church that I represented—the forgiveness of many Native peoples is not so swiftly extended. They are waiting to see whether we mean what we say when we say we are sorry.

And in the meantime, the prayer of the church must be the same as it was that August night in Sudbury,

> *Hide your face from our sins, and blot out all our iniquities.*
> *Create in us clean hearts, O God*
> *and put a new and right spirit within us.†*

For it is only thus, through the grace of God, that healing can come—to those whom we have wronged so deeply, and to us.

> *Robert Smith was moderator of The United Church of Canada from*
> *1984 to 1986. Now retired and living in Vancouver, he chaired*
> *the United Church's Seventy-fifth Anniversary Committee and is*
> *a spokesperson for the Healing Fund.*

*CANEC, 1986.
†Adapted from Psalm 51:9–10

"A Metaphor for Our Relationship…"
by Bill Phipps

A letter sent by the moderator to all pastoral charges

November 10, 1998

Dear friends:

I believe that the whole residential school system is a metaphor for the relationship of First Nations communities with those of us who are non-Native. Although the church was well intentioned in participating in this system, we have discovered that it resulted in horrendous damage, not only to individuals, but also to family life and communities at large.

I believe that this is a defining moment for The United Church of Canada as we are confronted by the abuses in the schools in which we were involved. The current trial with respect to our involvement in the Alberni Indian Residential School brings us face-to-face with the harsh realities of the total system.

As a Canadian of non-Native ancestry I enjoy untold blessings handed on to me by my ancestors. If I am to accept all these blessings, then I also need to accept responsibility for the wrongs which have also been handed down. The residential school system and all that it symbolizes in our relationship with First Nations peoples is one of those wrongs.

It was with this background that the United Church issued the apology of 1986, the repentance statement of 1997, and now has apologized for our participation in the residential school system.

I urge all of us to prayerfully reflect upon Canadian society and the deep fault line that exists between First Nations and non-Native peoples. I urge us to become aware of the residential school system and other manifestations of that fault line.

I believe that The United Church of Canada can give leadership to our country in facing some of the ugly realities of life for First Nations peoples in this land that was theirs. Indeed, I believe many beyond our church look to the United Church for such leadership. Because of the distinctiveness of First Nations communities throughout the land, that leadership needs to come at the regional and local level. It could involve such activities as making contact with First Nations communities near where you live and embarking on a process of dialogue and understanding so that our road to repentance can be meaningful for all.

The apology that the General Council Executive issued is but one step along the long road of repentance. There are no quick fixes to this issue which lies at the heart of Canadian life. Rather it is a road that requires diligence, faith, and hope as we come to terms with our past so that we can create a more hopeful future.

The Right Reverend Bill Phipps
Moderator

Opening an Uncomfortable Scrapbook

by Keith Howard

Resolution of the United Church's implication in residential schools will take a long time. But the experience of pain doesn't wait for resolution.

The involvement of The United Church of Canada in the residential school system resembles opening up a chest full of old scrapbooks. At first, there's excitement—the prospect of rediscovering tales almost forgotten, stories of sacrifice, adventure, and triumph against overwhelming odds. But other pictures also lurk in the trunk. Their discovery feels more like uncovering family secrets long buried in the dark corners of memory.

In this scrapbook, the earliest pictures go back centuries. They contain many members of the family: Roman Catholics, Anglicans, Methodists, and Presbyterians. In those times, the common wisdom was that the First Nations inhabitants of the new country would be best served by converting them to European manners, customs, and culture. The scrapbooks glory in scenes of men and women working sacrificially in difficult frontier settings.

The Institutional Solution

Soon though, the pictures change. Men in dark coats sit on horseback, Bibles in hand, looking down on workers, shirt sleeves rolled up, erecting walls and roofs. Personal sacrifice and evangelistic zeal shifts to institutional solutions. In the background we see tool sheds, work areas, farm animals, garden plots. Food, and funding, always seemed in short supply.

In 1915 church and government resolved the funding problem. Under a formal agreement, government would supply virtually all the funding for these institutions. Laws required Native children between the ages of five and sixteen to attend these schools. Non-attendance was not a legal option. Scenes of police and government agents coming to First Nations' homes and communities to remove children by force are burned into many hearts and spirits.

By the mid-1930s there were over eighty residential schools. The government had run the schools through the founding denominations of the United Church.

Dr. Jon Jessiman, legal counsel for British Columbia Conference of the United Church, reports:

> The number of schools...ranged from a high of thirteen in 1927, to six in 1951 and four in 1966. We also succeeded to a number of day schools, usually adjoining reserves where children were permitted to return to their parents at the

end of each day instead of only during the summer break which was the pattern for those who were transported, sometimes long distances, to the residential schools. In 1927, the United Church was involved in forty-two day schools in Aboriginal communities....It is estimated that over 150,000 Native youngsters were placed in residential schools over the period they were in operation....

Missing from the administrative picture and structural charts is the zeal. Mission bands collected pennies for "the Indian work." Units of the WMS across the country raised money for furnishing and supplies, energized by the call to provide education and training to children deemed poor, struggling, and in need of Christian guidance. Dedicated individuals gave up their careers in urban centres to serve in remote communities.

One of the fascinating characteristics of scrapbooks is what they reveal about the storyteller. Each storyteller chooses images and details that capture particular memories. In the first part of this century, the official story was of Indian missions, of the urgency of the work of education, transformation, and redemption.

Other Scrapbooks, Other Images

Others carry different scrapbooks, with different images dominating. They tell different stories of the experience, meaning, and impact of the residential school system.

In a courtroom in Nanaimo, B.C., in February 1998, some of these memories are shared.

The United Church of Canada is in the Nanaimo courtroom because thirty former residents of the Alberni Indian Residential School in Port Alberni, B.C., are suing the church as well as the federal government and several former principals of the school. The suit involves questions of liability of the church and government for the abuse suffered at the hands of Arthur Henry Plint, a dormitory supervisor at Alberni. (Plint was convicted of the abuses in 1994. Some say his case gained the most notoriety, but allege that his actions were not isolated. Indeed, the abuse of the boys by Plint has become almost symbolic of the abuse of many First Nations individuals and communities by the residential school *system* as a whole.)

In the packed courtroom, scenes sear the spirit.

Danny Watts of the Nuu-chah-nulth Nation on the west coast of Vancouver Island refuses to swear the oath of truth using the Bible. For him, the Bible remains linked forever to his abuse.

Willie Blackwater paints a vivid and horrifying picture of being led to Plint's room soon after he arrived at the school as an eight-year-old boy. He says that for the next three years he was raped almost weekly and when he tried to tell his story to school officials he was beaten.

The stories of terror pile up. Each survivor opens a personal, and painful, scrapbook of memories. Each story paints another part of the larger story of the residential school system.

There are stories of boys being forced into the bed of a supervisor to perform sexual acts and then, afterward, being forced to kneel and pray for forgiveness. Stories tearfully told of the great gulfs that emerged between the children and their families back home. Children grew up not knowing parents and so they never learned how to parent their children. Studies have shown that families often dealt with the loss of their children by turning their anger inward—with violence, abuse of alcohol and other drugs, and other acts of despair. As page after page of the scrapbooks turn, a larger, devastating picture of cultural abuse emerges.

In this too the church had a role.

Jessie Oliver comes to the Nanaimo courtroom to tell her story. In the early 1960s she worked at Alberni as a Christian Education Director. She describes those who came and worked and genuinely cared for the children. She also tells of those for whom "it was merely a job." She tells of students who seemed to adjust and students who ran away. She tells of the avalanche of emotions—"anger, shame, resentment, guilt"—that buffet her now in light of the stories recently revealed: "I was there at the time, but didn't realize such things were happening." She tells of an attempt to discuss conditions at the school with the Superintendent of Home Mission and being told, "Stop! I don't hear complaints about my administrators."

Shrivelling with Shame

Each day of the Nanaimo trial more images emerge. Church members who originally came to support their First Nations friends, shrivel with guilt and shame as stories of the schools are told. They struggle with their role as representatives of the church. First Nations folk endeavour to keep clear two different images of the church—one as corporate institution seeking to limit financial liability, the other as a company of compassionate and well-intentioned believers. Relationships twist and turn like a rope bridge in high winds.

Long-standing friendships between church people and many First Nations people strain almost beyond endurance as each wrestles with powerful feelings. Hallways become corridors of discomfort. Soon it becomes clear that those church folk are not there to support First Nation survivors—as many initially intended—but to hear the stories, receive the anger, and bear the shame.

A Burning Sense of Betrayal

Part of the issue, of course, involves broken trust.

In no small part, in the early days—before legislation forced people to send their children to residential schools—First Nations parents and communities entrusted their children to the schools because the schools were connected with the church, and the church came proclaiming Jesus as the giver of peace, a healer, and a teacher. The experience of many First Nations has instead been of shattered lives and communities. A sense of betrayal scorches the image of Christ, the bringer of new life, as fire shrivels old photos.

The residential school system scrapbook bursts with images. More continue to be added. Although the last school in which the United Church was involved, the Alberni school, closed in 1973, the legacy and the stories of the schools continue. The story continues because healing of individuals, communities, and relationships is far from accomplished.

Many who worked at the schools agonize over their role and the legacy now being sketched. Survivors of the schools and their descendants reach for ways to rebuild shattered lives. The church, as institution, struggles to admit responsibility and find a faithful role. The apology extended by the Executive of General Council in October 1998 marks another step, but the long road of repentance feels far from clear.

Charlie Thompson, a Nuu-chah-nulth counsellor, addresses a special meeting of Victoria Presbytery. He challenges, "How many sad stories do you need to hear before you believe?" Many believe but wonder how to respond. Gifts of money will assist certain healing initiatives. But money alone does not provide the answer. Intentional and persistent efforts to understand both the history and the fundamental perceptions that created the history sound right. But many currently in the church wonder why they need to repent for actions that took place before they were born, before they could have in any way influenced those policies and conditions. The facing of sin, personal or corporate, remains a daunting task.

The Painful Path of Repentance

Ron Hamilton is one of the historians of the Nuu-chah-nulth experience in residential schools. He angers many in the same meeting when he does not

An Intergenerational Experience
by Constance Deiter

This is an excerpt from the book From Our Mother's Arms*.

Because so many generations attended residential schools they have affected all First Nations individuals. For example, even though I was raised in the city, all my family members, including my parents, my grandparents, uncles, and aunts on both sides of the family attended these schools. Most of my friends also attended the schools, including my husband and cousins. As well, all of the people whom my parents associated with during my formative years were residential school survivors. To say that the school experience did not directly affect my life would be a denial.

*United Church Publishing House, 1999

respond with empathy or forgiveness to the fears of presbyters that legal suits, such as the one held in Nanaimo, may spell the financial end of the United Church. The path of repentance, forgiveness, and hope will not be easy.

But there are signs.

Many colours of the spirit run throughout the scrapbook. Shame and pride, sorrow and joy, despair and hope.

Increasing numbers of First Nations people stand ready to tell their story. And many congregations seem willing to hear. In what can only be described as acts of grace, many plaintiffs in the Nanaimo trial gather with congregations and church leaders to begin the healing. Like small pinpricks of light, such initiatives involve risk, confession, and searching for the next step towards a relationship that truly does reflect the One who came proclaiming, in the shadow of the cross, the possibility of a new heaven and a new earth.

Keith Howard is minister of Pilgrim United Church in Victoria and a member of B.C. Conference staff with responsibility for communications.

The Sound of a Church

by Kim Uyede-Kai

The pain of those of different racial and linguistic origins who have been excluded and marginalized needs to be heard with the heart, not just the head.

The first thundering boom of the barrel-size *taiko* drum startled the Thirty-fifth General Council into wakefulness in the darkened arena in Fergus, Ontario. Its steady, single drumbeat was joined by another different drum, then another, until the arena was filled with a clamorous tumult of throbbing rhythms.

Aboriginal sisters and brothers among the gathering knew the drum's rhythm even though it came from drums different than their own. The sound called even late-rising commissioners running from their beds to see what was happening. When they arrived at the arena, they saw the drums and the drummers they expected to see. They also saw a space filled with people throbbing with sound.

A Painful Resonance

When the drumming stopped, each person in the room had both absorbed the sound and been its reverberating sounding board. Each stroke of a drumstick on tightly drawn skin had called the commissioners to hear a new way of being The United Church of Canada. To hear with their ears, with their hearts, with their whole being. And to be fully in community in the presence of the One who is the Sound.

My son was just five years old when he first heard the sound of a Japanese *taiko* drumming troupe. "It hurts my heart!" he screamed, clutching his chest. He thought that he was having a heart attack. He heard the drumbeats as more than a pounding in his ears. He felt them with his whole body as a sound too painful for his heart to hear.

In the beating of the drums at Fergus in 1994, I, too, felt a sound too painful for my heart to hear. Echoed in the drumming I heard the sound of the stories of those whose presence in the church was not seen or heard or fully felt: First Nations peoples; gays, lesbians, and bisexuals; those who live with poverty; those who live with challenges of body, mind, spirit. And as I heard the sound of the stories of peoples of racial ethnic minority heritage, I heard my own story.

At that Council, the Feasibility Task Group on Ethnic Ministries proposed a model for a new national body to be called the Ethnic Ministries Council. Yet racial ethnic minorities with Methodist, Congregationalist, and Presbyterian roots had been members of the United Church since Church

Ethnic Blinders
from an item in Currents

Saundra Anierobi discovered that Canadians don't listen very well.

Saundra is Black. Therefore people assume that she must have come here from somewhere else.

At a writing workshop, she described a conversation with a couple of Canadians at a church supper in Montréal.

"What country are you from?" they asked her, showing polite interest. "Jamaica?"

"I was born in Montréal," she replied.

"Really," they responded. "And how long have you been here?"

"All my life. I was born here."

They didn't hear her, even the second time. Their minds had focused on the Caribbean and stayed there. "Do you miss the sun, these cold Canadian winters?"

"No," said Saundra firmly, "this is my home."

"We've been down to your islands a couple of times now, haven't we, dear?" They began reciting some of the resorts where they had enjoyed winter holidays, and their difficulties with the local dialects…

"Yes," Saundra interrupted at last. "You probably have been to my island. It's very easy to get to. You just drive along the Trans-Canada Highway. They speak French there. It's called Montréal Island…"

Union. Like other Canadians who journeyed to this new land from other homelands, Black, Chinese, and Japanese peoples added the richness of their heritages to the heritages of Anglo-European peoples to found The United Church of Canada. This is my history.

Unfounded Assumptions

When I tell people that I am a third-generation member of the United Church I am often met with shock, sometimes with disbelief. People with Church Union roots are not expected to look like me. My Japanese features are usually interpreted to mean that I am an immigrant or perhaps raised by immigrant parents. In fact, on my mother's side my roots in Canada go back to 1900. My father's father was a staunch elder of his Methodist church in Victoria, B.C., long before the formation of The United Church of Canada in 1925.

United Church history has almost always been told from the majority perspective. The stories of minorities like my grandfather and many other women and men have rarely been included. The assumption that the United Church at its beginning did not include my grandfather is a silence I hear with my heart.

I do not know how my grandfather came to be Christian, how he came to the Methodist Church, or why he was so loyal to his United Church congregations. I only know that his faith community was so important to him that even when bowed by arthritis in his eighties, he conscientiously attended worship every Sunday morning.

Unlike my grandfather and many of my relatives who were active in Japanese congregations, my faith was formed in a suburban mainstream United Church congregation. There, I was grounded in the *New Curriculum* (which places me in a certain generation), Robert Raikes Sunday school attendance certificates, and our junior choir's rendition of "What a Friend We Have in Jesus," accompanied by an acoustic guitar, a sanctuary instrument considered radical for its time.

I did not transfer my membership to the Japanese-Canadian English-speaking congregation that shared space with my grandfather's congregation until I was a young adult. There, the warmth of the community and its refreshing celebration of Japanese-Canadian culture in worship drew me. It was not unusual for the Rev. Ken Matsugu, the second-generation Japanese Canadian minister who was struggling to learn Japanese, to use his latest lesson in writing Japanese characters as the basis for his sermons. I knew that this, too, was The United Church of Canada.

Isolated by Language

My grandfather died over twenty years ago, before I could articulate questions to him to help me reclaim my Church Union heritage. Sadly, I remember few conversations with him while he was alive. I remember seeing him faithfully singing in his usual church pew every Sunday and sitting at his desk at home, writing award-winning haiku poetry. Language and words were important to him; they gave him life. Ironically, it was language that kept his church memories from me. His language was mostly Japanese. Mine is solely English because I was raised in an English-language home shared with my mother's Canadian-born, English-speaking, Buddhist father. The legacy of the English language classes and English language social services offered by the early church had so thoroughly succeeded, in tandem with post-war Canadian society's pressures for Japanese Canadians to "integrate," that few members of my generation can understand the Japanese of their grandparents.

Most ethnic minority congregations were initially formed for immigrants and their children, as a safe and comfortable place for community and family to worship in their familiar language and ethnic culture. In the early years of Christian mission to immigrants, English language classes and social advocacy in English-speaking Canadian society were the main tools of outreach. I felt a real moment of connection when I learned that the Welsh Dewi Sant United Church in Toronto shares this same history with the early Asian congregations who became United Church.

English language classes replaced fluent Japanese with fluent English. It also helped reshape transplanted Japanese culture to "Canadian" cultural expectations. One legacy I inherited from my grandfather was his choice of the non-Japanese pronunciation of our surname, to accommodate English-speaking Canadians who could not pronounce Japanese sounds properly.

My grandfather's faith was not Christian when he was born in Japan. Somewhere in his life, he became Christian. Like many early Japanese immigrants to Canada, he found the Methodist Church a community in which he could be sustained. His faithfulness to his church community and the God he came to love helped him through the very difficult years during the Second

World War when he experienced the internment and relocation of Japanese Canadians.

Since Church Union, many racial/ethnic groups formed ethnic minority United Church congregations to worship in their original languages. Today, on any given Sunday, God is worshipped in Armenian, Akan, Cantonese, Finnish, German, Hungarian, Italian, Japanese, Korean, Lingala, Mandarin, Spanish, Swahili, Taiwanese, and Welsh, as well as in English and French.

Racial ethnic minorities contribute more to the life of the United Church than the sound of different tongues. The cultures and histories these communities honour are as diverse and as life-giving to the church as their languages. Some have been Christian for several generations; some are new to the Christian faith. They all contribute to the creation of supportive communities that sustain their faith even in times of great struggle.

The Role of Racism

Although Christian conversion from non-Christian faiths was an overt expectation, racism was also a catalyst for congregational formation for many ethnic minorities. While common language brought Japanese and other non-English speaking immigrants together to form worshipping congregations, experiences of racism in Canadian society often forced them to draw on the strengths of each other. In their daily lives and in neighbourhood churches, racial ethnic minorities were made to feel unwelcome and marginalized. Over ninety years ago, Union United Church in Montréal was founded out of the experiences of Blacks who were blatantly not welcome in White churches. Today it is exciting to visit Union and witness a vibrant United Church congregation that welcomes people from many different places, especially several Caribbean Islands and Africa, celebrates their cultures, and provides outreach services to communities that still face racism.

Racial prejudice shows up in other less vicious ways. Several years ago, a high-profile minister preached at a Japanese-Canadian congregation. He told a second-generation Japanese Canadian, English-speaking couple that their ethnic church should be a "stepping stone" to a "regular" congregation. With language no longer a barrier, he assumed they no longer needed their ethnic congregation. He encouraged them to join a majority congregation since nothing was preventing them from being one of "us." The implication was clear—an ethnic minority congregation was inferior to a majority congregation; it was something to be outgrown, like a relic of childhood. (The couple occasionally feels pangs of guilt, years later, that they still haven't "outgrown" their ethnic congregation, even though they have visited congregations in their neighbourhood with a serious thought to joining. They remained in their ethnic minority congregation because they found community there.)

"Why do you stick to yourselves?" is frequently asked of members of ethnic minority congregations by both racial ethnic majorities and ethnic minorities who attend majority congregations. Racism can be heard in the paternalistic voice telling racial ethnic minorities that they have made it in the church when they no longer need an ethnic minority church. Racism says that United Church faith is expressed best in English or French vocabulary in the cultures of the Anglo-European majorities. Racism says that ethnic and cultural diversity is desired in majority congregations, provided that ethnic minorities never become that majority.

Racism internalized can be heard when ethnic minorities in mainstream congregations think themselves superior, or more culturally adaptable, comfortable with, and accepted by the majority. They think of ethnic minority congregations as glorified cultural and linguistic ghettos for those who do not want to learn to change and adapt to Canadian culture or church. This attitude denies the fact that majority congregations also have their own ethnic identity and cultures. It perpetuates the misconception that there is a hierarchy of importance in the United Church, with ethnic majority congregations at the top and ethnic minority congregations at the bottom.

Sticking Together

Faith has many different cultural expressions, and God's loving presence is in each one. The living faith that sustains and supports ethnic minority communities is no less vital than the faith that lives in any other congregation. The Ethnic Ministries Council was inaugurated in 1996, not to create more racial ethnic hierarchy in the United Church but to find new ways of empowering the voices of ethnic minorities, to value their faith and faith communities in the church, and to hear their stories with hurting hearts. The Council also invites the majority church to come close enough to these stories to share their own.

We can all choose to "stick together," in the broadest possible sense, if those we choose to stick together with are as diverse as the people of the church are. The drums used in Fergus were only able to sound because the drum skins had been tightly drawn; they had a tension great enough to sound a call when struck. In the same way, ethnic minorities in the Church have been

Denominational Geneology
by Ross Skuse

This congregation started in the 1850s at the request of German-speaking people in Hamilton, Ontario, and was recognized by the Evangelical Association in 1856. They met in houses until a church was built in 1860.

In 1909 the Association and the United Evangelical Church became The Evangelical Church.

In 1946, the Evangelical Church and the United Brethren in Christ Church became the Evangelical United Brethren Church, which it remained until becoming Linden Park Community Church, a congregation of The United Church of Canada.

challenged to take the tensions of their marginalization, to use them to call to one another, and to resonate in the hearts of others.

My grandfather, Umekichi Uyede, is not heard among the throngs in the historical photos taken at the Mutual Street Arena in 1925. His face has never appeared on any later photo telling the story of who represents the United Church. But my memory of him sitting in his church pew is as loud and as steady in my heart as the most insistent drum that calls me to come running to join the gathering at the source of the sound. It tells me that I need to learn to listen with my whole being until the listening hurts my heart.

Then I will hear the sound of all of The United Church of Canada.

Kim Uyede-Kai is a contract Program and Resource staff person with the United Church's Ethnic Ministries Council.

Young People

Overlooked, undervalued, and often invisible

Where Are All the Youth?

by Noelle Bowles

The United Church's ministry with youth and young adults didn't die with the 1960s. It just looks rather different today.

People all across the country look at the average age of those sitting in their congregation's pews on Sunday morning, and they ask, "Where are the young people?" "How can we bring young people back into the church?" They remember what it was like when they were young and they wish it could be the same again.

Many who grew up in the first half of our church's life can tell stories of days when the church was bursting at the seams with youth and young adults. They recall time spent in Young People's Union (YPU), the Canadian Girls in Training (CGIT), or the Boy Scouts. They remember that the church was the "place to be" when they were growing up, and they wonder why it is so different today.

The years between 1930 and 1960 were, indeed, glory days of youth ministry in the United Church. Initially, the Great Depression meant that jobs were few and far between. There was not a lot of money at home for recreation, nor was there much government money for community youth programs. Young people needed things to do and people to do them with. The newly formed United Church of Canada had the financial resources of three founding denominations, and was able to put more money into youth programming than many other churches or community agencies. The church provided the recreational and social opportunities young people were longing for.

Then the post-war baby boom produced a critical mass of young people who could take advantage of the programs established during the 1930s. Since Canada still identified itself as a Christian society, the church was, for many of those young people, the centre of their social world.

A Heartbreaking Absence

The church is not the same today. We are not bursting at the seams with youth and young adults. Many United Church congregations are hard pressed to find enough youth to put together a youth group at all.

For many in our church, the absence of young people is heartbreaking. It suggests to them that the church, which they have loved and supported all of their lives, may not exist into the next century.

Though it may seem that the "glory days" of youth ministry in the United Church have ended, this is far from the truth. Stories about the "good old days" in YPU or CGIT are important—not because they hearken back to a time when the church was filled with young people, not because they prove that the church was doing a better job of reaching young people at that time than we do today, not even because they tell us that youth in the first half of our church's life were more spiritual or more committed or more Christian than they are today—but because they tell us why the church was important in their lives. These stories tell us that, at church, young people felt they belonged. At church, they felt valued. At church, they felt connected to people who shared common experiences. And in that community, they met God.

Those experiences continue to be the experience of many youth and young adults in our church today—but in different places and in different ways.

In 1975 the church did something new and different. In honour of the fiftieth anniversary of The United Church of Canada, the Mission and Service department of the church organized "The Youth Exchange." During that year, about a hundred United Church young people were sent around the world and another hundred from overseas churches visited here. *The Observer* (August 1977, p. 8) reported, "Many young people will never be the same again. Their enthusiasm has infected a few presbyteries and many congregations."

National Youth Gatherings Begin

In the wake of the enthusiasm generated by that exchange, another idea was conceived. Ron Coughlin, then the chair of the National Committee on Youth Ministry, and Shelagh Parsons, the staffperson with responsibilities for youth ministries, wondered, "What if we could have a gathering of youth in Canada?"

Their "what if" turned into the first General Council Youth Forum. In the summer of 1977, eighty young people, between the ages of sixteen and twenty-one, met at the same time as General Council in Calgary, Alberta. To quote *The Observer* again (October 1977, p. 15) the members of Youth Forum "came from every Conference, travelling as cheaply as possible, bringing their sleeping bags. They slept on gym floors at a nearby high school, ordered late-night pizzas, put out a daily newspaper, and got to know each other." They participated in some of the meetings of General Council, but spent most of the time holding their own council. They elected a moderator and a general secretary. They debated issues ranging from sexuality and values to Québec's relationship to Canada, alternative lifestyles, and alcohol and drug abuse. As they learned about the work and governance of the United Church, they

Very Long Sermons
by Noreen Hull

Dr. George Pidgeon was the minister at Bloor Street Presbyterian Church which became, in 1925, Bloor Street United Church. At Church Union, he became the first moderator of The United Church of Canada.

I grew up in Bloor Street United. I was baptized there, attended nursery school, Sunday school, junior congregation, and finally church proper. I was married there by Dr. Pidgeon himself.

My earliest recollection of Dr. Pidgeon is of very long sermons. As time went on and I grew older, I began to appreciate those sermons. They were always deep in scripture, but Dr. Pidgeon had a way of fully and graphically explaining them. He was a great orator, and his interpretation of the Bible was very easy to understand.

My father served as treasurer of Bloor Street United Church for more than twenty-five years. My sister and I were often persuaded to help count the offerings after the evening service. Dr. Pidgeon dropped into the counting room to visit, since he and my father were good friends. In this way I got to know Dr. Pidgeon.

He was a great storyteller. I wish, after fifty years, I could remember some of those stories!

worshipped and shared faith stories into the early hours of the morning. They left Calgary, excited about the church and about their new-found friends. At that first General Council Youth forum, young people shared their lives and experienced the presence of God.

People wondered if Youth Forum would happen again. Would there be money? Would there be interest? Yes, there would. The Thirty-seventh General Council, to be held in Toronto in August 2000, will welcome the eleventh consecutive General Council Youth Forum. The present format of Youth Forum differs from 1977's, but the spirit is the same. Young people gather to be the church, to share their lives with one another, and to meet God.

Not long after the first Youth Forum, people started wanting more gatherings of youth and young adults from across the country. Conferences started to host their own youth gatherings to coincide with their annual meetings. Youth and young adults across the church wanted to get together more often than once every two or three years. In 1985, it happened. About three hundred young people gathered at the University of British Columbia in Vancouver. The event was called *Kairos*—a Greek word meaning special or significant time. And it was a special and significant time. It was the first time in decades that so many United Church young people had gathered in one place, and it was a resounding success.

Kairos, like Youth Forum, did not remain a one-time event. It generated so much excitement and touched peoples lives so deeply that it continued to happen in every year between Youth Forums. When General Council moved to a three-year cycle in 1994, British Columbia Conference organized the first Soulstice, a regionally planned young adult event. The youth and young adults in the church were determined that no year would pass without an opportunity to gather.

Experiencing the Presence of God
Events such as *Kairos*, Youth Forum, and Soulstice, as well as Conference and Presbytery youth events, have become the "young people's movement" of the seventies, eighties, and nineties. People talk about these times with the same

fondness and nostalgia as those who grew up in the forties and fifties talk about the Young People's Union. One young man from western Canada describes *Kairos* '95 as his best experience of church. He remembers one of the worship services in particular:

> We had been together all week. It had been an intense and emotional time. The worship service brought it all together. There were some people who had guitars and they led us out of the service singing. We just kept singing. Right there on the lawn, we kept singing and some people started dancing. I was just so happy. That's all I know.

A young woman from Winnipeg describes a Presbytery Youth Committee Easter vigil:

> We had been up all night. We should have been exhausted, but we were not. We experienced together the confusion, fear, and pain that Jesus must have felt. We sat together as he died. And then, somehow, in the midst of that death, in the midst of the pain and confusion of our own lives, there was new life. Resurrection! We had the biggest party. We shared bread we had baked together earlier in the evening. We ate fruit and cheese and crackers and cake. We sang and then we danced until dawn. That is communion! That is church!

In those places and in those times we, the youth and young adults of the United Church, share our lives, our faith, and our doubts. We encounter the Holy, and youth ministry continues to happen.

Cut Off by Their Own Churches

As important and transformative as youth and young adult events can be for people, the church's youth ministry must not only be about "big bang" events. For many young people, national events, even Conference and presbytery events, are inaccessible because of distance and cost. Indeed, for many, these events can be lonely places. They are painful reminders of what is *not* happening for youth and young adults in their local churches.

Even those who feel encouraged, valued, and uplifted at these types of events often feel disempowered by other experiences of church. They feel cut off by congregations that do not seem to understand or care about what it's like to be a young person today. They feel like there is no place for them in

Meeting Each Other on the Way
T. M. Russell Dunham

I was thirteen at the time of Church Union. In our village of Arkona, the Presbyterians didn't vote for Church Union, but several Presbyterian families joined with the Methodists anyway. The Presbyterian Church in nearby Lamon voted for Union and became a second point in the pastoral charge with Arkona. But another Presbyterian church in Centre Line, a few miles further east, stayed Presbyterian. So the strong Presbyterians from Lamon drove to Centre Line, while the ones for Union in Centre Line drove the opposite way toward Lamon, often meeting each other on their way to their respective Sunday services.

the worship life of the church. They are welcomed to fit into the way things happen, but "the way we've always done things" feels foreign to many youth today.

They offer leadership, they try to share ministry. But their gifts are disregarded because of their age. Financial resources are often available for buildings and for meeting expenses but not for youth and young adult ministry.

For many youth and young adults, church is alienating, disconnected, and boring. They are not in church on Sunday because, too often, what happens Sunday morning has no connection with what happens in their lives the rest of the week. They find "church" in their own separate communities such as *Kairos* or Youth Forum, or they simply stay where they perceive the church wants them to stay—away.

A New Vision for Youth Ministry

The church hurts when part of it is missing. Youth and young adults hurt when there seems to be no place for them. Between 1980 and 1994, the national church held a number of consultations to ask youth and young adults to help it be a church with room for all of its people. It asked young people to help it find, welcome, and encourage youth, young adults, and their ministries. The Thirty-fifth General Council established the Youth and Young Adult Task Group, made up of young people from across the country, with a mandate to help the church move from consultation to integration.

At the 1997 General Council, the task group offered the church this vision:

> Indeed, the body does not consist of one member but of many. If the foot would say, "Because I am not a hand, I do not belong to the body," that would not make it any less a part of the body. And if the ear were to say, "Because I am not an eye, I do not belong to the body," that would not make it any less part of the body. If the whole body were an eye, where would the hearing be? If the whole body were hearing, where would the sense of smell be? But as it is, God arranged the members in the body, each one of them, as God chose. If all were a single member, where would the body be? As it is, there are many members, yet one body.
>
> *(1 Corinthians 12:14–20)*

As a part of the body:

- We believe youth and young adult ministry is an essential part of the church.

- We believe youth and young adults need to gather separately within the church and together with the whole church.

- We believe that youth and young adults are active, vital participants in youth and young adult ministry.

- We believe that, for youth and young adult ministry to be effective, this ministry needs to be done in partnership with the whole church.

- We believe youth and young adults bring to the church a variety of gifts because of their life experiences.

- We believe that youth and young adults in the church, and beyond, hunger for spiritual nurture and pastoral care.

- We believe the church has much to offer to and receive from youth and young adults.

Your sons and your daughters shall prophesy, and your young shall see visions, and your old shall dream dreams.

(Acts 2:17)*

Along with this vision, the task group presented a twenty-two page report outlining ways in which the church could fully welcome and integrate youth and young adults into its life.

Waiting to See What "Yes" Looks Like

The General Council received this report. It affirmed youth and young adult ministry as a main priority of The United Church of Canada. It approved the twelve priorities outlined in the report as guiding principles for the United Church at all levels. It committed over $1 million to youth and young adult ministry over the next ten years. And it asked that a group be formed to help the church implement the strategies outlined in the report.

In principle, the church has made a bold move. In principle, the United Church has said a resounding "Yes" to youth and young adults. Yes, we are the body of Christ. Yes, we are the church together. Yes, we need each other. And yes, together we will meet God. The church's "Yes" carries with it the hope that no one will ever again have to ask why there are no young people in the church. For the church will be a place where we all are truly welcome to share our lives and where we come to know that God loves us.

So, now we watch and we work, waiting for time to tell us what this "yes" will really look like.

Noelle Bowles is a staff member of the Division of Mission in Canada, responsible for youth and young adult ministry.

Youth and Young Adult Task Group Report, 1997, p. 6

Young, Black, and Canadian

by Wanda West

Young people in the United Church have not given up their spirit of hope and optimism, despite circumstances that may make life difficult.

One of the blessings of youth is the gift of faith and optimism. The following article reports a conversation of a group of young Canadians of African descent, living at the turn of the millennium. The youth are all members of Union United Church in Montréal (one of the oldest Black institutions in the city).

Being a Black youth today is not always easy. In our cities and neighbourhoods we see minority groups confronted with prejudice and injustice. We have to deal with the problems of violence, sexuality, and drugs, and the media does not always project a flattering image of minorities.

The concerns of those between the ages of thirteen and seventeen are more or less the same for males as for females. Our biggest concerns relate to schooling—hopes of attaining grades high enough to gain acceptance into the colleges of our choice upon graduation. We also think of future careers, and wonder whether there will be jobs for us in the fields we want. Will we be happy with our career choices, or might we be pursuing fields that will later prove less than fulfilling?

Peer pressure is not a big issue for us. We are all trustworthy friends and will not put pressure on each other to do things that are not good for us. However, we can see how people who are insecure, not confident with their own identity, can be persuaded into undesirable situations.

Among those of us who are between eighteen and twenty-six, our main concern is job security. For those of us in school, the question is whether there will be jobs for us. And for those who already hold down jobs, the question is whether those jobs are secure, and whether we will be able to take advantage of promotions when opportunities arise.

The Fallout of Separatism

The future of Québec is a concern for all of us. If Québec separates from the rest of Canada, what future is there for us—young, Black, English-speaking youth—even though most of us are fluently bilingual? Will our families stay in Québec or move? If they move, will it be to other parts of Canada or other countries entirely?

Another concern faced by both genders is independence. We are trying to establish our own independence, but at the same time have little choice but to continue leaning on our parents or guardians for financial support and guidance. That a time is coming when we will have to take full responsibility for our choices is sometimes frightening.

We all have relationship concerns. Are we going to meet the "right person" to spend the rest of our lives with? We all, male and female, have anxieties about marriage, because of adultery and the high divorce rate. There is concern about sexually transmitted diseases, including the deadly AIDS virus. All this makes it hard for us to be optimistic about relationships. In a world where single parenting and absentee fathers are on the rise, we want to be good role models for our children, raising them to have good moral values. We hope to pass on the good we have learned from our own upbringing and to change where change might be needed.

Racism on a Daily Basis

Racism, injustice, and violence are major concerns for all of us. The persistence of racism is troubling. We experience racism particularly when we are in groups, with our friends. That is when we get watched by store owners, and when people cross to the other side of the street or clutch their bags more tightly or just drop their eyes. It happens so often, we have grown accustomed to it.

About violence, we feel we always have to watch our surroundings and be mindful of what people are doing. That we ourselves are peace-loving does not matter—the person who confronts us may not be. In the past, people would argue and then just walk away. Today, they have weapons.

In spite of all the problems, obstacles, and temptations it is refreshing to know that we are all generally optimistic and hopeful about the future. We have faith that all things are possible through God. We will continue to grow spiritually and to experience God's love, which leads to self-love and self-respect, making the second part of Jesus' summary of the law—"You shall love your neighbour as yourself"—possible.

We will remember to be the kind of people God wants us to be in every situation. We are learning to deal with our concerns as they arise rather than waiting until they become huge problems. We look forward to the challenges that lie ahead, understanding that change may not be realized in our lifetime.

Knowing that God will give us no more than what we can bear is what keeps us going.

Wanda West is a registered nurse who lives in Montréal, Québec. This article originally appeared in By Faith Sojourners: A Resource for African History Month, *published by the Ethnic Ministries Council.*

On Page and Screen

The United Church and the media—internal and external

The Mass Media and the United Church

by Jim Taylor

The United Church sometimes winces at the media coverage it gets. It has trouble relating the mass media with the gospel, the Good News of Christ. But you can't get good news out of no news.

"The United Church?" said Lloyd Robertson, famed anchor for CTV's national newscast. "Thank God it's there!"

I had called Lloyd, a member of the Presbyterian Church and currently on the board of its national magazine, the *Presbyterian Record*, to ask if he would write this article about the relationship of the mass media to The United Church of Canada. He didn't have time to write the article. Neither did about a dozen other media personalities I contacted. But they all spoke well of the United Church.

Unfortunately, I didn't have my tape recorder running, so the words attributed to Lloyd above may not be precisely what he said. But the gist was clear. He commended the United Church for its clear stands on issues. He praised Moderator Bill Phipps for having the courage to speak honestly about his Christian faith.

That may come as a surprise to those on the receiving end of the media's broadcasts and stories. Judged solely by the headlines of the last few decades, one might assume that the media had a grudge against the church. The church—any church—only seems to make a splash in the news when it has done something outrageous or controversial. When you pick up your paper, or turn on the evening news, and find the United Church featured, I suspect that you're more likely to wince than to beam with anticipation.

Straddling a Crevasse

In this context, I find myself in an awkward position, like a mountain climber straddling a glacier crevasse. Because I have a foot on both sides of the crevasse.

On the one foot, I'm a lifelong member of the United Church. I was born into it. My parents were United Church missionaries in India; my father was an ordained minister, and later principal of a theological college training other ministers. I've spent thirty years promoting the Christian faith as an author, editor, and publisher.

On the other foot, those thirty years, and another ten before that, were all spent in forms of the mass media. I'm a journalist. I write for the mass media.

So I am hurt when the media put out articles and stories that seem damaging to the church that I love deeply. But I know that if I had been assigned to those stories by the secular media, I would probably have said much the same thing.

To understand that, you have to understand the difference between "hard news" and "soft news."

Hard News and Soft News

The media, you see, live and die by hard news. Hard news means that something concrete and specific *has happened*. Someone has done something or said something. Soft news means that something *is happening*—but we don't know yet quite what it is, or how it will work out, or who's responsible.

I was once turned down for a job as religion editor for *The Globe and Mail* because of that distinction. The paper's managing editor, during the employment interview, said he wanted religion covered as hard news. I replied that religion was almost always soft news.

Think about it. The media want actions they can capture on film or videotape; churches have meetings and pass resolutions. The media want sound bites and memorable quotes; the churches issue carefully worded statements. The media want someone identifiable to focus on; the churches— and the United Church in particular—prefer the anonymity of committees.

Even when churches do something visible and physical—like throwing open their basements to homeless street people, giving sanctuary to refugees, or gathering relief supplies for a disaster somewhere around the world—we make it difficult to turn the story into hard news. Projects that work are rarely one person's efforts; things grow by a kind of consensus; no one knows who really started it and no one wants to take credit away from others; our efforts have more to do with our relationship with God than with achieving some measurable goal.

The real news in churches defies defining. Historians—with the 20/20 vision of hindsight—may be able to trace the evolution of the United Church's focus from personal salvation to social justice. But there was no single moment when this happened. Each step was a small one, often an insignificant one, building on other small steps that had gone before.

The mass media recognize these changes only they are dramatized and become hard news. When a J. S. Woodsworth leads a protest in Winnipeg, when a Lydia Gruchy is ordained, when an Al Forrest publishes editorials critical of Israel…or when a Bill Phipps draws the divinity of Jesus, almost as an aside, into an *Ottawa Citizen* interview on the United Church's justice stances. Then all hell breaks loose. Because the media are trying to catch up on news that has been going on under their noses for decades. And they've missed it. It was soft news.

Incarnating the News

I hope you noticed that all those stories centred on particular individuals. The mass media need to personify their stories. So the prime minister embodies the entire structure of government. Proposed bank mergers take place between two CEOs. The APEC protest zooms in on one RCMP officer and his pepper spray.

It's a very "incarnational" approach. We in the churches, of all people, should recognize it because it's intrinsic to our Christian faith, and to the Jewish faith from which we trace Christian origins. The psalms speak of "David" as a synonym for the whole people of Israel. "Moses" embodies the whole of the law. The universal God becomes a specific Jesus. Paul makes "Adam" represent the whole human race, and treats members of the church as "the Body of Christ." Literary critic Northrop Frye—himself a United Church minister—called this practice "metonymy," the vesting of the whole into an individual.

Strangely, the mass media may be more faithful to this tradition than the churches. The United Church—and perhaps all conciliar churches—tend to go the opposite direction. They vest the individual into the whole. The committee, the board, the presbytery, the conference, or the council speaks—not the individual member.

The mass media have trouble getting their cameras and tape recorders around a corporate identity. They recognize, quite rightly, that individual readers and hearers don't relate well to organizations or institutions. Corporations relate to other corporations; people relate to people. So, for years, individuals who could come up with catchy quotes *were* the United Church: Bob McClure, Ernie Howse, Jim Mutchmor, Ray Hord, Clarke MacDonald, Al Forrest, Bob Smith....Lois Wilson is probably the only woman who would make it onto that list. In part, that's because men dominated the United Church for so many years. It may also be that (at the risk of stereotyping) women tend to be more conciliatory, more sensitive to relationships, in their public comments.

Conflict, Conflict Everywhere

Unfortunately, conflict is almost intrinsic to hard news. Look closely at almost any day's newspaper or TV news, or any issue of a news magazine. Notice how many of the stories deal with conflict of some kind. Political parties attack each other. Labour and management square off. Civil wars rage. Thieves rob banks—or big banks rob customers, take your choice. Sports always involves conflict between teams or individuals. Even the "good news" stories have a thread of conflict running through them. The single mom with five kids survives welfare bureaucracy to get her university degree; the young man crippled by a bicycle crash regains the use of one hand; school kids clean up a river fouled by polluters.

And what does the church promote? Reconciliation. Peace. Harmony. Shalom. These things make headlines only when preceded by conflict, never on their own.

One time, while I was managing editor of *The Observer*, I covered a meeting between representatives of the Division of Mission in Canada and the Canadian Labour Congress. At the end of a day of talking, I concluded that there had been no progress on fundamental issues. The draft of my story said that the two sides seemed as far apart as ever in their goals and attitudes. Clark MacDonald, then Division secretary, gently corrected me. "The news is not that we failed to reach agreement, Jim," he said. "The news is that we talked together."

That focus on conflict means that dissidents within the church get more than their fair share of news time. It's hard news when dissident groups or aggrieved individuals come out swinging against the amorphous body of the United Church as a whole.

The media are also under pressure to be fair. "Fair," in their eyes, means presenting both sides. (Again, they assume conflict.) So even if the United Church says or does something that's endorsed by 99.4 percent of its membership—claimed as absolute purity in soaps, if not in churches—the media will not cover it, cannot cover it, unless they can find someone to represent that other 0.6 percent.

I saw this most obviously during the 1983 Assembly of the World Council of Churches, in Vancouver. There were something like eight hundred representatives, from four hundred churches, from two hundred nations. They represented every colour in the theological spectrum. The mass media

You Can't Win 'em All!
by Rod Booth

A word in defence of the much-maligned media reporter: those who, in the eyes of many a church spokesperson, never seem to tell the story we want told, who always go for the sensational in their headlines, who seem to miss all the critical nuances around our activities….I've done my share of complaining over the years.

But we need to understand the pressures and constraints under which reporters have to work—particularly in these days of shrinking news staffs. We need to appreciate that reporters do not write their own headlines. Nor can they be experts on everything. We also need to be humble enough to acknowledge that what may be very important to us may in fact be of very little interest to the general public—whose perspective needs always to be there in a reporter's mind.

An organization's publicist tries to make the connecting links. But even then one can fail. It happened to me while I was fulfilling a publicist role for the Sixth Assembly of the World Council of Churches in Vancouver in 1983.

Preparing the media
We went through the agenda with a close ear to the media wind, identifying items, personalities and features that we thought would interest their broader readership. We met with, and briefed, the editorial boards of both major newspapers and had some success—they assigned a reporter (whom we then equipped with backgrounders and a detailed "media calendar") to cover the event full time.

Opening Day! There was a great service of celebration in the Pacific Coliseum with Jean Vanier, liturgical dancers, Sir David Wilcocks leading the massed choir, a CBC national telecast, the works! Our reporter dutifully did his feature article, complete with pictures.

Oops!

Meanwhile, outside the Coliseum (in drowning rain—there is a God!), the Rev. Ian Paisley and a motley crew of protesters were parading with placards, decrying the World Council as the anti-Christ. Being a good reporter, our reporter could hardly ignore the protest—but he rightly treated it as a small sidebar to his main story.

But—and here's the rub—the night editor who was on duty that night had been on holiday at the time of our briefings with the rest of the editorial board. He took a look at the Paisley sidebar, looked at the story on a church worship service (albeit a large and international one)…and guess which feature was front-page news on Monday morning?

Our World Council colleagues were furious—with me, the Vancouver committee, the newspaper, and most of all the poor reporter, who threw his hat in the door next morning protesting: "Guys, it wasn't me!"

So we did it right, and I'd do it that way again. But in an imperfect world we need to accept that, even then, "you can't win 'em all"!

Rod Booth retired in 1999, after more than three decades of leadership in radio and television broadcasting for the United Church.

expected divergence of opinion to result in a vicious scrum, like a gang war, with everyone knifing everyone else in the back. It didn't happen. The mood was of a gigantic family reunion.

But if you weren't there, you'd never have known that. For the first ten days, the media were utterly baffled. They didn't know what to do with this situation. So they focused their attention on a few fundamentalists parading their placards in front of the Assembly halls.

Out on the Leading Edge

Given all that, though, I sense that most of the mass media are profoundly grateful to the United Church. If it weren't for the United Church, there would be no hard news to report in religion.

The United Church is at least the first to do things. That's always news. The first mainline church to ordain women. The first to openly ordain gays and lesbians. The first to elect a layman to its highest office, followed by a Black man, an ordained woman, a laywoman, an Asian man, and a Native man. It is usually the first to speak out for oppressed minorities, in Canada and elsewhere. And it is by long odds the most honest about its theology.

Unfortunately, the media usually distort theological differences by attaching misleading labels. They borrow from politics or labour or biology terms such as liberal/conservative, left/right, even, occasionally, dinosaur—and assume these terms also define religious viewpoints. They don't, of course. (Interestingly, I doubt if the media themselves would ever stereotype actors as liberal/conservative, or basketball teams as left/right.)

I think a better model of the church is an amoeba. Or, if you prefer, any creature that's free to move in any direction but has to feel its way along. Any part of it can be out in front at any time. That leading edge constantly encounters new situations. Some are sharp or painful—the creature retreats. Some are promising, hopeful—the rest of the creature follows along.

In the same way, the United Church has a leading edge and a trailing edge. The leading edge is constantly getting into trouble. It has to be—it's the only way to explore the unknown waters ahead. The trailing edge experiences pain each time the leading edge stubs its toe, so to speak; it keeps trying to pull back to safer ground.

We need both leading and trailing edges. A church with nothing but leading edges will disintegrate; a church with nothing but trailing edges will withdraw into itself, shrivel up, and die.

The mass media—those that have paused to think about it, at least— respect the United Church because it *has* a leading edge. It's not afraid to extend a tentative toe into uncharted territory. Of course it gets burned, sometimes. But sometimes it also finds new insights, new ways of working, new causes to commit itself to. And the rest of the body follows—sometimes cheerfully, sometimes reluctantly. But it does follow.

The hard news that the media seize on may be the leading edge, reaching out into unfamiliar places, or it may be the trailing edge, desperately sinking its fingernails into the sands of time to keep from being dragged along. The soft news, the part the media have so much difficulty recognizing, is the way the whole body moves.

Our Business Is Good News

But it does move. Indeed, it might be said that among the churches of Canada, the United Church *is* the leading edge. That's why Lloyd Robertson and others can say flattering things about the United Church. It gives them some news now and then. When I worked with editors of other denominational journals in the Canadian Church Press association, I found that other churches were grateful, too. They were rarely jealous of the media coverage given the United Church. It's less risky to hang back, to let the leading edge feel out the route. If it's safe to follow, they will, in their own good time; if not, they won't. But either way, it's not news.

The church's business is the Good News of Jesus Christ. You can't get good news out of no news. Remember that, the next time you see something about the United Church bannered across a newspaper's front page. At least our edges are being recognized.

Jim Taylor's mass media career includes private radio, CBC, The United Church Observer, *the clergy journal* PMC, *and Wood Lake Books.*

Much More Than Candy

by Mardi Tindal

The United Church's tentative entry into the world of television has had more impact than anyone expected.

It was the summer of 1988. I had just agreed to co-host *Spirit Connection*'s first season on Vision TV. And someone said: "Candy for the eyes—that's all television can ever deliver. The church should have nothing to do with it."

The comment touched some of my deepest fears. Like many in the church, I had not yet been converted to television.

When I first heard about plans to create a regular United Church television presence I was filled with dread. I doubted that we as a church knew enough about the medium to do anything better than embarrassing ourselves. I wondered whether it was even possible, no matter how skilled we were, to do anything beyond the superficial on television. Then I received the phone call asking me to audition to co-host the dreaded beast. A friend told me once that I should never say "no" too quickly, so I decided to meet the folks involved. Before I knew it I was sitting across from Bruce McLeod, sharing a couple of coffees in a restaurant meeting to see if we could get along well enough to co-host a television show.

Then, suddenly, we were on the air, far more aware of the skeptics than the supporters, and painfully conscious of the enormous amount we had to learn about how to "do television."

Meet the Family

At the time of our launch in the fall of 1988, there was a lot of tension in the United Church family. Relatives, friends, and neighbours found themselves fighting over General Council's decisions about sexual orientation and ministry.

The first step in my conversion to television came when I saw how the program immediately brought us face to face with one another, with all our warts and warring, to be reminded that we were still part of the same family. It's one thing to read the text of what someone said at General Council. It's quite another thing to filter those words through sadness in a voice and pain in a face. Television brought us into the same electronic living room, from across the country and from across a wide spectrum of belief. It provided us with a mirror in which we could see ourselves more clearly and in which others could see us too.

These unprecedented meetings through the medium carried the potential for better understanding. We might never meet those people of Gander, Newfoundland, or downtown Regina. But we could feel as if we had. In the fall of 1988 our television did not deliver the sweet distraction of candy. It offered substance and nourishment: it dared us to listen and learn from those who didn't always share our points of view. And we grew stronger because of it.

Something Worth Chewing On

The second step towards my conversion came in a church parlour in Cambridge, Ontario. A group of "moms" had invited me to talk to them about United Church television at their weekly gathering for friendship and learning. Rather than preparing a talk, I simply grabbed last week's program, thinking we'd watch and then discuss it. I introduced my plan and pushed the "play" button. I don't think we were into it more than three or four minutes when the chatter started. They were reacting to and discussing everything on the show! I kept pausing the tape so they wouldn't "miss anything." Then I realized that the action had shifted from the box to them. Clearly, it was possible to watch and discuss television simultaneously. In fact, they weren't able to watch without talking! The stories on the screen provoked comment for a full half-hour. Candy melts away, but they saw something worth chewing on.

The final story of that program profiled volunteers running a Maritime food bank. No sooner had I stopped the tape when lively discussion erupted once again. And after about fifteen minutes one of the women quietly said, "It's really hard to have to go to the food bank." I could feel a quiet shock ripple through the room. Until that moment, no one had guessed that they had been discussing a daily reality for anyone in their circle. The television story provided the spark for a courageous woman to tell her story, which ignited a discussion about what they could do to support local mothers. Before they left, they had a plan to provide babysitting and transportation for women who needed help to get to the food bank. And I was converted to television's potential to inspire heart-to-heart encounters and faithful action.

Showing the Media What to Look For

Another step towards conversion came at General Council in 1990. For the first time, we were able to broadcast nightly General Council reports. The

Should the Church Be Found in the News?
by Linda Slough

"There's a story in the newspaper about our church."

"Wonderful, how did we manage that? That story will attract attention and discussion."

"Oh no! Did you see that dreadful headline? Why did we have to say something so controversial?"

Those contrasting reactions accompany almost every foray the United Church makes into the public media. Does the church want to be found in the news? Should it be found in the news?

When our moderator, the Rt. Rev. Bill Phipps, became a controversial public persona during the fall of 1997, the effect of his public statements was astounding. Hundreds of messages poured into General Council offices; more than half were strongly supportive.

It was noteworthy, however, that the negative and worried messages most often came from members of the church. Many members also offered their support but a significantly large number of supportive messages came from people on the periphery or outside of the United Church. They indicated that they had been touched deeply and were excited by the faith perspective that Phipps offered. They could only have been reached through the public media.

It's risky to attract public attention of any kind; it's especially risky for mainline denominations where the range of opinions within the church membership is wide.

Nonetheless, it is becoming increasingly apparent that people, whether or not they are active in a religious institution, are very interested in a spiritual perspective on the issues we face today.

Is such a spiritual perspective news? Yes indeed. An articulate genuine spokesperson who offers perspectives beyond the mundane and trivial will be sought out by reporters and journalists. Mary-Frances Denis, Manager of Public Relations, received more requests from reporters for a United Church comment on a variety of issues after Phipps hit the headlines. And Phipps himself was able to move from stories about his personal Christology to stories about "faith and the economy"—a spiritual perspective on the economy and the government and corporate policies that affect it.

Is offering a spiritual perspective into public view a faithful way for the church to act?

If the church chooses to be in the public arena, it encourages public discourse. Professional journalists respond by digging deeper and writing stories that present faith perspectives on key issues such as health care, education, the taxation system, or any topic affecting community life. When people are better informed, more interested in dealing with issues in depth, and are hearing from a variety of faith perspectives, they will surely live out their personal and corporate lives with more loving care for their own and the global community.

Linda Slough is General Secretary, Division of Communication.

issues surrounding ordination and sexual orientation were as hot as ever and still on the church's agenda, so naturally we covered them in our broadcasts.

United Church members were still feeling bloodied and bruised by the events of the Victoria General Council and by the media coverage we'd received at that time. But the newspaper articles this time around didn't seem to be quite as uninformed or inflammatory.

And then a friend from *The Observer* told me something interesting. Every night, she said, when General Council *Nightly Update* came on, reporters in the newsroom all crowded around to watch.

I was surprised by their interest. After all, they'd sat through the debates already and knew what had happened. Then it occurred to me that there were at least two reasons for their interest in the broadcast. For one thing, it gave them a perspective on the day's events from a United Church understanding. In other words, it would help them to get it right—never easy for someone who lacks first-hand church experience. For another thing, they were no longer the only news game in town. If they filed reports that looked very different from ours, readers and viewers might doubt them. Questions might be raised about their accuracy.

And I was converted to the importance of having a media voice that would keep other media voices honest and informed. Viewer feedback told us that it was important to have us there as trusted reporters and commentators.

And beyond that, for the first time, church members had direct access to the debates, the tears, and the humour at the heart of our church's decision making. They had access to a broader range of information than they could get from secular media. Letters of appreciation for the nightly updates poured into the General Council offices. Many told me about how good it was to actually see their own representatives participating in the process. From that point onward, television (and other electronic media such as the Web site) gave us new opportunities for building understanding and trust about what exactly happens at General Council.

An Influence within the Church, Too

I'm convinced that United Church television has contributed to our church's evolution in several important ways.

It has enabled us to give voice to the voiceless in a media-dominated culture. Many of our televised stories have an unglamorous, gritty edge that rubs against what most television delivers. Our stories are also far less "mediated" than much of what you see in television news. For example, we spend far less time telling you what street youth say and far more time allowing them—and those who work with them—to say it themselves.

It has strengthened our credibility. Only those who don't care about reaching people would ignore the potential of television and other electronic media. If we and our partners have important stories to tell and if we're serious about telling them, then we must be on television. This is congruent with our history. The United Church has always been one of the first mainline religious groups to embrace the potential of new media and new ways of doing things, because we've been confident that our message is relevant and worth sharing with those outside of our circle as well as with those within it. A community that knows it has good news to share takes every opportunity to share it.

Television has helped us to rediscover that we have things to say that the world wants to hear. I remember the day, for instance, when we had a request from a parliamentary committee dealing with prisoners' rights. They wanted a copy of a story we'd done on prison ministry through the eyes of Rod Carter, a one-time convict and current United Church minister and prison chaplain. The story was compelling enough to be considered within the circles of government.

The Challenges Facing Us

Several important challenges face the church in relation to the media.

First, while the church's relationship with new media has in many ways been courageous, in many other ways it has been, to say the least, ambiguous. Church folks seem to have an automatic suspicion towards any technological advances invading the church—including those designed to improve communication. In the early eighties, when my husband Doug and I were working on a book about computers in the church, we encountered countless people who were skeptical about any use of computers. Along the way, we heard a lot of stories about how congregations dealt with new media, including one about a church that resisted installing a telephone. God only knew what evil could come of that!

I still hear about church folks who are proud to not own a television. Given that our entire history of faithfulness is one of discerning and challenging dominant cultural stories and of using the media of every age for our own storytelling, I find their position confusing and smug at times. It appears that they're not really interested in telling or hearing good news stories within today's context.

We need to become more self conscious of our attitudes—and their implications—towards new media. A couple of years ago Derrick de Kerckhove, Director of the McLuhan Centre at the University of Toronto, spoke to our Division of Communication. He spoke admiringly about the "open arches" of The United Church of Canada, open to the world rather than closed into itself. When someone from outside of our tradition makes this observation about what we've been doing in television, I think it's worth hearing.

Second, we have to become more appreciative of the power of images linked to the power of words. Our tradition is one of words. But as I've learned how to produce television and seen the reaction to that work, I've learned that images touch hearts as much as any words do.

Third, we have to be constantly vigilant about discerning which developments in television style we will adopt and which we won't. For example, mainstream media are addicted to controversy. They won't touch a story unless they can show a conflict. There are times when the church needs to bring more light than heat to an issue. We must find other ways to tell a good story or deal with an issue without reducing it to a simple fight.

Fourth, it seems that we don't have enough resources to continue doing television the way we have, so we'll need to continue to find other partners with whom we can produce nourishing programs. We need to continue our uniting tradition in the ways we join with others to produce good television.

Fifth, we need to be prepared for what will follow television as we've known it, and to be unafraid of giving up what we've been doing to do something new.

Food for the Soul

It started in 1988....Over a decade later, I think we have produced some "candy for the eyes" when conveying moments of beauty and grace. But together, as a church, we've done much more than that. We've produced food for the soul with honest debate, thoughtful documentaries, stimulating interviews, moving profiles, and faithful commentary. Millions of Canadians are hungering for spiritual sustenance. They're searching for help and buying chicken soup in various forms. They're looking for more than candy. With access to the most powerful media of our time, combined with the other resources of our church, we're delivering a lot more than chocolate.

> *Mardi Tindal, a co-host of* Spirit Connection *for its first nine years, is currently a freelance producer of religious television programming. She is also a congregational facilitator and mediator.*

A Faithful Record

by Patricia Clarke

Over the years, under various editors, The Observer *has helped the United Church discern what it was, what it is, and what it would become.*

When I first joined the staff of *The Observer*, more than thirty-five years ago, I was advised that it would be important in my work to have "a very becoming hat."

How times change. The current *Observer* editor, Muriel Duncan, does not even own a hat—aside from a Stetson, no doubt quite becoming.

It was a different church in the 1950s and 1960s—expanding, still influential, confident. That church was observed, and reflected, in a different magazine. The magazine eulogized the little country church. It inspected a new species, "Little Girl Minister." It profiled (and I plead guilty) four "great preachers," all male and, perhaps a worse sin, all in Toronto. Some changes—both in the church and in its magazine—are for the better.

But some things about *The Observer*—and, I hope, about the United Church—don't change. One is its prophetic witness. I think of its series in the 1960s by the late Rev. Arthur Ebbutt, exposing readers (some of them kicking and screaming) to biblical interpretations that were commonplace in their ministers' seminaries, its advocacy for neglected Native peoples, and its sensitive but candid reports on their suffering in church-run schools.

Over the years it has consistently been a major source of our sense of who we are as a denomination and of our connectedness outside the congregation. As a report to General Council in 1990 said,

> *The Observer* has faithfully recorded the journey of the United Church over the years...wondering and waiting for God's purpose to reveal itself in the debates and struggles...a place where our efforts, differences, behaviours, passions, faith-stories, joys, and angers are collected, noted and named, perhaps long before they are understood. The forum provided by *The Observer* allows dialogue to take place between different parts of the whole.

Taking an Independent Stance

And two other things have not changed: *The Observer*'s editorial excellence and its editorial independence. It has consistently taken more awards than any other Canadian church magazine in judging by the Canadian Church Press and the Associated Church Press (covering North America)—often including both organizations' top award for general excellence. A bedrock of that excellence is its independence, an independence reaffirmed by General Council as recently as 1990.

Editors have insisted over the years that their first responsibility is to their readers. *The Observer* has never been a house organ. The chair of its board of directors, the Rev. Albion Wright of Mississauga, Ontario, says, "*The Observer* sees itself as part of the total church family, but not in the back pocket of the leadership. There is a healthy distancing. It is a voice that can challenge, call the church to account, and enable public debate to take place."

A bit of history: *The Observer*'s roots go back to 1829, when Egerton Ryerson founded the *Christian Guardian* as the organ of the Canadian Methodist Church. At Church Union in 1925, the new denomination created *The New Outlook*, published by the United Church Publishing House. It acquired its present name in 1939.

The Observer was an arm of the publishing house, Ryerson Press, until the Press was sold in 1970. Then for a few years it lodged in the Division of Communication. At present it is a non-profit corporation, under a board of directors approved by General Council Executive and accountable to the corporation's members.

When the Rev. A. C. Forrest took over as editor in 1955, *The Observer* was a typical church magazine of its time, filled with speeches by the moderator and other worthy officials, sermons, Sunday school lessons, lengthy obituaries, and reports on church extension and overseas missions. Forrest later described the early magazine as "the handmaiden of the establishment," supporting in its articles and editorials the campaigns and crusades undertaken by the boards of the church. Even then, though, it played a role *The Observer* still plays— providing a voice for dissent. Letters raised questions about missionary policy. Other letters decried war and capital punishment. One criticized the paper for a "pussyfoot attitude to Communism and Communists." A reply called it "a sorry day when our church paper is denied the right to comment on matters of national importance."

Forrest changed the magazine almost immediately. He added cartoons, columns, the still-popular Question Box, and gave even more emphasis to letters. Instead of sermons, the articles in his first year were titled "Why I returned to parish ministry," "The unmarried mother," and "Breaking the race barrier."

His contribution was "historic," says the Rev. Kenneth Bagnell, who was Forrest's managing editor and who has contributed to *The Observer* for the last forty years. "His superior skills as a journalist and editor took *The Observer* to a new level. It was unsurpassed as a general interest church publication anywhere."

Albion Wright remembers *The Observer* of the Forrest years as "much like a small town newspaper." It kept its readers up to date on what was going on in the church, and helped them feel part of a community although they lived in very different places.

"The magazine was part of the family for readers," says Muriel Duncan, remembering people from across the country dropping in at *The Observer* who felt they knew Forrest, whether they had met him or not.

A Prophetic Voice

Although deeply pastoral, Forrest's *Observer* was prophetic as well. He spoke out for Palestinians when almost no one else did. His most important editorial decision, he wrote once, was to put Pope John XXIII on the cover, because he said "the single most important development in the Christian world during the century has been the ecumenical movement reflected in the new rapport between Protestants and Roman Catholics."

In a few areas, however, his *Observer* lagged behind. It came late to opposition to the Viet Nam War. Homosexuality was taboo until Bagnell fought for a piece in 1965 on the church and the homosexual, accompanied by a Forrest editorial saying it "cannot be condoned." It came late as well to the feminist revolution. Writers in the 1960s claimed that a working wife "unmans her husband" and advised wives, "If he hits you, do not take it too seriously." Males dominated its pages, as they did the senior posts in the church. The Rev. Shelley Finson of the Atlantic School of Theology remembers how she and other women in the 1970s kept count in each issue of the relative numbers of women and men photographed or featured. And because of his great love of the church and his own deep rural roots, Forrest was not able, Wright says, to help readers deal with the beginning of the church's decline.

It was a different church when Hugh McCullum took over as editor in 1980, following Forrest's untimely death. For a number of years, when both circulation and church membership were climbing, *The Observer* was one of the few North American church publications to operate without subsidies. Ministers put their jobs on the line for *The Observer*, telling their finance committees, "If you cancel, I go." But by the 1980s, old loyalties were fading. Society was becoming more secular; church membership was falling. Congregational budgets were squeezed, making it tempting to cut back on *Observer* subscriptions. Postal rates and printing costs zoomed. Controversy raged over the ordination of homosexuals, and objectors got even by cancelling the magazine that brought the news.

So since 1984, grants from the national Unified Budget have helped pay the bills. In 1998, *The Observer* received $265,000 from Mission and Service funds—slightly over 19 percent of its budget. Another 64 percent comes from circulation and 14 percent from advertising. (Many secular magazines get most or almost all their income from advertising.)

Afflicting the Comfortable

McCullum was a different person too. Reared in the Arctic, in an Anglican manse, he came with twenty-four years of professional journalism experience, including eight as editor of the Anglican Church's national publication. His passion was social justice, especially in Latin America and among Canada's Native peoples. Almost from the beginning, he says, "I tried to challenge the church on global issues—poverty, environmental distress, violence—in which Canada was complicit. I was often accused of more concentration on what went on in Africa than at First United."

It was a valuable passion. McCullum's *Observer* told the stories of the powerless and the oppressed, stories few readers would find in other publications, and challenged them to apply the words of scripture to the world around them. Not everyone was comfortable with that. "When I used to visit the presbyteries, one question that was nearly always asked was, 'Where is the hope?' My view of the world then and now would not be called hopeful or optimistic. Hope as I understand it is the church struggling to challenge the world and to have a view of scripture that sees God with the powerless and the poor."

McCullum admits now that perhaps he wanted change too fast. "We tried to afflict the comfortable, rather than only comfort the afflicted." Nor is he sure now how effective the challenge was. "My perception is that the church is still captive to society, not very prophetic, not on the cutting edge."

An equally important part of his contribution was his organizing skills. General interest secular magazines were already in trouble across North America. The leading publications of three major U.S. denominations had collapsed. McCullum changed *The Observer* to a news magazine. He set up national reporting links with a network of contributing editors. He promoted Conference-edited news inserts. He foresaw the coming financial crunch and searched for ways to meet it. He moved *Observer* offices outside the national church building, emphasizing its independence from the national structure. McCullum's staff tried to make as many decisions as possible based on journalistic principles: this is news that readers have a right to read. Some of those decisions were not popular, particularly when it involved criticizing the national church.

Emphasizing the Congregations

Muriel Duncan, another professional journalist who had been on *The Observer* staff since 1975, became editor in 1989 when McCullum left. Like Forrest and McCullum, she has a rural background, growing up on a farm in Ontario and with a grandfather and two uncles who were United Church ministers.

Having worked under both Forrest and McCullum, she has tried to combine the things she liked best about both, while gradually shifting to a more reader-centred magazine. She wants to maintain both the intimacy and community that readers felt with Forrest, and McCullum's vision and passion for justice. But as well, *The Observer* now emphasizes how congregations and individuals get involved in making a difference. "We're still trying to hold out hope. We want to keep the pastoral and prophetic in tension, holding up the possibilities of hope in large issues as well as in our own lives."

One of the important conscious decisions Duncan and her team made was to make room for different voices and report all sides of an issue. What you read in *The Observer* today—and this has been true in varying degrees throughout the last forty-five years—may not square with the decisions of national policymakers, or even with the views of the editorial staff, but it does provide a forum for those who feel marginalized by those decisions. Another conscious change was to emphasize what goes on in congregations, and make more room for reports on healing, prayer, and other spiritual issues.

So how did we get from there to here? The path was forged by a chain of outstanding journalists and dedicated church people as editors and staff striving for excellence, a network of devoted circulation representatives in the congregations, and a commitment to editorial independence on the part of church leaders.

And what lies ahead? The future looks scary if church membership and money continue to fall. Yet in an increasingly congregational church, *The Observer* is one of the few clear and visible links with the denomination. Without it, Albion Wright says, we would lose not only the opportunity to converse with one another, we would lose "the sense of who we are as a church."

Patricia Clarke has served The Observer *as associate editor and later as a contributing editor under three editors: Al Forrest, Hugh McCullum, and Muriel Duncan.*

Delivering Resources

by Margaret Nix

As the world keeps changing, so do the ways that the United Church finds to make information available to members and congregations.

After the Second World War, all resources came from the United Church Publishing House, at 299 Queen Street West in Toronto, the large white stone building on the corner of Queen Street and John Street that currently houses CITY-TV. The two top floors of the building, farthest away from the great rumbling presses on the ground floor, were the offices for the national church. All the rest was taken up with printing, publishing, and distribution.

Distribution included Ryerson Film Services, with its 4" x 4" glass slides and some filmstrips. Kenneth Beaton provided slides of overseas work for mission education; Anson Moorhouse provided films, filmstrips, and slides of Canadian work.

Christian education materials also came from "299"—the Sunday school quarterlies and Sunday school papers, the program materials for Tyros and Explorers and Messengers, the Young People's Union papers….

Decentralization began in the 1950s, when Berkeley Street United Church was purchased to become a production house for United Church audio-visual resources. It continued when the national offices moved out of "299" to a new building at 85 St. Clair Avenue East in Toronto.

The Birth of Audio-visual Distribution

In Winnipeg, in 1946, Dr. Peter Gordon White was Secretary for Christian Education. He was the total staff—one person. Peter travelled the conferences with filmstrips and a projector. Congregations seemed willing to buy a filmstrip projector of their own, if they had a library of filmstrips available. The first library had just ten filmstrips in it, and it cost $5 to join. But twelve congregations signed up, and AVEL (the United Church's Audio Visual Educational Library) was born. Peter had to keep buying more filmstrips from Ryerson, at about $25 each, to keep his customers satisfied. AVEL existed in a recipe box on Peter's desk.

About that time, my husband and I went to a small charge north of Edmonton. Barrhead had four preaching points in 1947. We were among those early members of AVEL. I had no idea that thirty years later, I would be responsible for AVEL distribution across the nation.

During the 1950s, audio-visual resources expanded enormously. We still had two separate women's organizations then—the Woman's Missionary Society and the Woman's Association—and both were distributing materials, including children's resources and missionary study packets with slides, filmstrips, even movies. Peter Gordon White, by then working out of 299 Queen Street, was distributing resource lists to every Sunday school superintendent across the country.

Publishing Empires Crumble

The 1960s brought the *New Curriculum*, and all the controversy that went with it. The publishing house maintained the old *Quarterlies*, perhaps unsure how the new materials would sell. But the *Quarterlies* piled up in the warehouse, while orders for the *New Curriculum* shot up 90 percent. The publishing house hadn't counted on this popularity. They worked nights to fill the orders. Their old equipment couldn't handle the pressure—new equipment was necessary. They had a choice between traditional technology (called "letterpress," using poured hot metal plates) and the newer offset presses. They made what turned out to be the wrong choice—a huge investment in obsolete letterpress technology—just when orders for the *New Curriculum* declined as congregations re-used student books instead of buying new ones.

By the late 1960s, some assets had to be sold to pay off debts. So in 1970 The Ryerson Press, a Canadian publishing institution since 1829, was sold to McGraw-Hill. Later, the 299 Queen Street property was sold to Moses Znaimer and CITY-TV. In the words of Frank Brisbin, then the Secretary of the Division of Communication, "It was a sad time."

The United Church Publishing House continued, but—in the hope of encouraging other denominations to use our services—changed its name to CANEC, the "Canadian Ecumenical" publishing house. The ecumenical effort never happened so, after some twenty years, CANEC reverted to UCPH, the United Church Publishing House.

Resource Centres Begin

In 1973, a new entity emerged—the Resource Centre. It started in London Conference. At the time, I was Program and Resource Officer for Montréal Presbytery. In 1977 three of us from Montréal and Ottawa Conference travelled to London to see these new centres for ourselves. Morley Clarke and Ev Smith took us around. We met Muriel Neice, who had started the first Resource Centre in Windsor. She was trying to convince the church there should be a Resource Centre in every presbytery. We visited Marilyn Durham in London. We went to Lambton, to Chatham....By the time our Montréal group headed home, we were really excited about possibilities.

A year later, I found myself at the national offices at 85 St. Clair, responsible for the distribution of AVEL resources, working with thirty-five Resource Centres and seven AVEL outlets.

The Television Age Arrives

By the 1980s we were handling films, filmstrips, slide sets, and moving into videotapes. We ran workshops and provided users guides, to help congregations learn creatively from the resources they showed. To encourage more people to use our resources, I produced *The Media Resources Bulletin* as both a promotion piece and a working tool.

At first films and videotapes were expensive: $500 to $900 each. (Even more if we produced them ourselves!) The various divisions of the national church designated a portion of their budgets to purchase these resources and place them in AVEL. We needed ten copies of each title to service the national church, which meant that one title could cost $9,000. Over time, these costs have come down.

In 1988 the United Church began broadcasting nationally, through *Spirit Connection* on Vision TV. These programs also became available through AVEL on a loan basis, and were sold as cassettes, individually or by subscription.

Currently, the change seems to be a move into partnerships and co-operative relationships. In the early days, every department or division developed and promoted its own resources. The only common ground was distribution through UCPH, Resource Centres, and AVEL. Today, diverse groups work together for production, promotion, publicity, and marketing, as well as distribution. Partnerships are constantly growing.

In fact, if it had not been for partnerships, we would not have had Vision TV here in Canada. It was the United Church's agreement to broadcast on Vision that made it possible for Vision to come into being. Since then, other

We Have Faith in Our Books
by Beth Parker

The United Church Publishing House is Canada's oldest publishing house. There is a direct link between our founding in colonial Upper Canada and what we refer to today as UCPH. And certainly we have a rather impressive history in the story of Canadian publishing.

In a piece of unsent correspondence addressed to Irving Layton, Jack McClelland wrote about what he refers to both as the United Church Publishing House and Ryerson Press: "I think that they have done more for Canadian literature than any other single publishing house through the years."

Another history expresses similar sentiments*:

A list of titles published by this House fills a large book. It is interesting to speculate what the writing of history and biography and literary criticism in Canada would have been without them. What would have been the history of art, poetry, belles lettres, and education in this commonwealth had not this House sought out and published the long lists of titles in these special categories? The entire list had a sense of timeliness about it, even of urgency. It is all now part of the maturing culture of our country, or growing sense of identity, our understanding in our own eyes, and in the eyes of the world.

The General Managers, Editors and Managers have in varying ways made a continuously important contribution to this Publishing House, and to the publishing Houses of Canada generally. In a very real sense this is the Mother Publishing House of Canada, not merely because it is the oldest, but because its trained personnel have gone out to establish Houses of their own, some of them among the leading publishing concerns of Canada.

As expert printers, book craftsmen, and publishers, The Ryerson Press stands in the forefront of the great book publishing Houses of the English Speaking world.

When Canadian Methodists severed their ties with their U.S. counterparts in 1827, they immediately set out to secure a printing press so that they could begin a journal and a book room. Originally founded in 1829 as The Methodist Book Room, Ryerson Press was named in honour of its first editor, the Methodist minister and educator, Egerton Ryerson.

Ryerson was known for his social and political concerns: democratic government, religious equality, free schools, one law for the rich and poor, and a working partnership between Catholic and Protestant, French and English. From the beginning, the book lists of Ryerson Press reflected these interests, even though its catalogues covered a broad range of history, biography, travel, science, business, literary criticism, and religion.

Ryerson Press became the United Church Publishing House, and has continued to serve as a distribution and retail store operation, as well as a denominational publisher, even after the sale of the actual press, as well as the sale of the name "Ryerson Press" to McGraw-Hill in 1970.

In June 1996, after almost a decade of rebuilding a Canadian "publishing" presence, the United Church Publishing House made its Canadian debut at the national Canadian Booksellers Association trade show, alongside other small and large Canadian-owned or operated publishing houses. The declaration heard most often from our Canadian publishing colleagues at that first show was: "Welcome…you're Ryerson Press, right?"

In the same tradition fostered by Egerton Ryerson 170 years ago, the United Church Publishing House continues to publish a variety of spiritual and religious books that hold up the values of equality, social justice, history, emerging social issues, and religion.

Our catch phrase for the past few years, and as we move into the next century, is a strong declaration that we still, indeed, "have faith in our books."

*Source unknown

agreements have happened. Increasingly, our church is looking for ecumenical and interfaith partners to produce video and print resources, and to exchange ideas on production and promotion.

New technologies in distribution improve customer service. The stock of the United Church Book Rooms is now on a computer database, making it simpler and quicker for staff to respond to customers' requests. Lending resources—such as AVEL—should soon be on a comparable system. Already, you can check out much of what's available on the United Church's Web site, www.uccan.org.

Things have changed since the 1940s. Ways of providing information to members and congregations of The United Church of Canada will continue to evolve.

Margaret Nix was national staff person responsible for AVEL and Resource Centres from 1978 until her retirement in 1989.

The Forgotten French

There is a part of the United Church that doesn't speak English

Une journée mémorable à Belle-Rivière

by/par David Fines

Le soleil disparaît lentement à l'horizon. Reste-t-il la promesse certaine et irréfutable, offerte par Dieu, de l'aube du Shalom? On se pose la question : y aura-t-il un futur pour une Église unie francophone?

En un frais dimanche de la fin du mois d'août 1982, une rencontre bien spéciale rassemble toute une foule bruyante à la vénérable église de Belle-Rivière : des gens d'Afrique, d'Europe, d'Amérique du Sud, du Québec, de l'Ontario...Une fête y a lieu—mais une telle fête n'a-t-elle pas aussi eu lieu en bien d'autres temps et bien d'autres endroits?—pour souligner la clôture de l'Assemblée générale de l'Alliance réformée mondiale (ARM) qui vient de vient se dérouler durant les deux semaines précédentes à Ottawa, à quelque 100 kilomètres de là.

Les débuts de l'église de Belle-Rivière

L'église de Belle-Rivière est un lieu très particulier; empreint de multiples souvenirs, elle raconte et symbolise une histoire précieuse, souvent ignorée. Toujours solennellement debout sur ces imposantes pierres des champs, c'est l'une des plus anciennes églises protestantes françaises en Amérique du Nord. C'est tout juste après la Rébellion populaire contre l'autorité britannique de 1837–38, alors que plusieurs des « patriotes » avaient été excommuniés de l'Église catholique, que sont envoyés à Belle-Rivière, en 1840, deux missionnaires, le pasteur Daniel Amaron et sa femme; ils avaient été mandés de Suisse par la « Société Missionnaire Franco-Canadienne, » tout récemment créée par les principales Églises protestantes et qui s'était donné pour but de « pourvoir aux besoins de répandre l'Évangile parmi les Canadiens français » à travers les campagnes québécoise, notamment par le colportage de Bibles et l'évangélisation. Selon l'habitude coutumière qui remonte à la Réforme, madame Amaron réunit quelques enfants pour leur faire la classe : pour pouvoir lire les merveilles de Dieu contenues dans sa Parole, il faut savoir lire! Les débuts ne sont pas faciles, malgré quelques conversions. Les Amaron quitteront Belle-Rivière en 1844, remplacés par le pasteur Jean Vernier. L'école qui s'était rapidement développée et dont la renommée amènera bien des familles catholiques de la région à y envoyer leurs enfants, sera transportée à la Pointe-aux-Trembles sur l'île de Montréal et continuera son œuvre d'éducation auprès des générations d'enfants franco-protestants. Vers 1858, la congrégation est assez importante pour songer à construire une église; elle sera consacrée en 1860, et depuis lors, elle est toujours debout et sert toujours; surtout pour des occasions spéciales comme la célébration d'aujourd'hui.

L'Alliance réformée se rassemble

L'atmosphère est à la fête et au partage fraternel pour les quelques soixante-quinze participant-es, dont une vingtaine de délégué-es de l'ARM. Les pasteurs Jean Porret de l'Église presbytérienne et Jacques Labadie de l'Église unie animent le culte. Les deux prédicateurs sont Edmond Perret, de l'Église Réformée de France, le secrétaire-général de l'ARM et M. Tshimungu, délégué presbytérien du Zaïre. Marthe Laurin et quelques autres membres de la paroisse se regardent et sourient; alors que pour les quelques cultes d'été seulement, elle n'accueille qu'une douzaine de personnes « plutôt grisonnantes, » leur église est aujourd'hui envahie, pleine à craquer, par ce groupe coloré, bigarré, de gens de tous âges et de tous horizons : des Églises unie, presbytérienne, ou réformée, de l'Armée du Salut, de Tchécoslavaquie, de Madagascar, du Mozambique, d'Angola, du Sénégal, jusqu'à un théologien de Madrid! Il y a tant de monde qu'il a fallu sortir, pour permettre aux gens de s'asseoir, les longs supports en bois qui servent à recevoir le cercueil lors de funérailles!

Une communauté unique

L'histoire du secteur francophone de l'Église unie, c'est beaucoup ça : des gens d'une grande diversité de cultures, d'origines, de nationalités, de langues parlées; des familles immigrantes, européennes surtout, des personnes d'ici aux lointaines racines protestantes, des visiteurs, des étudiantes….Chacun, chacune, à sa façon, y a apporté un peu de sa personne et des ses origines, y a offert un peu de sa foi et de ses espoirs, pour que se façonne, au long des décennies, une communauté unique à laquelle ne colle pas facilement une étiquette précise; une communauté vivante, en marche, remuante, ruant dans les bracards, supportant mal la bride, et trop régulièrement, au cours des soixante-quinze ans de l'Église, oubliée par les instances institutionnelles anglophones; une communauté hétérogène, insoumise, le plus souvent délaissée, laissée à elle-même parce que mal comprise….Et de la même façon qu'on se demande quelles impressions ces visiteurs de l'ARM rapporteront-ils de leur voyage à Belle-Rivière, sans doute peut-on se demander comment cette communauté francophone complexe a-t-elle été perçue au cours de ces années de routes communes, en parallèles, par le reste de l'Église unie? Quelles impressions de perplexité ou de commisération aura-t-elle causées? Quelle part de ce parcours, qu'on ne saurait lui enlever, aura été la sienne, qu'aura-t-elle apporté d'ineffaçable à l'histoire de l'Église unie? En a-t-elle toujours constitué un élément essentiel dès l'Union? Après soixante-quinze ans, quel regard le reste de l'Église y porte-t-il? Un rendez-vous a-t-il été manqué quelque part? Quel dialogue, quelle fête n'a pas eu lieu? Quelle ouverture, quels pas de rapprochement auraient-ils pu, pourraient-ils aujourd'hui et demain être faits?

Le temps froid, un pique-nique chaleureux

C'est sous un ciel nuageux et de plus en plus menaçant que cette joyeuse communion se déplace à travers champs et bois, pour un pique-nique animé et une période plus informelle de partage et de discussions, vers les Bois de Belle-Rivière, centre d'interprétation de la nature gouvernemental qui vient tout juste d'être inauguré il y a quelques semaines. Pour se faire, il faut passer par le cimetière de l'église. Nul ne remarque la tombe anonyme de monsieur Therrien qui y a été enterré au milieu des années 1920 : quelques membres de sa famille n'ayant jamais accepté sa conversion au protestantisme, et craignant vivement pour le salut de son âme, viendront, de nuit! déterrer son corps pour le transporter dans le cimetière de l'église catholique. Scandalisés d'un tel procédé, les membres de l'église de Belle-Rivière iront la nuit suivante, le déterrer et le replacer là où il désirait reposer...en paix! Ils le veilleront jusqu'à l'hiver, pour éviter tout nouveau déménagement!...Le pique-nique est fort animé notamment par diverses chorales, certaines polyphoniques, d'autres d'enfants, de chaque groupe de nationalité différente. Le temps se rafraîchit considérablement et si les gens du Québec savent que l'hiver est encore loin, si les visiteurs d'Europe admirent les paysages, si les Chiliens, Gonzalo et Rosa, sourient bien emmitouflés dans leurs ponchos, les Africains se mettent à frissonner, à grelotter pour vrai, à sautiller sur place pour se réchauffer quelque peu, se demandant quelle peut bien être cette malédiction que leur envoie le ciel, et si une avalanche entière de neige ne va pas leur tomber subitement sur la tête et les ensevelir à tout jamais.

Le Consistoire Laurentien

Son statut de minorité, et même de double minorité—religieuse dans la société environnante catholique-romaine et linguistique dans une Église anglophone—a fait de cette communauté franco-protestante du Québec un groupe fragile, vunérable, semblant constamment être menacé de disparition....Et pourtant il est toujours là; en bien des luttes pour sa survie, il a résisté à toutes les intempéries. Est-ce un exploit? Les francophones de l'Église unie, dont les prédécesseurs sont venus en Nouvelle-France même avant Samuel de Champlain fondateur la ville de Québec en 1608 et qui y ont toujours été présents, savent qu'ils sauront toujours revendiquer et trouver leur place. Peut-être faut-il souligner que les années qui ont suivi l'Union ont été les plus dures. Sans leadership local, sans possibilité de formation, n'étant pas considérée comme prioritaire dans la vision initiale universaliste des fondateurs de l'Église unie, le déclin du secteur francophone de l'Église unie semblait inéluctable. Faute de relève, les gens partaient; ou s'anglicisaient, faute d'écoles. Les églises, les lieux de cultes fermaient; de quarante-cinq en 1925, il n'y en aura plus qu'une demi-douzaine dans les années 1960, éparpillés sur un territoire plus grand que la Suisse (chérie), isolés, sans pouvoir de décision, sans prise sur leur destinée. En 1985, elles se regrouperont alors que sera constitué le premier consistoire francophone de l'Église unie, le Consistoire Laurentien. Ce ne sera pas une panacée miraculeuse à toutes les difficultés, car si la formation du consistoire a eu de bons côtés comme permettre une prise en main des processus décisionnels et un partage des ressources, elle en a aussi eu de moins bons comme des responsabilités considérables pour un très petit nombre de leaders, pasteurs et laïcs. Il faut être bien conscient que le secteur francophone de l'Église unie restera toujours fragile. Il faut être conscient des limites, de l'impossibilité ne pas pouvoir tout faire, de l'obligation d'établir des priorités—formation des laïcs, développement de leadership local et constant questionnement identitaire; s'associer en partenariat avec d'autres consistoires au niveau des paroisses ou des missions, ou d'autres organisations, caritatives, sociales ou œcuméniques, tout en préservant ses particularités propres, c'est la voie de son avenir. Défi ecclésiologique et communautaire considérable et exaltant.

Tard dans l'après-midi, les gens se quittent, par petits groupes; dans les au-revoirs, les félicitations, les remerciements réciproques, les sourires sont mélés à quelques larmes, les accolades aux reniflements. Certaines personnes se reverront, d'autres non, mais resteront néanmoins dans les cœurs et les souvenirs qui s'ajoutent à tous ceux incrustés dans les murs de cette vieille église. Le soleil disparaît lentement à l'horizon. C'est la fin d'une belle et mémorable journée à Belle-Rivière, mais aussi, et surtout, la promesse d'un autre jour, d'une autre fête; la promesse certaine et irréfutable, offerte par Dieu, de l'aube du Shalom.

David Fines est rédacteur-en-chef du mensuel Aujourd'hui Credo, *publié par l'Église unie, pour offrir une optique chrétienne, réformée, et œcuménique.*

The Ministry

**The kinds of leaders
we have and how
we regard them**

Still a Mystery

by Jean Hamilton

Despite all the changes of recent years, we still struggle with what it means to be a minister, and with what a minister does.

When I was a child, I was a little Anglican. The minister had a black suit, a white collar, rimless glasses, snowy hair, and a kindly face. We knew him as "Mister Harris." If any adults called him by his first name, they didn't do it in front of the children.

I stopped being a little Anglican and became an intermediate United Church person when my parents moved. I brought with me my grandfather's prayer book, the Creed, the Prayer of General Confession, a respect for language, an abiding love of right liturgy, and a sense of mystery at the heart of things. It was only later that I realized the sense of mystery was closely connected to the liturgy and the holy hush of my first church.

The minister at the United Church was also named "Mister." He had a tweed suit with a vest, glasses, a kindly face, a car named Owen (because, well, you know), and an ability to deal with adolescents with humour and respect. He engaged us in genuine theological discussion, and I became a theological junkie in his Sunday school class.

Eventually, I became chairperson of a presbytery, a lay commissioner to General Council in Guelph where the church's Task Force on Ministry was reporting, and thus a member of the enlarged task force. And then, after all these years, I was asked to write about changing attitudes to ministry in the United Church.

Déjà Vu All over Again

When Rip Van Winkle awoke from his twenty-year nap, he found his world greatly changed. I expected to have a similar experience when I began to explore issues around ministry twenty-four years after I first joined the Task Force. Certainly the world has changed. And the face of ministry has changed, with women numbering over half of all candidates for ordination and a proliferation of categories of church personnel. For this and other reasons, the political landscape of the church has changed—and not always peacefully. But the issues bear a stunning familiarity. It's déjà vu all over again!

The story of ministry in The United Church of Canada is a story of repeated studies and debate. In 1960, for example, we find ongoing studies on ordination, lay workers, and deaconesses. In 1964 the Commission on Ministry in the Twentieth Century was formed. It was followed by the Task Force on Ministry, in 1972, expanded in 1974. This was followed by Project

Ministry, which reported to General Council in 1980. Meanwhile, there were studies on lay theological education, women in ministry, feminist theology, sexism, sexual orientation, lay pastoral ministers, and staff associates. And another task force is now at work studying the implications of various categories of designated ministry personnel.

Yet the questions remain the same: what does it mean to be ordained? More specifically, what does it mean to be ordained in a church where the term "ministry personnel" might mean diaconal minister, diaconal supply minister, lay pastoral minister, lay pastoral minister in training, student supply, or staff associate? What does it mean to be ordained to a ministry of Word, Sacrament, and Pastoral Care, when any of the above may preach, administer the sacraments, and perform all of the duties involved in pastoral care? Similarly, what does it mean to be trained and commissioned to a ministry of Education, Service, and Pastoral Care, if you then are placed in a ministry of Word and Sacrament? And among all these "ministries," how can we recognize, develop, and make accountable the gifts of lay people in congregations, church courts, and secular occupations? How can we ensure justice and equity in salaries, benefits, and hiring practices for these many categories of ministry? Trickier still, how do we do this without losing our emphasis on an educated clergy?

Differing Views of Ministry

Successive task forces have spelled out the alternatives. By one view, the logical outcome of a doctrine of the *laos*, the "priesthood of all believers," is to do away with ordination altogether. This view is not widely embraced by the clergy.

Another view holds that there is one ministry, given by God. Within that ministry are various functions, recognized and made accountable by ordination, commissioning, or baptism and confirmation.

Still another group has recommended that all candidates for ministry should be ordained, and the various functions be distinguished at the time of induction.

There has been fairly consistent agreement on the definition of three functions of ministry: *presbyteral*, the ministry of Word and Sacrament; *diaconal*, the ministry of service; and *episcopal* (or oversight), which in the United Church falls mainly to presbytery and is exercised within church courts.

The matter of "who does what," though, became more complicated when congregations in some areas, notably Newfoundland and Saskatchewan, found

One Union Leads to Another
by Annie Crowell

In 1925, the year of Church Union, I attended Methodist Church services in a one-room school in Norris Arm South, Newfoundland. My mother, Harriet Cox, was superintendent of the Sunday school, and my father, William Cox, was one of the lay readers and occasionally preached sermons that he had personally prepared.

I was twenty-three and the church organist. We had a choir of ten or twelve members, and practised every Friday evening. A favourite hymn was, "The Day Thou Gavest Lord Is Ended." The congregation sang it with great gusto.

One Sunday each month, a student minister conducted services at Norris Arm. As a student, he baptized, married, and buried, but he was not permitted to administer Holy Communion. Communion was restricted to the ordained ministers from Grand Falls, and only rarely took place.

Church Union came to our small Newfoundland community without fanfare or celebration. It really came in name only. The older members of the congregation were not pleased when told they were no longer Methodists but now belonged to The United Church of Canada. Whatever consultation occurred with the Newfoundland Methodist Conference, it did not reach this little town. They felt they were not involved with the decision.

The first United Church in Norris South Arm was built around 1927, by Saunders & Crowell from Carbonear. That had implications for me, because in 1929 I was married in this church to Randolph Crowell. The Rev. Charles Howse, father of former moderator the Very Rev. Ernest Marshall Howse, came from Botwood to perform the ceremony.

that they were unable to attract or support an ordained minister. They identified leaders within their own communities. These persons were subsequently recognized as lay pastoral ministers—there is some question about whether it was ever intended that these persons would be open to "call" to other congregations. Other congregations hired staff associates, usually lay persons with particular skills, to do Christian development work, hospital visiting, or other tasks.

And still the question, "What does it mean to be ordained?" continues to nag at the church, takes on new dimensions and, for some, new threats.

Status or function?
Some denominations hold that ordination changes the essence of the person, and is therefore indelible. This view would not find wide acceptance in United Church circles—although sometimes we come close to it in our hearts.

One response to the 1977 Task Force report stated: "By Christ's appointment there is within this Church such a given indispensable [sic] as the Ministry of the Word and Sacraments and the celebration of these Christian mysteries pertains to the Ministry and to it alone." As Archie Bunker used to say, "End of argument."

Repeated studies insist that we ordain, not to status, but to function. In other words, the community recognizes, trains, and ordains or commissions persons with particular gifts to do the things that need to be done, to ensure that the faith is taught and nurtured, that the sacraments are celebrated, and that pastoral care is provided, which is not far from the Presbyterian concept of the minister as "teaching elder." This concept has certain attractions. The current moderator's unguarded comments to journalists about the divinity of Christ raised questions about how much teaching of theology had actually been going on in congregations all these years. In this view, ordination realizes that one among us has been given the privilege of spending an extended period of time studying the scriptures and the theological thoughts and insights of the centuries, and is responsible for putting that theological competence at the disposal of the congregation.

It is common to hear ministers preface their remarks with the disclaimer, "I'm no theologian, but...." For me this is analogous to hearing my physician, whose skill and knowledge I have trusted through all the ills to which the flesh is prone, suddenly stand up and say, "I'm no doctor, but...." What they mean, of course, is that they are not academic theologians. But theology is not the sole preserve of the academic. It is the very stuff of Christian life.

We are all theologians. The great questions of life are theological questions, and the decisions we make every day are affected by our theological understanding. That does not mean, of course, that our theological assumptions are always considered, informed, or grounded, or that theological understanding is automatically conferred at baptism. What we believe about God and ourselves must be nurtured and worked out, if not in fear and trembling, at least in contemplation and study.

It is leadership in this quest that we have a right to expect from our ministry, and this is why we cherish and continue to insist on an educated clergy.

Like Exiles to Babylon
from the unpublished memoirs of William S. Taylor

The most traumatic event of my university life was the unhappy exodus from Knox College in 1925. The tension and bitterness that developed in the Presbyterian Church over Church Union was certainly reflected in the student body at Knox College, but it was not as strong as in the church at large. For the next year after Union, we continued to eat together, live together, and play together on the same teams. Then the blow fell. The provincial government decided that Knox College should remain in the possession of the minority Presbyterian Church, which had stayed out of the Union. That meant we had to get out of Knox College and go across the campus to join the Methodists.

What a shock that was! At that time, the Presbyterian students did not love the Methodists. Our decisions to go into Union had nothing to do with any liking for them. We went into Union because we felt that God required it of us, for the good of the church and its witness in the nation. God seemed to say, "You join the Methodists." And we could answer, "Yes, God, we hear you, but please excuse us this time, God. Ask us to do something else, and of course we will, but please excuse us from joining people we don't really like."

But a sincere Christian can't answer God that way. God seemed to say "Go," and so we had to go.

More Than What Simply Happens

The second "authority" conferred at ordination is the administration of the sacraments. It is frequently said that we let anyone preach, a highly skilled activity, but we are careful about who we allow to perform the beautifully simple act of celebrating communion. Even when permission is granted to some other categories of ministry to administer the sacraments, there is always some sense of discomfort. Why? What happens in the sacraments that many people feel belongs rightfully to the ordained alone?

In fact, what is it that happens at communion? When I asked that question of a variety of people, I received a variety of answers. It is simply an act of remembrance, and yet....It is a family meal, within the congregation, and yet....It's a symbolic act, in which the body and blood of Jesus becomes our body and blood, and we become the body of Christ, and yet....

And yet, and yet, and yet....

But we felt like the Israelites being carried off into Babylon. How could we sing the Lord's song in a strange land? The Lord's songs were, of course, for Presbyterians, the metrical psalms. Our steps lagged and our hearts were heavy as we crossed the campus to Emmanuel College.

To our Methodist hosts at Victoria College, we must have seemed like a bunch of spiritual snobs. We were. We thought we were bringing with us, in the Presbyterian tradition, the pearl of great price that the others had missed. Deep in our hearts we believed that when our Lord finally assigned someone to the heavenly seat on his right hand, it would not be the Pope, the Archbishop of Canterbury, nor even John Wesley. It would be John Calvin.

Looking back on those first couple of years after Union, I have nothing but admiration for the way in which the Methodists received us. We must have seemed an indigestible morsel. But I cannot remember any coldness or unfriendliness on their part. They were gracious and welcoming in a way that I doubt if we could have managed had the situation been reversed, for our coming inevitably upset their way of doing things. The clannish aloofness that we brought with us quickly evaporated in their warmth, and we became better people.

W. S. (Bill) Taylor was principal of the United Church's Union Theological College in Vancouver and the first principal of Vancouver School of Theology.

As with ordination itself, our rational formulations fail to satisfy. Perhaps in this age of reason, this Newtonian universe, we are driven to explain and codify to the point where we leave no room at all for that Spirit that we invoke at ordination, no room for that grace of which communion is a means.

Missing the Mystery

Certainly, we have removed the sense of mystery from Sunday worship. Perhaps that is why our efforts to "bring the young people back to the church" seem all doomed to failure.

Pastoral Relations people tell me that search committees still look for two things: good preacher, "good with the young people." That is, someone who, by attracting those who apparently viewed confirmation as graduation, will ensure that their beloved church will carry on when they are gone. Yet the way to "bring back" those young people continues to elude us. The "contemporary worship" of the 1970s didn't do it. Our efforts to adopt the language of teenagers and be cool doesn't do it. Making children and youth part of the courts of the church doesn't do it either.

Still, the Spirit moves where she will. And what may bring people back to the church is already evident. There is a great spiritual hunger in this generation, and they fill the gap with a variety of "-isms," of which consumerism and technology-ism are not the least. And still the hunger is unsatisfied. When and if they do come back to the church, what will they find? Will they find serious consideration of the questions that drive them? Will they find a willingness and ability to bring a theological perspective to their search? Will they find worship that does not patronize, that does not deal in outworn formulations, but addresses and touches their craving?

Much will depend on how we answer the questions about ministry.

Living Organisms Grow and Change

I am retired now, and back in that first United Church I attended. The minister has a first name, which everyone uses. He has a wardrobe of golf shirts, a few clown costumes, and vestments for ceremonial occasions.

Have attitudes to ministry changed much within the congregation? Not much, I think. The life of the community still centres around the churches and the sports facilities, and our minister is at home in both. His style of community ministry suits very well. The children who gather at the front of the church on Sunday mornings experience the church as a warm and friendly place. Maybe they will stay around. We still gather to hear the word, and to be fed at the table. And we know there is an open door to the minister's study when we need it.

Occasionally, I go back to that little Anglican church—usually for family funerals. The minister, a young man, struggles to bring inclusiveness to the archaic language of the Prayer Book. But the heart of the liturgy is timeless. The little church no longer looks like a cathedral to me. There are six pews on each side of the aisle and one stained glass window above the altar. But the sense of mystery is still there. And when I hear that young man's voice from the back of the church saying, "I am the resurrection and the life," things just fall into place.

Questions about ministry, about ordination, about justice and equity will go on, as they should, because the church is a living organism and to live is to change. Perhaps we will never arrive at consensus, at satisfactory formulations.

At sixty-six, I think I know why. It is because there is still a mystery at the centre of things.

Jean Hamilton is a lay theologian who lives in Brookfield, Nova Scotia.

The Spiral of Diaconal Ministry

by Eric King

Many members of the United Church know little or nothing about diaconal ministry. For diaconal ministers, invisibility is a continuing problem.

Jessie MacLeod

Jessie MacLeod had no idea that the influence of her ministry would be felt from the east to the west coasts.

She began her work at Chalmers United in Ottawa in 1950. When she helped found the Ottawa Lay School of Theology, she could not know that it would continue for fifty years. In British Columbia she served with the Board of Christian Education and the Board of Women. She helped develop volunteer leadership; she worked with Native communities. In 1970 she moved to Sackville, New Brunswick, as Associate Director of Student Affairs at Mount Allison University. She came to national prominence in the Division of Mission in Canada as Associate Secretary for Leadership Development and later as Deputy Secretary in the Office of Christian Development. Despite heavy administrative and supervisory duties, Jessie never relinquished her belief that lay people needed to be intimately involved in church leadership.

Halifax drew her east again as pastor-in-residence at the Atlantic School of Theology. What she had learned in working with Mount Allison University undergraduates came in handy in chaplaincy with theology students and their families. Prior to retirement in 1990 she returned to congregational ministry in Sydney, Nova Scotia, where she worked in a multiple staff ministry. She supported Sunday school teachers and mid-week leaders; preached and gave leadership in worship and adult Christian education; and performed pastoral responsibilities such as visiting, marriages, funerals, and grief work.

Edith Radley

Edith Radley was a registered nurse as well as a diaconal minister. She worked first with the Woman's Missionary Society in Angola and later with the Division of World Outreach in Angola and Zaire. As a nurse, she taught and supervised public health, trained midwives, and assisted those with leprosy. As a deaconess (the name used prior to 1981), she worked with pastors, deacons, other deaconesses, and students in rural schools helping them understand and participate better in public health programs. It was always her goal to transfer her skills and knowledge to Angolans so they could assume leadership when the missionary went home.

After she was deported to Canada by the Angolan government after spending three months in prison with her friend Dr. Betty Bridgman, also a

207

missionary, the two returned to neighbouring Zaire (now the Democratic Republic of Congo), to work with Angolan refugees.

Don Reid

Don Reid was the first man designated as a "certified employed churchman" in 1963. Thankfully that title did not last long. Don worked at Brunswick Street Mission in Halifax on the congregation's extensive outreach work in the inner city. There were summer camps for children who could not normally leave the city in the summer, along with more traditional services such as a clothing depot and emergency food assistance.

In 1965 Don became director of the recently established Atlantic Christian Training Centre in Tatamagouche, Nova Scotia. These lay training centres provided programs in educational design and personal growth, and had an active winter course for young adults who wanted to explore their future from a faith perspective. Don stayed there until he moved to Windsor, Nova Scotia, to be director of the Windsor Elms, a seniors residence with nursing care. He retired from this ministry in 1990.

Barb Elliott
by Betty Marlin

Barb Elliott lived touching, relating, building community as no other person I have ever known. She built strong relationships with people far and near, offering support, encouragement and appropriate challenge to move beyond the status quo. Barb was a woman of vision and strength, working tirelessly for justice and compassion for any who were marginalized. Her thoroughness to detail and her commitment to networking strengthened and supported the work of women and men within the church in Canada and throughout the world. She touched the lives of many with gentle compassion. Her sensitive probing questions helped many to both expand current thoughts and begin to develop a broader understanding and appreciation for justice and compassion throughout the world.

As she listened to the frustrations, trials, and concerns of her colleagues and friends; we felt heard, cared for, and pushed to think new thoughts and act in new ways. She also did her share of raging and yearning for a world that cared for each person, a world that affirmed the contributions that each person or group brought, regardless of orientation or gender, colour or race, age or ability. She lived "action–reflection" in her own life and invited those of us who considered her a friend to do the same. She could ask the hard questions in a way that was not judgemental.

Men and women, young and old, gay and lesbian and straight—it did not matter, all were of equal importance to her and claimed her full attention when in her presence. Justice was her vision and compassion her response. This was a strong woman, with clear vision and determination. Her strong feminist commitment as well as her many friends and

Education, Service, and Pastoral Care

I could have chosen many other stories, but these three illustrate the three dimensions of diaconal ministry. Their ministries weave education, service, and pastoral care into almost every aspect of their work. Their example and vision of diaconal ministry continues in the lives and work of over two hundred United Church diaconal ministers.

Diaconal ministry started with Jesus. The Greek verb *diakonia*, literally "to wait on table," would include Jesus' healing of the sick, feeding of five thousand, and washing his disciples' feet. As a noun, *diakonos* was used to describe the work of Phoebe (Romans 16:1–2), Dorcas (Acts 9:36–42), and Stephen (Acts 6:8–7:54) as they served the needs of the widows, orphans, poor, and foreigners; and prepared people for baptism. Paul uses *diakonos* to describe colleagues throughout the world nourished her vision and propelled her to action.

Barb loved the nights. Sitting at home with her telephone to her ear, keeping in touch with friends and colleagues or inviting someone to struggle with her on an issue that was troubling her at the moment would be a typical evening for her. As Barb's bronchiectasis became more debilitating, her telephone became her lifeline to family, friends, and colleagues. And she loved the church that had shaped her, even as she challenged it. She worked tirelessly to make it a place of justice and right relation.

Some would say that diaconal ministry is alive in the United Church today because of her. Her belief that the gifts of diaconal ministry were essential to the well-being of the church, her ability to read between the lines, and her commitment to read minutes as a political act helped to alert both the church and the diaconal community that action was needed. Barb, who never did anything on her own that would be more authentically done by a group of people, helped to mobilize the diaconal community to come together and claim in a new way the place of diaconal ministry within the church. In her memory we have established the Barbara Elliott Trust for Innovative Ministry, a fund available to people doing ministry that finds difficulty securing funding and yet is a valid ministry.

We will remember her for her integrated life, her insight and her strong determination to bring justice and right relation into the world. Barb's work towards justice for herself and for all whose lives she touched, and there were many, is a legacy that we will carry in our hearts and in our lives for many years to come.

Betty Marlin is one of the two co-ordinators for the Western Field-based Diaconal Ministry Program.

himself and other leaders. As Elizabeth Schussler Fiorenza points out in *Women of Spirit*, biblical scholars later translated *diakonos* as minister, missionary, and servant in reference to men, yet used only deaconess for women.

By the end of the first century, church roles became more rigid. There were restrictions put on the role of the deacon (and deaconess). The most notable restriction was that women could only serve and teach other women. There still were numerous deaconesses in the fourth century; forty deaconesses worked with Bishop John Chrysostom of Constantinople.

The diaconate for both women and men fell into disuse as the monastic way of life became more established around the year 600 and did not reappear in until re-instituted in Germany in 1836. In that year, Theodor Fliedner and his wife Friederike Munster established the first mother house and trained women to carry out ministries of nursing, teaching, and social work. It was an effort to respond to the social upheaval caused by the Industrial Revolution and to utilize the ministry of a growing number of women who wanted a significant role in their church.

The Canadian diaconal ministry grew out of the British deaconess movement. Women there were not in a mother house or hierarchical structure. They were an association of independent women affiliated for professional development and mutual support. Canadian women in the Methodist Church were the first to organize themselves. In 1894 the Methodist Deaconess Order was formed. The Presbyterian Church of Canada formed Ewart Missionary and Deaconess Training School in Toronto in 1897 and, by 1909, had established a Deaconess Order. In 1926 the Methodist and Presbyterian Deaconess Orders came together to form The United Church of Canada's Deaconess Order.

In 1928 the *Report on Employed Women Workers in the Church* recommended that a new diaconate be formed, which would be recognized as an order of ministry, with the authority to preach and baptize where necessary. However, not until 1964 were deaconesses accepted as members of presbyteries and other courts of the church.

A Minister by Any Other Name…

Those in diaconal ministry have experienced many name changes. If you belonged to the Deaconess Order, you were a deaconess. There were also missionaries employed by the Woman's Missionary Society. When the first men were admitted, they were initially called certified employed churchmen. Only after 1968, when all of the above were recognized as members of the Order of Ministry, did the term commissioned ministers came into use. However, there was no consultation with anyone involved. So in March 1980, General Council Executive took the unprecedented action of calling a consultation of all deaconesses, certified churchmen, and commissioned ministers. For two years the Task Force on Commissioned/Diaconal Ministry consulted with regional clusters of their colleagues. A second consultation in February, 1982, made a consensus decision to call themselves diaconal ministers.

The consultations also resulted in the Division of Ministry Personnel and Education establishing the Committee on Diaconal Ministry, to develop meaningful and effective diaconal ministry, to recommend policies, and to address issues still facing diaconal ministry.

One of these issues is whether they should be ordained or continue to be commissioned. For outsiders this may seem a trivial question, but for diaconal ministers this distinction is important. They fear that if diaconal ministers were ordained, the church would soon forget the unique and valuable gifts diaconal ministry offers the church.

A Virtue Creates Its Own Problems

One characteristic of this diaconal identity is its flexibility. When the world needed social workers during the Industrial Revolution or the Great Depression, diaconal ministers took training and offered themselves as pioneers. When the baby boomers came to Christian education programs and Sunday school in unprecedented numbers, educational design, curriculum development, and leadership development became major emphases for candidates. When personnel were needed to work with overseas churches or Native or remote communities in Canada, they became missionaries.

As the United Church moves into a new century, it has to find ministry personnel willing and able to serve churches in remote areas of the country, or churches that are transforming themselves into something yet to be determined. With lay pastoral ministers, who often serve remote churches, and ordained ministers, who take special training in interim ministry, diaconal ministers have been moving into both.

The dilemma for diaconal ministers is that these churches require ministry personnel who can administer the sacraments and be licensed to conduct weddings. Although this permission is much easier to obtain today, it still is resented by some lay people and ordained ministers, who feel that the line between ordained and diaconal ministers is being blurred.

Training for a Different Drum

From Church Union, when the United Church Training School was created, to today where students attend the Centre for Christian Studies, most diaconal ministers received their education at a single theological school. It has gone through its own history of name changes. In the early 1960s it was called Covenant College. In 1969 it amalgamated with the Anglican Women's Training School as the Centre for Christian Studies. At present all non-Native students attend the Centre for Christian Studies, now located in Winnipeg; Native students attend either the Francis Sandy Theological Centre or the Dr. Jessie Saulteaux Resource Centre.

The wisdom and cost to continue a separate educational institution for diaconal ministers has been debated for at least the last forty years. In 1974 the Centre for Christian Studies developed a program quite different from what theological schools offered candidates for ordained ministry. The Centre's model is based upon adult education principles. Students take primary responsibility for their own learning. While they take courses in theology and ethics, biblical studies, church history, and pastoral care (including worship, Christian development, and church policy), they are also engaged in field education in a congregation or social ministry. The learnings are drawn together in a self-directed learning group. This action/reflection spiral of educational and learning has become symbolic of diaconal ministry, representing the educational dimension of our work.

In Partnership with Lay People

Given diaconal ministry's diverse and valuable resources, what does it have to offer the United Church, Canada, and the global community in the future? Recent assessments done by the United Church indicate that the church needs ministers who are adaptable to changing needs—who can both assess needs and respond with sensitivity and vision. If finances continue to be restricted, making it more difficult to have paid ministerial staff, there will be even more need to work alongside educated and empowered lay people. The group-learning model of diaconal education will serve the church well to assist it in valuing the wisdom, experience, and knowledge many lay people have.

Diaconal ministers' commitment to and skills in shared leadership are not only sought in congregations and the community. The courts of the church also recognize its value. The General Secretary of General Council is a diaconal minister.

Ironically, just as the larger church clarifies its need for ministry personnel with the skills and training of the diaconal minister, diaconal ministers are experiencing more difficulty in finding settlements, calls, or appointments. Diaconal ministers all have stories of having to explain diaconal ministry to ill-informed discernment committees, to education and student committees, and to pastoral relations committees searching for a new minister. It would be easier if these groups were aware the church has personnel especially trained in education, service, and pastoral care.

Western Field-based Diaconal Ministry Preparation Program, 1989–1996
by Betty Marlin

During the 1980s the church continued its many reflections on ministry in The United Church of Canada. There were conversations and papers about ordered and lay ministries. There were considerations of new models of ministry to serve a changing church and world; this included exploring different models of theological education to meet the needs of the people called to ministry as a second or third career. As well as focusing the attention on the ministry of the whole people of God and, within that, the specific roles of diaconal and ordained ministries, the documents for the first time considered field-based theological education as an alternative to the traditional residential theological programs. At one of those consultations, in 1982, the Centre for Christian Studies and the church made an agreement to explore the possibility of a model of theological education for those called into diaconal ministry where the opportunities for preparation would be dispersed in two or more locations.

Meanwhile, in Alberta and Northwest Conference, people interested in diaconal ministry were gathering to talk about ways in which they might have a program that would meet their needs. Before long a group composed of those in diaconal ministry and those who felt called to diaconal ministry began to explore ways in which this kind of preparation might happen in western Canada.

The group met with the Centre for Christian Studies and St. Stephen's College as together they began to develop a program for diaconal ministry in the west. The program was developed in consultation with the Centre for Christian Studies, the Dr. Jessie Saulteaux Theological Resource Centre, and St. Stephen's College.

The Invisible Ministry

Does this mean that after all the energy of the early 1980s, diaconal ministry still is unable to make a place for itself in the life of the United Church? Is its future questionable? This assumption could have been made with some confidence if another significant series of events had not taken place early in 1998.

In the closing months of 1997, there was great turmoil over a proposal to move the Centre for Christian Studies from Toronto to Winnipeg. The wider diaconal community was drawn into the discussion. After two months of preparation, a special meeting was called. Over a hundred members participated, many through telephone conferencing. Again, the diaconal

After considerable work and planning, it was agreed that a program would begin in the fall of 1989, out of St. Stephen's College in Edmonton. St. Stephen's had been involved in non-residential programming for several years, which was a definite asset to the program. While this dispersed and field-based program for diaconal ministry was not a program of the Centre for Christian Studies, there was always close contact with the Centre with much support and wisdom from the experience of the staff.

In August of 1989 the Western Field-based Diaconal Ministry Preparation Program was inaugurated with thirty participants in the initial program. It soon became evident that there were many people, primarily women, who were interested in a program that enable them to remain in their home community while they studied for ministry. Thus, in the fall of 1991, a second intake of this one-time pilot project began. Program participants, with the exception of one person from the Bay of Quinte Conference, were all from the four western Conferences of the United Church.

In all, forty people have now completed the program and are active in ministry in the United Church of Canada [two are deceased]. Several of these thirty-eight people in diaconal ministry were involved in getting the program started. And these people will, we anticipate, be welcomed as permanent Friends of the Centre at its next annual meeting.

The program was a full-time, five-year program, with the expectation that half of the participant's time would be in field experience and half in study and reflection. It was a program rooted in the call of the gospel to justice and compassion within a ministry that understands the inter-connectedness of our global context . It was a program that encouraged growth in understanding of self and self in community, as we strived for right relationship, person to person, community to community, and nation to nation.

community gathered chose to make the decision by consensus. Although there was not unanimous support, over 90 percent finally supported the proposal. Most of those who could not support the decision still felt heard and continue to support the decision.

This experience indicates that when the diaconal community is pressed by circumstances, it still responds with creativity and commitment. It also shows that the diaconal community wants to be involved in determining its future in the United Church. It is not satisfied to have others making decisions for it.

As we move into a new century, the challenge before the diaconal community is to help the church seriously own the contribution this ministry has to offer in the church's future.

Eric King is a diaconal minister and a staff person for the United Church's Maritime Conference.

Passing It On

Education for our children and for ourselves

Who Will Teach the Children?

by Anne Squire

Looking back, the United Church's revolutionary New Curriculum *proved a turning point for the church as a whole, and for many individuals within it.*

> "Theological college had taught me to have nothing to do with Christian education. Then my life was turned around by the *New Curriculum*."

> "When I first read the *New Curriculum*, I asked my minister why he didn't preach this stuff!"

> "The Observation Practice Schools, initiated to supplement the *New Curriculum*, reframed my understanding of Christian education."

> "I think we abandoned the *New Curriculum* too soon."

These were a few of the comments made by the people brought together in 1996, by Wehn-In Ng and Phyllis Airhart of Emmanuel College, to evaluate the impact of the *New Curriculum* on The United Church of Canada. For a day we sat and reminisced about our own experience in that exciting venture of the 1960s. The group included Peter Gordon White, editor-in-chief of the new resources; Norman McNair, editor of the senior books; and Gordon Freer, Robin Smith, and George James, all involved in the publishing effort. Wehn-In Ng and I were there as writers of supplementary materials, along with Audrey McKim who had been involved in the *Uniform Curriculum* that preceded the new materials. Yvonne Stewart was present as part of the team that developed the *Simplified Curriculum*, which followed the *Core Curriculum* (as the *New Curriculum* came to be called).

Present, too, as educators who had first introduced the material in their congregations or in their conference roles were John and B. J. Klassen, Don Bardwell, Bill Blackmore, Stuart Bell, Bill Lord, and Marion Best. Anne Bell was the only person present who had still been in the church school as a student when the material was introduced.

Present in spirit were many others like Olive Sparling who had shepherded the nursery, kindergarten, and primary materials through the process; Bob Wallace, Bob McLean, and George Johnson who had written some of the material; and Donald Mathers who wrote *The Word and the Way*, the first book to be published. It was a groundbreaking introduction to theological reflection. All were remembered as pioneers involved in developing that three-year cycle: *God and His Purpose, Jesus Christ and the Christian Life*, and *The Church and the World*. The curriculum had been years in development. Its presuppositions had been examined by congregations and by educators travelling across Canada for consultations. It was a mammoth undertaking, and one that changed the church forever. The writers developed readers for every age level and teachers' guides.

The Beginning of Forty Years of Teaching

That reunion at Emmanuel College led me to reflect on my own faith journey. I had been part of church school for longer than I could remember because, I am told, as a baby I sat on the teacher's knee while my mother sang in the choir. My earliest memory is the day some men changed the sign on our church from "Wesley Methodist Church" to "Wesley United Church."

I am not sure what curriculum the Sunday school of my childhood used, but I know that some things changed when a new superintendent took over. Until that time we had moved through the classes as we moved through school. He insisted on age-graded classes. That meant that I, as a thirteen-year-old product of a system that encouraged children to skip grades, was entering grade 11 in high school but at church I was moved back with a class of grade 7s. I stormed, I sulked, but I went. And I hated it, until the teacher in the kindergarten class recognized my predicament and asked me to help her.

That was the beginning of forty years teaching in the church school. Even though I had read through the Bible many times since my first perusal at the age of nine, what I read raised more questions than provided answers. I could only be called biblically and theologically illiterate. And theology was for ministers!

A Mind-blowing Experience

The *New Curriculum* was, for me, a mind-blowing experience. By the time it appeared in the early 1960s, I had been teaching in the church school for over twenty years. None of the courses I had taken through those years had ever made a connection between theology and teaching children. To be introduced to the excellent materials on child development, the theological backgrounds, and the carefully prepared lesson plans, was a breath of fresh air.

At that time my congregation was erecting a Christian education building, and the insights from the curriculum were incorporated into its very structure. Before beginning to teach the *New Curriculum*, our whole contingent of teachers, who would be working with over six hundred children, took fourteen weeks of training under the guidance of our minister, Don Bardwell, using *The Word and the Way*. Education was for teachers as well as children!

The sixteen kindergarten teachers who worked with one hundred children met for a whole morning twice each month. We soaked up child psychology, theology, Bible study, and methodology, and we saw how they were intrinsically related. Our minister often spoke of this experience as a watershed in his career. The same was true for me.

The *New Curriculum* offered me more than leadership training; it made me part of the leadership team. The papers I submitted for a "Christian Leadership Education Honour Diploma" and an article that I had written for *Christian Growing*, a Canadian Council of Churches periodical, had brought me to the attention of editors in The United Church of Canada. They invited me to write some supplementary material for the curriculum—for parents in *The Christian Home*, for kindergarten teachers in *Focus*, for the back pages of the children's kindergarten leaflets, and for *Sunday School in the Home—By Mail and Air*.

Because I was working not only with the Sunday school but also with Explorers (the mid-week group for junior girls), I was asked to be a reader for the junior material of the *New Curriculum*. This led to an invitation to write some of the Mission Study material and "Explorations" for Explorers.

When I switched from teaching kindergarten to teaching juniors, I began to recognize some of the problems inherent in the *New Curriculum*.

The Decline and Fall of the *New Curriculum*

The people present at the 1996 Emmanuel consultation agreed that the *New Curriculum* failed to get full co-operation of parents who were not accustomed to devoting time to reading to their children. As a practical problem, *New Curriculum* lessons were geared for ninety-minute classes while most churches had less than an hour. And, according to the one participant who had been a child when the curriculum was introduced, it seemed "too much like school, with homework!" Even the teachers complained that it was too much work.

It did not help that the media seized every opportunity to fan flames of discontent.

When it became evident, after a few years, that the *New Curriculum* story books were not being used effectively, that they were being recycled rather than being left with the families as intended, and that shorter stories were needed, the church tried to salvage what it could. I became involved in writing material for juniors in *Wow*. I was expected to write not only stories and articles for children, but also the session plans and biblical and theological backgrounds for teachers. At this stage I realized I needed more religious education myself. I returned to university, a move that eventually led to me being invited to teach in the Department of Religion at Carleton University.

The *New Curriculum* helped me own my own ministry. Much later I finally realized that everything I was doing in the church was ministry, whether working on Project: Ministry, being part of a feminist group, writing curriculum, acting as General Secretary of the Division of Ministry Personnel and Education, or serving as moderator. I also came to understand that educational ministry was at the heart of the life of any effective congregation, and that education need not be limited to a formally approved curriculum.

The Main Beneficiaries

When the group came together at Emmanuel College to evaluate the impact of the *New Curriculum*, I learned that my own experience was mirrored in many others. B. J. Klassen spoke of her experience in a communicant's class where the questions in the Catechism were not her questions, and how she learned to teach using students' questions. Stu Bell discovered that the teachers were the main beneficiaries of the *New Curriculum*. Marion Best realized how deeply influential the curriculum had been when she entered into discussion about the Bible with her grandchildren.

By 1980 Marion and I, like others involved in educational ministry, knew the curriculum was already out of date. For us, that realization was painful. The curriculum had meant so much to us. For many, it seemed that the questions had once again changed. The curriculum needed to be re-framed to be more inclusive of different types of families, different types of experience, and a very different world, a world where "multicultural" and "multimedia" became the buzz words.

What made the curriculum so valuable to the church was a solid theological background appropriate to its time. As Gordon Freer said at the consultation, "Theology is central to the life of the church, and theology involves education. A credible theology must be rational."

Was the *New Curriculum* too rational? Was it without sufficient spiritual base?

The next generation of teachers would develop more experiential material. But the *New Curriculum* had proved that those who were ready to teach the children were themselves ready to learn.

Anne Squire was moderator of The United Church of Canada from 1986 to 1988. Prior to that, she had been General Secretary of the national Division of Ministry Personnel and Education. She is now retired and lives in Ottawa.

From One Thing to Another

by Yvonne Stewart

The United Church seems to go through cycles—from wide acceptance of a single curriculum, to freewheeling experimentation, to wide acceptance, to....

"Church school will be cancelled for the next six months!" That startling declaration came from John Sullivan, the minister of Chapel in the Park United Church in the late 1960s, because we were having so much difficulty recruiting teachers. We had been using the *New Curriculum* but, despite good training opportunities, leaders were not coming forward with enthusiasm.

That announcement started me on a journey that led to working in Ministry with Children in the Division of Mission in Canada.

Numerous meetings led us to try a six-week, two-and-a-half-hour Sunday afternoon program, each fall and spring, plus a two-week summer program. I volunteered to help develop the curriculum. John Sullivan arranged a meeting for me at Church House with Olive Sparling, the staff person for Ministry with Children. Olive was excited by the concept and contributed many hours planning these programs and training leaders. I had no idea that I would one day take the place of this tireless dynamo.

A Wealth of Programs Emerge

When I began work in the Ministry with Children portfolio in 1975, I overlapped with Olive Sparling for six months before she retired. Olive was the driving force behind the Observation Practice Schools and Demonstration Schools. She taught me much about the development of the *New Curriculum* from her first-hand participation in its development. She compared it to the preceding Sunday school *Quarterlies* that she had helped plan with other denominations in the United States. I also had the luxury of time to visit the United Church archives to review other Christian education and church school material, including the wonderful *Canadian Girls* and *Canadian Boys* papers.

The *New Curriculum* had acquired a new name by this time—the *Core Curriculum*. A *Simplified Curriculum* (based on the themes of the *Core Curriculum*) appeared in response to complaints about the complexity of the *Core Curriculum*. Writers such as Anne Squire, Marian Brillinger, Audrey McKim, Anne (now Wehn-In) Ng, Robbie Salter, and others created material for *Surprise*, the primary material and *Wow*, the junior. My job was to continue producing *Wow* and *Surprise* and to create updated *Core Curriculum* lesson outlines in *Children's Bulletin*, a publication for church school superintendents.

To get an impression of how the grassroots were feeling about these United Church curricula, before I actually started editing the material, I was invited to accompany Gordon Freer, editor-in-chief of Christian education materials, on trips across the country to participate in an evaluation process. I remember, particularly, sitting in a dim church parlour in Winnipeg, listening to stories from ministers and church school teachers. Some were thrilled with the creativity of the *Simplified Curriculum* and the theological soundness of the *Core Curriculum*. Others, I was shocked to hear, didn't like these materials at all. They didn't like "being told what to believe." The resentful tones still ring in my ears.

Into a "Babel Period"

Statistics indicated that even with this excellent *Simplified Curriculum*, even with leadership training workshops, the use of David C. Cook material (the nemesis of denominational curriculum and sometimes the gospel!) was increasing dramatically. I can't remember the exact percentage but it possibly ran as high as 50 percent of congregations. Although outstanding leadership was emerging because of the *New Curriculum*, Christian education in our church was far from "united."

Consequently, a task group, made up of creative Christian educators from each Conference of the United Church, was put to work.

A historical review revealed that since the beginning of curriculum development, people have debated

a) its content—doctrine, scripture, or life experience;

b) its methodology—memorization, experiential, uniform, or graded lessons; and

c) its goal—relationship with God, understanding of scripture, moral formation, development of the religious life of the child now.

We began to think we were in a "Babel period" of curriculum development. Denominations in the United States came to a similar realization. They started an ecumenical enterprise, called Joint Educational Development (JED) to create a selection of curricula to meet varying needs in their constituencies.

The task force finally sought approval to offer choices to the United Church constituency. The *Core Curriculum*, supplemented by updated lessons, would remain; sadly, the *Simplified Curriculum* would not. It was replaced by an ecumenical curriculum, called *Joy* (that later included a United Church insert). A third stream would be a resource called *Loaves and Fishes*. Although many were not happy with having a choice of curricula (they wanted just one—their preference, of course), the positive result was a decline in the use of David C. Cook and an increase in United Church materials.

Loaves and Fishes gathered materials developed by local leaders in response to children's questions. It was intended to address resistance to material created by "head office," and to add some balance to the more rational base of previous curriculum. Teachers were trained to talk with children, to discover their questions about life and faith, their fears and joys, and then to develop sessions in response that brought in biblical, theological, and social resources. New *Loaves and Fishes* material was distributed twice a year from congregations all across the church with suggestions on how to put the resources together into a church school program. The sessions seemed to group naturally under the three themes of the *New Curriculum*—God and [His] Purpose, Jesus Christ and the Christian Life, and the Church and the World.

The Whole People of God Arrives

Possibly inspired by *Loaves and Fishes*—or perhaps disgruntled by the lack of a standard curriculum—many congregations across the United Church experimented at this time with developing their own educational curricula. Soon they discovered this was not as easy as they hoped.

A group in Regina, led by Marilyn Perry, decided to go farther than planning a single lesson or unit. They wanted to develop an extensive curriculum. They asked Ministry with Children to support their request for General Council experimental funds to get them started. Little did we (or they, for that matter) know where this project would lead.

Their constituency wanted something that didn't involve creating or stitching together their own curriculum. They wanted something more organized, with a biblical focus (in this case, the lectionary readings), that addressed the children's need not only to know, but also to live their faith in worship and in their daily lives.

This local initiative quickly developed into a national and ecumenical curriculum. *The Whole People of God* took off, the United Church bought and used it enthusiastically, and David C. Cook usage dropped as dramatically as it had risen earlier.

Multiple-choice Questions

Currently, the church seems to be moving again towards a choice of curriculum. Some folk want something that teaches the biblical stories in more depth. Some seek materials that incorporate radical new theological understandings of God, Jesus, and the church. Others search for a way to combine knowing our story and being in relationship with God and Jesus and the hurting world. Still others desire an orthodox view of faith. And so on.

Consequently, the United Church will be participating in an ecumenical, infant-to-adult story-based curriculum called *Bible Quest* starting in 2000. The denomination will also continue to support the lectionary-based *Whole People of God*, which will be revamped by 2003, and *Dancing Sun*, an ongoing ecumenical curriculum for First Nations people in Canada. The United Church will also produce *Resources for 21st Century Christians* that whole congregations can use for worship, mission, and education.

Tippling in the Furnace Room
by Philip A. Cline

My grandfather, John Wesley Cline (no secret to his heritage!) was an example of Methodist moral and spiritual rectitude. His Methodist scruples were put to the test one Christmas Eve, just a year after Church Union.

The superintendent of the Sunday school and the church caretaker arrived at the church early that afternoon to light the furnace. While they waited for the church to warm up, a blizzard blew in. It was some hours before anyone arrived for the Christmas Eve service.

These two worthies whiled away the time by nipping on a bottle, which one of them had thoughtfully brought along in case of just such an emergency, as they sat by the furnace waiting for the storm to abate.

Unfortunately for them, the first person to arrive was my grandfather. His Methodist sensibilities were so enraged by the sight of the superintendent of the Sunday school consuming alcohol in the church basement that he promptly dismissed him from his position—and just as promptly replaced him with his son, my father, Charles Wesley Cline. Charles remained superintendent of that Sunday school for the next thirty years.

United, yes—but Methodist under the skin forever!

Listening to children moved the church to think more seriously about what children want or need to learn for a faithful life in relationship with God (as opposed to what adults think) and even influenced the inclusion of children in worship and communion. In "Who Will Teach the Children?" Anne Squire describes the transforming influence of the *New Curriculum* on many— particularly adults. Curriculum resources such as *Loaves and Fishes* set a tone that freed some people to develop their own learning programs. It enabled them to explore scripture, theology, and spirituality for themselves, to see how they give meaning to the lives of young people they work with and to their own.

Knowing our Judeo-Christian story and being in relationship with God and the community of Jesus is essential to give meaning to the life of Christians today. Without Christian education programs, church members will not know who they are. They will not be moved to live and act the healing, compassionate, and just way of Jesus in the world today. The dream of both the *New Curriculum*, of having all ages studying similar topics over a three-year cycle, was an appropriate ideal for a relatively new United Church still forming its identity. *The Whole People of God* similarly attempted to have all ages focus on common themes, this time derived from the ecumenical lectionary.

It may be that in times of great theological transition, we can only hold together by offering a variety of approaches to Christian education within some common boundaries.

Yvonne Stewart has held a variety of positions in educational ministry. She is currently director of the Five Oaks Centre near Brantford, Ontario.

More Than Just a Tool

by Karen Hamilton

Although the Bible lies at the heart of our Christian faith, the United Church sometimes has trouble keeping it there.

There was dust everywhere....More piles of rubble than the high priest Hilkiah would have thought possible....But Temple renovations were like that. And in the midst of the dust and piles of rubble, the discovery of the book of the law. Hilkiah touched it with great trepidation because of its fragility and sacredness. Was the book of the law, found under layers of Temple history, an authentic revelation from God? The prophet Huldah would know; she was the one to ask. Huldah's answer was prompt and direct and pulled no punches: "Thus says the Lord...." And scripture was authenticated. (2 Kings 22)

There were people everywhere....More excitement than the dark-haired woman singing in the choir would have thought possible....But the inauguration of The United Church of Canada was like that. On June 10, 1925, at a worship service in the Mutual Street Arena, Toronto, The United Church of Canada officially came into being. My grandmother was there, adding her voice to the paeans of praise and celebration. At that time, the *Basis of Union* was formally signed by the chief officers of the supreme courts of the uniting churches.

The *Basis of Union* speaks about scripture in its section on Doctrine:

> We affirm our belief in the Scriptures of the Old and New Testaments as the primary source and ultimate standard of Christian faith and life....We receive the Holy Scriptures of the Old and New Testaments, given by inspiration of God, as containing the only infallible rule of faith and life, a faithful record of God's gracious revelations, and as the sure witness of Christ.

A Means Or an End?

If we journey with The United Church of Canada in the years since 1925, years including the Great Depression, the Second World War, a tendency to anti-Semitism, the affluence and church-growth of the 1950s and 1960s, and an emphasis on social justice and courageous social stances, a subtle shift can be seen in the way scripture is understood and used. The nature of that shift, in a sweeping generalization and over-simplification—which is so often the way in which we imperfect human beings understand ourselves and our context—is that scripture that was said by the church in 1925 to be "the

Unsuitable for an Auditorium
by Grace Tuer Jacklin

When the various Presbyterian Churches in Stratford, Ontario, voted on Church Union, both Knox and St. Andrew's decided to remain Presbyterian.

This left minorities in both churches that together formed the nucleus of a new congregation. They joined with the members of Trinity Methodist and the Congregational Church. Dr. Martin, formerly the minister at Knox Presbyterian, left with the minority to become minister to the new congregation.

They began holding services in the City Hall auditorium and, at times, in the Majestic Theatre (now the famous Avon). When the time came for the first communion, however, it seemed unsuitable to hold the service in an auditorium. Central United Church offered their sanctuary for the service, to be held on a Saturday evening.

Several new members were confirmed at that service, including the writer of this piece. I was fifteen.

Plans for a new church were made. A building fund was set up. Even the teenagers contributed 25 cents a week from their meagre allowances. The new church—St. John's United—was built and paid for in two years.

primary source and ultimate standard of Christian faith and life…" comes, over the years, to be seen as in the service of the church and the church's ministry.

When the confirmation class, of which I was a member, gathered in a circle in the church parlour for its first meeting, I was glad that we were using a brand new confirmation resource. The new book had a bright and relevant-looking cover. It was much of an improvement, to my teenage mind, from the little blue *Catechism* that the previous year's class had had to use. And not just the previous year's class.

I was confirmed in 1972. Long, long before, on April 7, 1942, R. B. Y. Scott of the United Church's Commission on Christian Faith suggested that scriptural passages be used in the new catechism that the commission was drafting. The final version of that catechism, however, used scriptural language rather than quoted passages. Not until the third section, on salvation, did explicit references to the Bible occur. The Ministry, the Bible, and the Sacraments—in that order, according to the *Catechism*—are given to the church by God as tools "to equip the church for its work."

The Power of Biblical Story

Ironically, the "new" confirmation resource that I received with such teenaged enthusiasm has tumbled to obscurity in The United Church of Canada. Not only have I never come across it again, but I cannot even remember its name! Meanwhile, the questions and answers of the little blue *Catechism* are readily accessible as a historical document of the church.

On the other hand, I think that I will remember all my life, the figure of Lot standing high on a lookout, pointing with an imperious hand to the land he has chosen for himself and his people. Lot who, when offered by his uncle Abraham the choice of all the land, chooses the very best for himself and his own. That scene was printed in brilliant red, yellow, and blue on the cover of *God Is Always With Us*, the primary book of the *New Curriculum*. I even remember where, on the bookshelf of my childhood bedroom, my copy of the book resided. It made that much of an impression on me.

Teaching the Bible to the Church

In any discussion of the way in which The United Church of Canada has understood scripture in its life and work, the *New Curriculum* is a major topic—because of the multiple volumes of material involved, because of its official promotion as Sunday school curriculum in the church, and because of the vast number of United Church people who came in contact with it as clergy, Sunday school teachers, or Sunday school attendees.

The *New Curriculum* was convinced of a need to bring to all the church's people an understanding of the faith of the Bible and its relevance to their world. It was also convinced that many people had given up hope of understanding the word of God in the Bible because they found its language and thought forms too difficult. It saw itself as a fresh and radical alternative to this need and problem. My own experience indicates that it was highly successful in its purpose.

Such thinking also betrays, however, a tendency to believe that the Bible belongs in the hands of leaders who will translate it according to the people's need for relevance and meaning. The Bible can, therefore, still be seen as a tool in the service of the faith. The implication is that without the help of the church, scripture either has little meaning, or little meaning that can be understood.

The *New Curriculum* also tended to speak in deprecating and supersessionist terms about the Old Testament as a kind of preamble to the New Testament. This way of thinking about the Old Testament has been a part of the history of the church. It is, in fact, still common today. However, if one part of scripture can be described as having a lesser value than another part, then human judgement becomes the norm for what is authoritative. Once again, scripture can be perceived as a tool in the service of the faith.

A Passionate Belief

It was also in my teenage years that "she" swept into my life. "She" was a Sunday school teacher. She was not only young and vibrant, but she believed passionately in the relevance and meaning of the Bible and the Christian faith in my urban context. We made brightly coloured banners with office towers on them! These banners spoke of Jesus' care and concern for the world in which we lived our daily lives. We hung them in the traditional chapel of our church. And so I saw, in vibrant and passionate colour, the truth of the song: "Jesus loves me, this I know, for the Bible tells me so!"

In 1974, when I was still a teenager, the Twenty-sixth General Council of The United Church, meeting in Guelph, Ontario, requested the Committee